SIREN SONG

Seymour Stein

with Gareth Murphy

SIRE

Side A

WITHDRAWN

SIREN SONG
(My Life in Music)

ST. MARTIN'S PRESS   NEW YORK

Warner publicity shots, found on pp. 10–16 of the photo insert, are courtesy of Warner Music Group.

www.stmartins.com

Designed by Steven Seighman

The Library of Congress Cataloging-in-Publication Data is available upon request.

ISBN 978-1-250-08101-8 (hardcover)
ISBN 978-1-250-11685-7 (ebook)

Our books may be purchased in bulk for promotional, educational, or business use. Please contact your local bookseller or the Macmillan Corporate and Premium Sales Department at 1-800-221-7945, extension 5442, or by email at MacmillanSpecialMarkets@macmillan.com.

First Edition: June 2018

10 9 8 7 6 5 4 3 2 1

Siren Song is dedicated to my beautiful daughters, Samantha and Mandy, to my dear friend, Richard Gottehrer, and to the incomparable Syd Nathan.

Samantha was taken way too soon, on February 8, 2013, after a long and brave battle with brain cancer, leaving behind a most beautiful and brilliant young daughter, Dora Wells, and scores of friends who flooded the chapel at her funeral.

My younger daughter, Mandy, a film producer / director, is a constant source of inspiration, whose help and support while writing my story was invaluable. She also took on the responsibility of finding and selecting the photos for the book from noted photographers Bob Gruen, Roberta Bayley, and Bobby Grossman, as well as some family photos, most of which were taken by my dear late cousin, Brian Weisberg.

Richard Gottehrer and I started Sire together and were partners for seven years, which were among the roughest but also some of the best. Richard had already built up quite a name as a songwriter or producer on such hits as "My Boyfriend's Back" by the Angels, "Hang On Sloopy" by the McCoys, "Giving Up on Love" by Jerry Butler, and his own band with Bobby Feldman and Jerry Goldstein, the Strangeloves, with "I Want Candy." Richard is probably the closest thing I ever had to a brother, and our friendship has endured for well over half a century. I'm being honest and fair when I say I don't think I could've done it without him. Much love and many thanks to him and his lovely wife, Anita.

Syd Nathan was far and away my greatest mentor. The founder of King Records in Cincinnati, he was a music man through and through. Syd saw something in me, and it was that belief and the training and knowledge he passed on that saw me through, especially during those earliest and toughest years at Sire Records, and right up until today. I've tried, throughout my career, to pass on what I have learned and mentor and help in any small way to ensure that great music men move forward and take on the responsibility as mentors to ensure the continued growth, importance, and success of music around the globe. That, above all, was my main purpose in writing this book.

CONTENTS

SIREN SONG

PROLOGUE

I can't imagine a world without music.

The best songs of every generation make society stand up and walk into the light. In my own lifetime, I've seen how popular music has helped improve human rights, racial equality, sexual equality, and inspired so much love and hope where once there was only ignorance and injustice.

Songs have influenced the course of modern civilization, as in the case of "La Marseillaise," written soon after the French Revolution. Unlike "The Star-Spangled Banner," written nearly forty years after the American Revolution, "La Marseillaise" was a battle cry for French citizens to rise up and defend the first Republic from invading tyrants. Or consider "Over There" by George M. Cohan during World War I. Also, on the British side, "Keep the Home Fires Burning," by Ivor Novello. Two of America's biggest national holidays, Fourth of July and Memorial Day, celebrate our freedoms and our fallen soldiers in war. What is life all about except for freedom? There's no denying: it took wars to win them.

I remember participating in several civil rights protests and singing "We Shall Overcome." That song and others helped to change so many people's minds and lift the civil rights movement into national consciousness. "Eve of Destruction" by Barry McGuire was another. "Like a Rolling Stone" and so many songs by Bob Dylan, "The Sounds of Silence" and "America" by Simon & Garfunkel, "Woman" by John Lennon, "Teach Your Children" by Crosby, Stills, Nash & Young, and "I Am Woman" by Helen Reddy, all carried these classics' important messages. And so did a Sire release, "Scatterlings of Africa" by Johnny Clegg and Juluka, a racially mixed band from South Africa during the last days of apartheid back in 1982.

The inspiration to write the story of my life in the music business was stirred in large part by concern over the decline in sales and what appears to be a dwindling interest in pop music, culturally. Music has played a central role in life, history, and religion for thousands of years. It's bigger than any of us, and it belongs to us all.

I'm the man who signed the Ramones, Talking Heads, Madonna, the Pretenders, the Dead Boys, the Replacements, Ice-T, Brian Wilson, k.d. lang, Lou Reed, Throwing Muses, and many more. I've also been the indie community's number-one transatlantic operator. Across fifty years of high tides and economic troughs, I've tracked down and shipped into America a whole bloodline of British bands, from the Climax Blues Band and Barclay James Harvest to Depeche Mode, Echo and the Bunnymen, the Cult, the Smiths, the Undertones, the Rezillos, M, the Cure, Madness, the English Beat, Soft Cell, Yaz, My Bloody Valentine, Ride, Primal Scream, Seal, Aphex Twin, and many others.

Sire is my label, still afloat, still trading, and just celebrating its fiftieth anniversary. How I'm still alive is the greatest mystery of all. Yes, I'm still hobbling around the deck of the good ship Sire, refusing to give up on the giant beast that almost killed me all those years ago.

Before I begin my story, I have to warn you that I have no easily definable skills or talents. I'm a hit man, a record business entrepreneur. But what I'm not is a producer like Phil Spector or Quincy Jones. I can't play any instrument, I can't operate a studio, and I definitely can't abracadabra something into a gold disc. My exact job description is A&R—*artists and repertoire*, the old show business term for talent hunting. But the word I tell myself when I look in the mirror is *fanatic*. What I really am is an extremist. Every happy accident I provoked in pop music happened as a result of my zeal bumping into originals whose lucky stars only needed to be seen, believed in, and, most of all, supported.

And because I wasn't a musician with any formal notion of technique or virtuosity, I was often able to spot the genius black sheep—the rejects and mavericks who couldn't sing or play by conventional standards but who possessed something unique the world was waiting for. If my life and legacy means anything, I hope it's something about so-called losers playing to their strengths and winning big. I've been wrong far more times than I've been right, but I'm still here.

I still don't know if the ability to spot talent in others actually counts as a talent in itself. The one weird gift I do seem to have is a photographic memory, which, strange at it seems, is how I developed an ear. Since I was a boy, I've kept devouring names and adding to a personal collection of old tunes the world has long since forgotten. My head is a giant jukebox. It's also a ghost train of long-departed showbiz characters who I've never let die. They're all in here, screaming down telephones and cracking jokes. I can impersonate every Ahmet, Syd, and Jerry down to their accents and mannerisms. You see, I always saw the music business as something between comic folklore and an adopted family. And the more I learned from the old school, the more clearly I could see the new one walking past me on the street.

So, here I am, one of the last-standing lifers, aged seventy-five and still looking. The thing about getting old is that the truth doesn't even hurt anymore. I know I was born damaged in some way, not that my condition was immediately evident or was ever diagnosed. I don't even know if sixty years in the madhouse of rock and roll made my condition better or worse. Excess definitely made me crazier, but success brought me relief. In songs and adventures, I found both solace and purpose, and just as importantly, I met people like myself.

It's amazing how things look when you reach my age. The cruel test of life is that we're set free into a world that doesn't really need us. We're lost souls stuffed into these suits of skin we can't take off. From our first lung-opening scream, the pressure is on to get a grip, invent a persona, join some gang, and come up with a plan. For the rest of our lives, our daily ritual is to repeat this birth sequence. We wake, we ache, we look in the mirror and ache some more. Then we start to medicate. On goes the radio while the coffee is percolating. With songs to lift our spirits and caffeine coursing through our veins, we slowly turn our minds to the lowly chores of hunting and gathering.

No matter what way we choose to explain the mysteries of life, the only way to get through it all is to keep our spirits *high*. Music is one way to do it, and there are many others, but that emptiness follows us every step of the way. You know you're lucky to be alive, you know you should be making the most out of it, but the sinking feeling that you're not seizing your precious time is the great human killer. Every one of us suffers from it, wealthy tycoons and pop stars included. In fact, the best among us get there *because* of it.

As you'll see, due to design faults beyond my control, I was a crash landing that had no choice but to run and keep running. In doing so, however, I learned how to harness my mad, hungry dissatisfaction into rocket fuel. Okay, so my ass was on fire without a

Stop button, but at least I wasn't sitting around stewing in my own burning frustrations. My curse became my crusade. My unemployable craziness became my entrepreneurial strength, my solitary nature became my indie spirit.

My hope is that between the lines of this book, you will better understand how hits are landed, how stars are born, and how you make money out of what is basically thin air. For a fanatic, you'll see that I'm very practical when it comes to running a tight ship. My prayer is also that you will invest in your local music community and pass on all these old-school secrets to children coming up behind you. Talent is constantly *out there*, but it'll always need to be found and helped in practical ways. Boiled down to its basic ingredients, the music world runs on discovering exceptional people and great songs—the two key substances that create musical explosions.

Whether you're going to gigs, buying stuff, or actually making a living out of music, we are all participating in the ancient ritual of helping talent rise. On a collective level—gigs, charts, playing records at parties—it's a modern variation of a pagan ceremony, but in personal ways, it's more like a street corner. You seek, you score, and you get high on your own. In our modern world of screens, most listeners now get their daily hits by pressing buttons. I'm a believer in the collective high and rarely signed a band unless they could play live. But has anything really changed? Does it matter if your daily hit is acquired digitally or if it's needled up from a vinyl platter? Different people have their own traditions and rituals; all we really want is the spirit the songs evoke.

With the growth of streaming services, it seems we're now moving from the old system of bottled medicine to the brave new world of hits on tap. All *ways* can coexist and will keep evolving, because underneath it all, it's still the same old trade of medicating millions of people who, like you and me, are just trying to get out of bed and cope with the mixed emotions of living. That's why I can't stand the endless debates about technology. I know I'm an old guy, but believe me, it'll always come back to songs. Stick to the substance and people will line up.

The job of the label is to source the dynamite, to *know* what'll take people's heartache away, and, every once in a while, land the legendary whale. In a dense marketplace where timing is key, our imprints provide the guarantees that the dealers and connoisseurs can easily recognize and run with. Labels will always be needed, because only maniacs like me are insane enough to roam the globe, trawling through miles and miles of shit to just every now and then pick out a tiny diamond. It's a needles-in-haystacks treasure hunt driven by sheer obsession. As for the supposedly endangered species of copyright, don't panic. While there are lawyers stalking the jungle floor, music rights will be defended with a never-ending hail of well-aimed writs and judges' hammers.

All that's changed is distribution and how we listen to music, which has done nothing but change since I was a boy, anyway. The new dons of Silicon Valley have largely taken over the dirty business of selling the stuff to people, and most of my old friends who ran warehouses or drove around with boxes in the trunk have been undercut, bypassed, outmaneuvered, and—in the end—proverbially whacked. It's been a turf war, but the joke is, the new dons still need the old labels. Through mutual dependency, peace is slowly breaking out.

A hundred years from now, no matter how future generations listen to music, it will still boil down to song writing. A&R is basically a big, French-sounding way of saying *people and writing*. Hits need to *hit*. Only great music can raise the stakes by truly expressing what we all feel but cannot explain ourselves. The greatest artists are often the greatest writers, and even though you've never met them, they've always been your best friends. When we need a shoulder to cry on, our dearest, most treasured songs are like penny candles. They bring us to tears in a good way and put us back in tune with our true selves. They make us *better*.

I may not have any great talent as a musician, but I've seen and heard enough to know what it is. A lifetime of seeking out and then serving great artists has taught me that this precious madness we all suffer from is both a burden and a blessing. Depending on our character, it's an energy that can consume us or be put to good use. Talent is simply the gritty business of channeling all this inner spirit into the real world we all have to survive in.

The magic of recorded music is that we can all reach the highs that great artists reach. And even better, as witnesses of other people's true genius, we all get to elect the best minds of our generation. I take no bows. I never *made* any of these stars famous; we all did. In our own different ways, we felt something, we put our money on the table, and we lifted these kids up with a million arms. Long may this tradition last!

So, my travel companion, it's been a long, wild voyage. Yours now begins where mine must surely end.

1. SHELLAC IN HIS VEINS

On April 18, 1942, I was born Seymour Steinbigle, the only son of Dora and David. Considering my life's obsession would be to *get there* first, it's funny how late I arrived. Mother Nature's stork dropped me down the chimney just as the biological clock was closing in on midnight. My forty-one-year-old father was the last Steinbigle, who'd almost given up praying for a son to carry the ancestral name. My only sibling, Ann, was already six years old and might have already resigned herself to being an only child.

My birth was greeted with sighs of "At last!" The question was, would I last? I was born with a cardiac defect, a hole between the left and right heart chambers. In those days, they called it a *murmur*. As we now know, that little heart kept beating like a drum all the way to the pages of this autobiography, but who'd have bet on it? It was my destiny to begin life as the fragile boy, the defective model, exempted from sport and spoiled rotten by a mother who always heard a time bomb ticking in my chest and did what any mother would have done in such a situation. She held my hand tight, hoped for the best, and tried to savor every precious moment.

It had been the gloomiest winter in living memory. Since Japan's attack on Pearl Harbor the previous December, America was in a state of shock watching the whole world sliding irreversibly into war. The very day I was born, however, marked the turning point when finally, Uncle Sam stood up and hit back. Literally hour for hour, while my mother went into labor in a Brooklyn hospital, sixteen B-25s took off from USS *Hornet*, an aircraft carrier in the West Pacific. To avoid radar detection, they had to fly fifty feet above sea level for a nail-biting eight hundred miles. Off the Japanese coast, they split into squadrons and bombed ten military and industrial targets in Tokyo, Yokohama, Yokosuka, Nagoya, Osaka, and Kobe.

Throughout life, my mother always joked that the tremors from those bombs were what made me turn out crazy, but what always struck me as insane was that after they'd dropped their bombs, all eighty airmen couldn't turn back and had to keep flying west. By the time they reached the coast of Free China, it was dark and turning stormy. Some planes managed to crash-land on airstrips, but most of the raiders had to bail out into the paddy fields and let their unmanned planes crash. Three died, and eight were captured, four of whom were executed. One plane with a leaky fuel tank was forced to take an early right turn to Russia. About sixty airmen, however, managed to get home with the help of villagers, guerrillas, and missionaries.

The chief pilot behind this ramshackle adventure sported the unlikely name of Jimmy Doolittle. He got home to discover that every last target had been missed, and he was expecting to be court-martialed. But it's a measure of how depressing our situation was in the first months of the war; the sheer daredevil heroism of this "Doolittle Raid" was a direct hit with newsmen and succeeded in lifting American morale off rock bottom. In the end, the powers that *were* awarded Jimmy Doolittle the Medal of Honor.

It was the stuff of comic books in an otherwise terrifying reality. Unfortunately, smiling Doolittle and the American public had no idea what kind of wasps' nest he'd just rattled. Gripped by national panic, Japan's imperial forces traced the wrecked and abandoned bombers scattered around coastal China to a trail of parachutes, cigarette packets, coins, and aviation gloves that the American raiders had given locals for their help. With hitherto unimagined levels of extreme violence, the Japs began torturing, slaughtering, and raping the entire region. They burned down every home, destroyed every farm, and even flew in biologists to poison wells with the bacteria of plague, anthrax, cholera, and typhoid. Within weeks, the Pacific front was plunged into a steaming hellhole of terror, starvation, and disease.

Meanwhile, across Eastern Europe and deep into Russia, something was happening on a scale that my Jewish ancestors couldn't have imagined in their worst nightmares. All four of my grandparents had emigrated from Galicia just before the turn of the twentieth century, a rural region that had formed the northeastern edge of what used to be the Austro-Hungarian Empire until it was broken up into Poland and the Ukraine in the interwar period. Annexed by Stalin in 1940 and then invaded by Hitler the following summer, our ancestral land had just disappeared behind a deathly silence.

I was too young to remember anything of the war, but as any war baby will tell you, its shadow is stamped on your identity for life. A thousand times in my adult daydreams, I'd be sitting in a plane or a hospital waiting room, and get caught by that "1942" on whatever visa or medical form I'd be filling out. It's like a giant tombstone staring back at you, and yet, it's weirdly empowering, almost like the terrible truth you learned as a teenager was still being shot at and avenged by the little boy's comic book hero.

I've long wondered how so many genius originals were born during the war. Never in the history of music have so many heavyweights come from the same crop: Brian Wilson, Bob Dylan, all four Beatles, Jagger and Richards, Jimi Hendrix, Jim Morrison, Aretha Franklin, Joni Mitchell, Paul Simon, Smokey Robinson, Arthur Lee, Ray Davies, Jimmy Page, Pete Townshend, Roger Waters, Jerry Garcia, Otis Redding, Janis Joplin, Curtis Mayfield, Sly Stone, Randy Newman, John Denver, Scott Walker, Carole King, Neil Sedaka, Stephen Stills, David Crosby, Eric Clapton, George Clinton, Donna Summer, Dr. John, Captain Beefheart, Ian Dury, Diana Ross, Leon Russell, Robert Wyatt, Frank Zappa, Neil Diamond, Neil Young, Tammy Wynette, Bob Marley, Lou Reed . . . all war babies. Coincidence? I doubt it. We were born under a giant black cloud that I think made us run faster through life to wherever the lights were brightest. I obviously can't compare myself to all these artists, but I do know that I went through life feeling intensely lucky, and maybe that's what made me take so many chances.

Luck isn't solely about timing, of course; it's as much about being in the right place. When the credits roll at the end of my journey, the top of my thank-you list has to be the city where it all began—Brooklyn. Forget the hipster suburb it's since become; the Brooklyn of my childhood was such a human zoo, it's fitting that almost every cartoon character of my generation spoke in Brooklynese. Bugs Bunny, Popeye, Tweety Bird, Porky Pig, Daffy Duck, Heckle the talking magpie, Fred Flintstone, Barney Rubble. In fact, Popeye's famous line "I yam what I yam and dat's all what I yam" laughed me through a thousand embarrassing situations in adult life. Anytime I was made to feel like a halfwit from the gutters of the Third World, I used to pull that line out like a water pistol.

You see, as well as every other quirk and irregularity you're about to discover about me, I was a natural-born klutz. The hole in my heart caused me serious health problems later on, but what made me a playground misfit was my clumsiness. I had ten butterfingers attached to a jittery, left-handed nervous system. I was the red-faced kid who got so excited telling you all about his latest obsession, he tripped on his own shoelaces and accidentally squirted mustard down your shirtfront. To put it another way, I was the kind of boy that only a mother could love. I was difficult, impatient, I needed attention, people got dizzy just looking at me. Theoretically, my life should have been the thundering disaster that I physically am—but try defining "normal" in a place like old Brooklyn. We weren't polite, we weren't pretty, and we definitely weren't up our own asses.

What Brooklynites didn't have in wealth, beauty, or education we made up for in character. We were the world's most multicolored, multicultural multitude of mutts whose only common denominator was that just about everyone was working class and had an immigrant background. We had Puerto Ricans, blacks, Asians, Irish, and at least a million Italians, but I don't think there was anywhere like Brooklyn outside the new state of Israel. We had every flavor of Ashkenazim—Russian, Polish, Baltic, Romanian, Austrian, Hungarian, German, and Czech Jews, including about fifty thousand survivors from the concentration camps. We had lost Jewish tribes you didn't even know existed—Syrian, Iraqi, Persian, Yemeni, Ethiopian, even some Sephardic Jews whose family trees had curled through Spain, North Africa, the Middle East, and South America. I'm sure any unsuspecting goy driving through Brooklyn on a Saturday afternoon would have seen all the black yeshivish hats and lumped us together as one big, unhappy family. But among ourselves, each Jewish community was distinct, often with its own native food and language.

We even had our own time zones. For example, Galicia hadn't been on any school atlas since my parents were children, but many thousands of families like ours *never* said they came from Poland or the Ukraine—that dubious honor was generally reserved for camp survivors. When my Yiddish-speaking elders immigrated to America in the nineteenth century, neither Poland nor Ukraine existed, and in those days, Ukrainians were an ethnic group called Ruthenians. It's no secret that our Galician ancestors steered well clear of those vodka-swilling, pitchfork-poking schlubs of the east who, in the bitter end, evolved into the Ukrainian nationalists that lined up to do Hitler's dirtiest work.

No, thank you—we wanted nothing to do with the Ukraine. We were proud Americans descended from Galicia, a specific time and place under the respectable Hapsburg kings of Vienna. The old Galician cities like Lemberg had been the birthplace of the Haskalah, or the Jewish Enlightenment, a century when Jews embraced science, literature, art, and the liberal professions and even filled the ranks of the Hapsburg civil service. There's not a lot that Jews value more than noble kings and prosperous times, and *Galicia* was a word that expressed so much without having to explain.

The Italian community of Brooklyn also had its own tribes and clans pocketed around different neighborhoods. The thing to remember, however, is that Brooklyn and New York, although joined as one metropolis back in 1898, were still distinct, especially as you moved east toward the coast. Unlike the Brooklyn Heights and Williamsburg side, which looked at Manhattan, the bigger half of Brooklyn from Bay Ridge, Dyker Heights, Bensonhurst, and Sheepshead Bay down to Coney Island had its back to New York and faced the ocean. Most inhabitants either worked locally or wanted to live near the beach—which in those days was clean, spectacular, and *the* place to be in summer.

We lived in a small, two-bedroom apartment on Dahill Road, just off King's Highway near a predominantly Syrian corner of Bensonhurst that was otherwise Brooklyn's Little Italy. By trolley, we were twenty minutes from Coney Island and Canarsie, where my grandparents Benny and Esther Weisberg ran an Italian-American grocery and Grandma's elder sister Rose had a similar store nearby on Cropsey Avenue. Their brother, my great-uncle Morris, was the family bigwig who ran a successful olive oil importation business. Maybe I've watched too many Al Capone movies, but for a Jewish guy who made it on Italian turf during the thirties and forties, old Morris always struck me as suspect. I shouldn't judge because it was Uncle Morris who helped his sisters set up their grocery stores, which in turn put great food on my plate and provided a key part of my education.

My mother had grown up above my grandparents' store on Neptune Avenue, between Fifteenth and Sixteenth Street, and still considered Coney Island as home. Visiting my grandparents, which we did all the time, you could almost smell the Atlantic Ocean getting nearer just by the avenue names—Neptune, Mermaid, Surf. You'd see the Wonder Wheel, the Parachute Jump, and Cyclone from three or four blocks back. Europe wasn't just over that big blue horizon; it was visible everywhere in our daily lives. But to simply call Brooklyn a *melting pot*, as so many do, is a terrible insult to the high standards of cooking. We were gourmets. Our store imported every delicacy known to Roman civilization. We had every type of pasta and olive oil, we had a hundred condiments and those scary-looking dried cod, or *baccalà*, hanging off the ceiling like giant mummified bats. For a start, when you pushed open that heavy glass door into the store, you'd get knocked backward by the smell of cheese. We stocked every imported variety of obscure, steaming *formaggi* that could practically follow you down the street if you whistled.

A few doors down was Totonno's, the most famous pizzeria in Brooklyn. Like a great pop record, a world-class pizza is a deceptively simple art, and Totonno cracked a hit formula in 1924 that's been drawing a loyal audience ever since. He was a dark, burly Neapolitan who spent his life in a white tank top because whether it was winter or summer outside, a hardworking day was always oven temperature. He was an opera fanatic who applied the same level of passion and perfectionism to the science of dough and hand-made mozzarella. Always freshly kneaded—never refrigerated—he sourced only the tangiest, firmest handmade mozzarella. He tray-baked his fifteen-inch pies sprinkled with fine olive oil so thin and crispy, the slices crunched between your teeth in an explosion of divine savors.

Totonno's masterpiece pizzas drew, and still draw, crowds of drooling Italians from all over Brooklyn and New York. His eldest son, Jerry, was taking over the restaurant by the time my legs were dangling off their seats, but their whole family was constantly running into our store for supplies because, as I learned only recently, my grandmother gave them credit, which wasn't something the Italians always accepted among themselves. In return, we were welcome to grab a pie whenever we wanted. Tabs would be divvied up and paid on Fridays.

In Brooklyn, Jews and Italians didn't just work side by side—we actually *liked* each other. I think they respected our family values, but there was our self-discipline, too. Jewish men generally didn't drink to excess, didn't beat their wives, and most of all, we minded our own business, literally. My grandmother Esther was a tough cookie, but she was innocent in the way that ladies were supposed to be in those days. I remember her chasing Puerto Rican kids away from the store with a broom because she thought *they* stole. How-ever, when it came to her beloved Italian customers, she never knew what it really meant that some of them were distinguished repre-sentatives of the local garbage union. Grandpa knew but didn't want to. His name was Benjamin, and he was the quiet one, especially when it came to other people's business. Whenever he saw a gang of Italians kicking some poor fella around the pavement, he'd pick up a newspaper or disappear into the stockroom.

I remember these rough-looking Sicilian characters who once

pulled up and bought some groceries. A minute later, two cops ran in. "See anyone suspicious getting into a truck?"

"What truck?" said Grandpa. When the cops ran off down the street, he turned to me and smiled. "If your grandmother were here, she'd have given them the license plate."

And for us, the Italians had by the bucketload the one quality neither the Yiddish nor the English languages even had a term for—*arte di vivere*, which translates as "the art of living." It wasn't just their cooking, the way they sang their hearts out while they worked, the way wore their fedoras and Sinatra-style suits. They were the original Brooklyn hipsters. We forget how decades before Jews built Hollywood, America's first entertainment superstar was an Italian opera singer, Enrico Caruso, who, along with Sinatra, Perry Como, Dean Martin, Tony Bennett, Vic Damone, and others in my time, taught the twentieth century how to sing. Pop music owes so much to black people, of course, but we must never forget the Italians who brought high culture to our streets.

Their lady-flirting, pleasure-appreciating attitude to life certainly took a lot of the stiffness out of whatever Waspy Victorian culture dominated nineteenth-century America, and I'm certain it had a profound effect on Jewish immigrants, too. I can just picture all those Coney Island Jews, still carrying all their Ashkenazi baggage, pickled in centuries of fear and sorrow. How they must have suffered in kosher torment resisting Totonno's pepperoni topping. They mostly gave in, of course. "Go thy way and eat bread with enjoyment"—Ecclesiastes 9:7. Peace at last between the Romans and the Jews.

In this seaside world of Italian cooking, my father, David, was the outsider who, God bless him, never once succumbed to the temptation of prosciutto. Father was born in 1901 and grew up on the Lower East Side practically under the Williamsburg Bridge in a German and Jewish tenement slum, where rag sorting was the local industry. It was called Sheriff Street until it was bulldozed into a housing project in the 1940s. My father never forgot where he came from, but I suspect the complete demolition of his childhood habitat was a something of a relief. Compared to my mother's side of the family, where everyone owned a business, Father was somewhat embarrassed about his humble origins, which partly explains why we didn't see his brothers and sisters and their families as often.

He worked in the city at J. F. Ditman's showroom in the Garment District in the upper Thirties and Seventh Avenue. Like a man with two jobs, he was also vice president of our local synagogue, the Congregation Shaarei Tefilah on the corner of West First Street and Quentin Road, just a street down from where we lived. Every day, he'd drop by the synagogue at six in the morning and then take the train into Manhattan, where he'd sell ladies suits and coats all day. On the way home he'd always stop by the synagogue for evening prayers.

Outwardly, he looked like the typical well-dressed Orthodox Jew, but in his own way, Father was an original who'd been nicknamed "Happy" by his oldest friends because of his sharp sense of humor. The joke was, he hadn't always been so religious. In his youth on the Lower East Side, he dated girls, ate in Chinese restaurants, and went out to vaudeville shows. He was the eldest of three sons, so when his father, Asher-Zalki Steinbigle, died, he felt it was his duty to carry on the old traditions. He put on his father's hat and looked after his widowed mother.

That's why my father was a late starter. Thankfully, one of his older sisters set him up with my mother, who for similar reasons was a late starter, too. You see, Esther wasn't actually my natural grandmother. My mother's real mother had died giving birth to what would have been her sixth child. To cut a long and tragic story short, my grandfather Benjamin ended up remarrying his dead wife's sister, Esther. Sounds bizarre, but hey, Esther loved those motherless kids as any heartbroken aunt would. The family had to be saved, and she stepped up and eventually fell in love. The daughter of her remarriage to Benjamin was stricken with polio and needed constant care, so my mother had to help out with the store. By the time I was born in 1942, Mother was thirty-six, and Father was forty-one.

Although he signed up, Father was deemed too old to fight in World War II, so they made him an air raid warden, a duty he thankfully only had to execute in drills. Neighbors already knew and trusted my father as a community man, even the nonreligious ones on account of his canvassing for the Democrats. Many Brooklyn Jews in those days were communists, but my father was a staunch anticommunist who loved America with all his heart. Without ever lecturing or condescending people on their own doorsteps, he just felt sorry for those communist Jews, sensing they'd been easily led astray because of the Nazi trauma. He even shared some of their concerns. In the Garment District, he worked closely with black people and felt very strongly about their mistreatment in society.

I never thought we were poor. Full-blown poverty was a common sight in Brooklyn and downtown Manhattan; it meant going hungry and never knowing where your next dollar was coming from. However modest Father's salary must have been, we were the very definition of lower-middle class. While he was off at his steady job in the city, Mother was always there to greet us after school and tend to our every need. Plus, we had our grandparents' store nearby to feed us like Roman nobles. That said, for as long as I can remember, I understood that money was precious. Anything I earned or was given, I saved religiously.

We were a family of four squashed into a two-bedroom apartment, but even that had its hidden advantages: we all went out and did things. If it wasn't the synagogue, the store, or school, it was

the beach, the amusement parks, the movies, the city, or just playing on the street. Even at night, we never missed an opportunity to
get out. Most every Tuesday evening in summer, my sister and I
would head up to the roof of our building to watch the fireworks
over the amusement parks in Coney Island.

My obsessive hobby was collecting stamps, bottle caps, and
trading cards, anything interesting and flashy. Unlike most boys at
school, I didn't care about those baseball cards sold with Topps or
Bowman gum. What I liked were the educational cards you found
in cigarette packs or bread. "Horrors of War" cards from World
War II were my favorite. The ultimate piece of treasure, however,
was an authentic foreign stamp. Mother knew that I loved nothing
more than to take the train into Manhattan with my best friend,
Brucie, whose father had been my father's childhood best friend on
the Lower East Side. She'd hand me a few coins, and off Brucie
and I would skip to explore the stamp department of Gimbel's.

It was around that toothy age that my future career as a talking
freak show got its earliest breaks. Any time my sister brought her
friends home from high school, their running joke was to have
little Seymour recite the Gettysburg Address. Like a disturbed
child prodigy, I'd stand up and rattle off verse after verse. When I
ran out of steam, they'd quiz me on state capitals, which I'd memo-
rized down to every last Salem, Bismarck, and Providence. Or,
when my parents went out, one of my sister's babysitting tricks was
to quiz me on the presidents while I was half-asleep on her lap in
the TV room. "The twentieth president of the United States?" she'd
whisper softly, and I'd apparently mumble, "James A. Garfield," or
whichever other number and name she was testing me on.

I don't remember ever being a good student at school—which,
by the way, was not a serious crime in Brooklyn. Going to university was not what people did or expected of their children. My
appetite for information, or my "photographic memory," as my

sister called it, made me something of a nerd in the eyes of my parents and wider family, whose opinion was all that really mattered to me. Those who knew me best, and especially my older sister, thought I was brilliant, so who cared about what my math or science teachers thought?

I also have to thank my sister for the foundations of my musical education. Because she was six years older and we had to share the same bedroom, I heard the soundtrack to her teenage years, which partly explains how my ears grew up faster than the rest of me. The dominant fashion in the early fifties was orchestrated country, and Ann's favorites included the stunning "Tennessee Waltz" by Patti Page, "Your Cheating Heart" by Joni James, and "Cold, Cold Heart" by Tony Bennett—the latter two of which were originally by Hank Williams. Another was "Goodnight Irene," a Lead Belly song covered by the Weavers. Its B side was "Tzena, Tzena, Tzena," a rousing, banjo-plucking tribute to the new state of Israel complete with a verse in Hebrew. Even my parents sang along to that one. I was only about nine or ten and wasn't consciously listening, but all these old standards hung in the air like cigarette smoke and yellowed my eardrums for life.

My earliest memory of musical obsession was running home from the synagogue on Saturday to catch the week's Top 25 hits on *Make Believe Ballroom*, a hugely popular radio show presented by Martin Block. I didn't know there was such a thing as the music business, but Martin Block's magic world of songs and scoops was like watching the conveyor belt rolling straight out of an imaginary song factory. One lasting memory was the way he doffed his cap to Patti Page's "Tennessee Waltz," which remained number one for thirteen weeks in early 1951. "How's that for consistency?" asked the master of ceremonies, as if to say that *durability* was the highest value in music.

Whether I knew it or not, I was falling in love. It wasn't just the lyrics I loved memorizing, it was the weekly thrill of the charts. Often, my father had to stay on at the synagogue, so I'd sit at the kitchen table with a notebook and pen and write down the show's playlist with chart numbers and notes. Watching my obsessive behavior with some concern, my mother whispered to my sister in the next room, "What's going to become of him?"

Ann, however, was my greatest believer and always reassured my mother, "Just you wait and see, Mom; Seymour's going to be a big success."

The unbearable weekly suspense of Martin Block's chart was probably accentuated by the other weekly ritual of my father wanting me to keep Shabbos. When he came home from synagogue, I'd have to hide under my blankets and hold the transistor against my ear with the volume turned down low. In the intense atmosphere of a traditional Saturday, I'd lie there almost breathless, taking in every new tune and piece of news like it was life's honey seeping through airwaves.

It almost bothers me to paint such a stern portrait of my father, because had he ever caught me, I doubt he would have ripped that radio from my ears. He was a gentle soul whose orthodoxy was vastly outweighed by my mother's side of the family. Being proud traders of fine Italian produce, most of my family rarely ate kosher, didn't rate Ashkenazi food, and only went to synagogue for special events. We were a mixed family. Our home was 100 percent kosher, but outside, my mother could be easily tempted. On Saturday afternoons, she would always hand me fifty cents and quietly slip me out the front door to catch the movie matinées. Father never forbade this or passed any comments. For the unbeatable value of forty-five cents, I'd get a soda, a hot dog, a bag of fries, a screening of *Flash Gordon*, and five color cartoons. This was Mother's reward for my respecting Father's piety.

Our big family gathering was not Friday-evening Shabbat but a

big fat Italian lunch above the store on Sundays. On the way to
Coney Island, Father would stop by a kosher delicatessen to take
away a corned beef sandwich, which he'd politely nibble at the table
amid a tangle of uncles, aunts, and cousins devouring Esther's legendary spaghetti and tomato sauce. Pizzas from Totonno's would
arrive to whoops of joy, and Father, being good humored, always fit
effortlessly into this almost Catholic riot. I'm sure scenes such as
this weren't uncommon in Brooklyn. Most Jewish families were a
mix of Orthodox and secular. The unspoken rule was to let each
other be and always put family harmony first.

The only thing my father insisted on was Talmud Torah classes
for my bar mitzvah, which was standard procedure for twelve-year-
old boys. After school, I'd walk to the synagogue and sit down
beside other fuzzy-faced prepubescent boys from around the neighborhood. Our teacher was the inspirational Rabbi Rosenfeld,
something of a mystic who'd recently discovered a branch of Has-
sidic Judaism called Breslov. These were the teachings of Rebbe
Nachman, an eighteenth-century Hassid who had developed revolutionary ideas about happiness that had resonated among Jews in
feudal, czarist Russia. It didn't matter if you were poor or oppressed;
by choosing to be happy, no matter what, you would slowly take
control of your life. As well as certain philosophical ideas, Breslovs
emphasized joyous rituals like singing and clapping.

Needless to say, such Jewish evangelism was lost on a lot of
Brooklyn mothers who clamored around my father, because as vice
president of the shul, he was the one person who could rein in the
strange new teacher. "We only sent our son to Hebrew school to get
bar-mitzvah'd," they'd complain. "I didn't want him to become
an ultraorthodox!" Twelve-year-old sons were coming home still
wearing tzitzit and yarmulkes and would sit silently in their bedrooms observing Shabbat, while in the living room, their fathers
were watching TV and pigging out on popcorn. In his jovial way,

Father would reassure all these concerned mothers that their sons weren't being brainwashed. A bar mitzvah was an education in the principles of Judaism, and yes, it was a rite of passage when a son stops acting like a kid and gets working for the Man Upstairs. It was not just a gold-framed photo for Mom's dressing table.

I'm sure such debates were common in the midfifties, a boom-town era when a growing majority of Jews were second- and third-generation Americans who wished to keep their Jewish identity but ditch all the heavy rituals. My father's crew running the local synagogue was skeptical of this "secular" fashion. To them, Judaism wasn't like an old song you mumbled along to; you learned the words and understood what they meant. You either lived Judaism or you didn't. And if a twelve-year-old came to his local synagogue to learn the religion of his forefathers, he was going to be taught properly by teachers who cared. What that young man did with his life thereafter was his own business.

On the day of my bar mitzvah in March 1955, I remember so clearly being escorted to the synagogue by my future brother-in-law, Martin and his father, Lou Wiederkehr, racked with fright. My father was already there at 7:00 A.M. It was the Saturday before Passover, and the building was packed to the gills with the entire neighborhood, including my entire extended family squashed into the front benches. I stood petrified on that stage for almost two hours as our community leader, Rabbi Kahane, read from Prophets and pulled out various passages about sacrifices, tithes, and the duty of charity. When my big moment came, I stepped up and sang the long *Shabbat HaGodol*, trying hard not to look at my mother choked up in the front row.

My voice was changing, and so was America's. "The Ballad of Davy Crockett" was number one that week, a novelty folk number about a comic book hero who chopped down trees, ran for Congress, and "died at the Alamo." Down South, a kid called Elvis was starting to make noise on Sun Records, still just a local stir that hadn't reached New York, but in every big city, R&B was already the fast-growing craze among white teenagers. Then, just a few months after my bar mitzvah, my sister got married and left home. Suddenly, I was alone in my very own bedroom, a man in God's eyes, just as my balls dropped and rock and roll began erupting. And that's when everything started to spin out of control.

I had already been exposed to doo-wop like "Gee" by the Crows, "Sh-Boom" by the Chords, and "Hearts of Stone" by Otis Williams and the Charms in 1954, but when I heard great rhythm and blues, I was hooked for life. The first hits I couldn't stop playing over and over were "Ain't That a Shame" and "Going to the River" by Fats Domino. Another obsession was "Shake, Rattle, and Roll" by Joe Turner. Whatever sound first hits you like a bolt of lightning at that mutant, mumbling, blanket-staining bar mitzvah age is generally what will tune your ears for the rest of your record-listening life. For me, it'll always be doo-wop and the raw sounds of Chuck Berry, James Brown, Sam Cooke, Little Richard, Hank Ballard, Ivory Joe Hunter, Lloyd Price, Johnny Ace, Ray Charles, Little Willie John, and without doubt, my favorite of all those early rockers, Fats Domino.

All these originals weren't just singers; most wrote their own songs and pushed their routines to the very edge—literally, like Fats, who pushed his piano around the stage, or Little Richard, who ran in and out of camera, or Chuck Berry, who strutted about like a duck. I had no idea, of course, that stage theatrics were all part of the black vaudeville traditions that had mixed up with the evangelism of rhythm and blues. All I knew, aged thirteen, was that nobody else on TV was daring such crazy antics.

I had to collect all these records, so I began selling ice cream or lugging deck chairs on the beach, which turned out to be an education in itself. In those days, if you could have held Manhattan upside down and shaken it, Coney Island is what would've dropped out. A summer heat wave could draw a million in one day—people as far the eye could see, crammed like sardines into the amusement parks, all over the beach, all the way down waist deep into the water. And I mean *everybody*: kids of all ages, mothers, fathers, senior citizens, sailors, soldiers, fortune-tellers, shoeshiners, thousands of blue-collar Romeos showing off to young ladies dolled up in bright red lipstick—every face of American life, swimsuited, bare-chested, overdressed, drunk, sunburned, asleep under newspapers, the lost, the found, and the still looking. Later in life, if I ever needed to visualize The Public, all I had to do was think of Coney Island on a hot summer's day.

Surf Avenue was the main subway terminus where all these swarms of people poured in. It was also the main drag for bars and curbside vendors. And like the choice of rides in the parks, there was every variety of steaming, greasy, sticky street food, most of it disgusting but perfectly edible when you're thirteen and carrying a pocketful of change. When it came to food, variety was the name of the game in Coney Island, which had inherited the "world's fair" tradition of the nineteenth century. Stalls sold everything from fried clams and crabs to knishes, sauerkraut, kebabs, chow mein, pizzas, hamburgers, crinkle-cut fries, steamed corn on the cob, roasted peanuts, waffles, doughs, cotton candy, toffee apples, marshmallow sticks, root beer, malted milk, and slices of fresh watermelon or pineapple. Hot dogs, or "franks" as we Brooklyn insiders called them, were even invented on Surf Avenue when the parks opened in the late nineteenth century. Some bright spark realized that a bread roll was the handiest way of serving frankfurters to passing crowds at ten cents a pop. A squirt of mustard, a funny name, and *bingo*!

For those of us who lived nearby and could get odd jobs, it was like growing up beside the circus. My grandparents had witnessed Coney Island's golden age in the twenties when wealthy Manhattan families would stay the night in plush hotels. The rich had long since moved down the Long Island coast, but in the fifties, Coney Island still had magic, albeit of a more working-class flavor. When I was a kid, Woody Guthrie lived just a block off the beach, where he wrote "Mermaid Avenue, that's the street where all the colors and the good folks meet." He was so moved by Coney Island's carnival atmosphere, he also wrote a collection of kids' songs, even a few tributes to Jewish culture.

On a busy day, I could make up to ten dollars on the beach— serious dough for a teenager—which I of course squirreled away into one of my secret holes. I make it sound easy, but I promise you, it was exhausting and embarrassing work wearing a heavy ice cream box in flesh-melting temperatures. To buy records, there were a few stores in Brooklyn, but for a full selection of R&B, I'd take the subway to Record Shack, or Bobby's Happy House in Harlem, and later Cousins' in the Bronx. In those days, the 45 and 33 formats had almost taken over, but many R&B records were still being pressed as 78 ten-inches—big heavy biscuits made from a substance called shellac, the precursor to vinyl. I much preferred the 45 RPM speed.

The first step in any teenage ambition is to fake the persona you wish to become; the next is believing it yourself. I started taking my new records to my grandparents' on Sundays and jiving like Martin Block to any cousin or aunt who'd listen to me. I'll never forget one Sunday lunch when my great-uncle Morris heard my plans to take over American show business. He smiled, gave me some sound advice, and put his finger straight on that idea of *durability* that Martin Block had referred to about "Tennessee Waltz." Uncle Morris may have been an olive oil importer, but he understood how New York operated. "Anyone can get into show business for a while," he warned, "but the true kings of Broadway are all about staying power."

It was time for me to investigate the machinery behind Martin Block's *Make Believe Ballroom*. I knew that *Billboard* compiled his charts, so on one of my city expeditions in the summer of 1956, I called into *Billboard*'s office, which was part of the Palace Theatre on Forty-Seventh and Broadway. "Excuse me, ma'am," I said to the lady at the front desk. "I'm really interested in your charts and was wondering if you need interns."

She kindly called out *Billboard*'s charts man, Tom Noonan, who was no more than thirty years old and surprisingly friendly. Knowing that I was far too young to get a job, I explained that I just wanted to copy his archives as a sort of school project. To my delight, he pulled out a pile of bound volumes, made space on the corner of a desk, and let me copy away in my left-handed scrawl.

I doubt anybody cared about my *project*, not even my mother. Fortunately, Tom Noonan let me come in during the holidays and after school to delve further and further backward to the very week I was born. I just kept copying and copying, learning names, watching Tom, and basically seeing how long I could last. Who knows what he and the other writers inside *Billboard* were thinking. Most of them were poor, unmarried music fanatics who practically lived in the office. Whatever sick obsession I had, they suffered from, too.

Lafayette High School was a giant four-story building on the west side of our neighborhood and had about four thousand kids. It's not that I didn't find the lessons interesting, but compared to *Billboard* or selling ice cream on Coney Island, the classroom felt like a straitjacket. I always sensed there was something different about me, but it took me a long to time realize what it was. I don't know what makes a person gay; I just remember standing on the side of the field, staring at our school's best athletes. Because I couldn't play sports, I just presumed it was normal to be so awestruck by other guys' strength and agility. I wasn't turned off by girls, and I had no problem picking out the pretty ones, but I was also becoming aware of the special camaraderie between guys that I think even the straightest of men can recognize is so strong. As the teenage merry-go-round started to spin faster, all these threads laced into an ever-tightening attraction, but it wasn't something I let *myself* think about. All I knew is that it would *kill* my father if he ever found out.

My eureka moment was watching Ricky Nelson on TV performing Fats Domino's "I'm Walking." That's when I *knew.* There was nothing camp in my mannerisms, no giveaways. If I ever got called names at school, it was because of the pranks I used to pull, like pretending a tiny transistor earphone was a hearing aid so I could listen to music during class. I knew I was tragically clumsy and something of a weirdo, but I also knew that the coolest thing about me was my record collection. Our school produced a lot of baseball players, including Sandy Koufax, Dodger Hall of Famer, but there'd actually been one pop star who'd graduated in the forties; Vic Damone was his name. He proved it could be done, so I just wanted other kids to know that I was riding into whatever stage-lit sunset Fats Domino and Ricky Nelson were singing in. I don't think anybody suspected I was gay, because in that era of Eisenhower and Doris Day, homosexuality was not something people would suspect, not even us dirty-mouthed Brooklyn brats. Even for me, it was buried so deep, I truly believed that if I ignored it long enough, it might go away, like the hiccups or a door-to-door salesman.

My secret probably caused me isolation, but I can't say that anything specific hurt or that I suffered. It was only when the music began flowing through me that I could feel something medicinal happening. I suddenly felt *better* without ever knowing there may have been an *unwellness* in the first place. I'd lie on my bed studying the small print on the sleeves: King, Apollo, Mercury, Aladdin, Excelsior, Atlantic, Miracle, Sun, Chess, Vee-Jay, Modern . . . all these castles and flags from across the land. Whether I was sitting at my desk in school or eating dinner with my parents, the only place I wanted to be was nearer the source of it all.

My obsession for records didn't seem to overly worry my parents, because a young man had to learn a trade, and officially, I was an intern at a respectable New York publication. The guys at *Billboard* had even given me a press card, which enabled me to bullshit my way into shows like Hank Ballard, Jackie Wilson, Lloyd Price, and others at the Brooklyn town hall. Plus, I was taking home scoops, like the day the Country Music Association paid a visit to the *Billboard* editor, Paul Ackerman, to complain about Elvis being put on the country chart. Paul Ackerman was an amazing teacher. He would tell me things, like the time folks from the Country Music Association came up to complain about Elvis Presley's Sun records hitting the country music charts, which in those days only ran to about ten or fifteen positions. They said to him, "Paul, you know this is nothing but nigger music." He felt ashamed that he didn't just throw them out of his office, but those folks carried a lot of weight. Paul was a sensitive intellectual and a true crusader for R&B and black people.

My father saw I was good with money and still harbored hopes of my becoming a doctor or a lawyer; however, to his credit, he let me find my own path and just watched over my shoulder from a respectful distance. He befriended Tom Noonan, which was easy because although Tom wasn't Jewish, he was a devout Irish Catholic whose extended family included a few nuns in Boston. My father showed his gratitude to Tom for taking me under his wing by inviting Mrs. Noonan to the garment center. In those days, Tom was probably earning as little as my father, so it was no small gesture to fit Mrs. Noonan out in a beautiful new suit and coat.

It was editor in chief Paul Ackerman, however, who made the biggest impression on my father. Ackerman wasn't religious, but he was a fine specimen of the upright, Jewish intellectual mensch. He was educated, principled, and viewed *Billboard*'s daily work as serving a higher cause. Paul had personal interests, such as poetry and horticulture, but it was his crusade as a music writer and belief in editorial substance that made him a renaissance man of the twentieth century. There's usually a rich businessman in every Jewish family, sometimes several; they're common species in any synagogue. For religious Jews like my father, the highest rank of man was the outstanding rabbi or community leader who stood up to be counted. Paul Ackerman was clearly one of these.

My father respected *Billboard* and was proud of the connections I was making; what frightened him was that I'd gotten sucked into music so young and had all but abandoned school. Paul Ackerman had studied English literature at Columbia, so there was little chance of me turning out like the boss. Even by Brooklyn's working-class standards in the late fifties, I was a freak. What my parents couldn't have known was that *Billboard*'s charts were nonetheless providing me with a solid education for the career I was about to embark on. Among many things, I was learning how TV and radio concentrated public attention on big-name stars, whereas sales reports revealed how vast and diverse the marketplace really was. As well as compiling figures from all over the United States, Tom received European charts, too. Watching him figure it all out was like biblical class. Names, names, and more names. You had to remember as many names as you could—artists, song titles, labels, publishers, songwriters. But once you could piece together all the little references, interesting patterns appeared.

I'd noticed all the foreign songs when I copied *Billboard*'s archives backward into the forties. Every month, a surprising number of entries were records directly licensed from Italy, France, or Germany. Some were localized cover versions that had been translated or totally revamped on Tin Pan Alley. The same was happening abroad, where American hits were being translated or repackaged into foreign language mutations. So, the very first golden rule I learned about the music business was that good songs fly around the world just as easily as food recipes or fashions in the garment trade.

This came as no major revelation to a Brooklyn child. You'd be hard pressed to find a better symbol of the music business than Luna Park or the Steeplechase—a swarming, multicolored amusement park with its big rides that draw the crowds, and all its smaller curiosities and foreign-themed food stalls that added an element of wonder. At the end of the day, people don't care where things originally come from. The fact that something might at first seem a bit strange is probably what hooks them. If it hits the spot, they'll soon make it their own.

Billboard's charts in those days were as accurate as they could be. There were three separate charts reflecting record store sales, jukebox plays, and airplay; there was also a separate chart for sheet music sales, which was quite important back then. There was also a chart that combined it all, called the "Honor Roll of Hits," but as Top 40 radio started to really take hold all over the country, Tom came up with an idea of using the Top 40 charts, combined just with sales, to make a Top 100 chart. The Top 100 became an invaluable tool at a critical juncture when speed and timing became the essence for getting the news out with regard to hits.

Tom Noonan and Paul Ackerman were my first mentors, but of all the lucky breaks I got at *Billboard*, there was one freak encounter that changed my destiny like no other. I was sitting in a music review session one Wednesday evening when I first laid my eyes on this potbellied, buffalo-shouldered force of nature. His name was Syd Nathan, the owner of Cincinnati label King Records. He was about fifty-five, although he looked closer to seventy and was so borderline blind he had to wrap these Coke-bottle glasses around his head or risk bumping into every doorpost. I'd never seen glasses like his. Set in reinforced frames, the lenses were so heavy and bulbous, when he moved his head around, his eyes appeared to zoom in and out in different sizes.

When Syd Nathan spoke, which he liked to do, it was best to focus on his mouth, where this fur-balled wheeze, a result of chronic asthma, emitted the most fabulous show business spiel I'd ever heard. His lungs and vocal chords were so shot, he had to strain at his highest register to get the words out. Syd talked and talked this high-voltage chaos of knowledge, gags, and anecdotes, stuff coming in from all angles. For every writer in *Billboard*, and especially Paul Ackerman, the old man was an American legend. He'd sold tens of millions of records in hard times to mostly country and black customers. He was the prototype record man whose crazy genius left me spellbound.

He'd dropped into *Billboard* to present some new releases, which, if reviewed favorably, would probably sell him about seventy-five thousand copies among jukebox operators alone. But unlike all the other label toppers who'd always talk up their dreck, Syd just played his records and hung around for hours to chat, pick up news, and hear to what the competition had to offer. "Load of crap" seemed to be his catchphrase for all the cheap talk the music business has always produced in vast quantities—back then, as today and always.

In that session, the reviewers were sifting through stacks of new releases when one writer muttered, "Oh, let's not bother with these Jubilee records. I hear they're going out of business." Syd sat up straight and peered out of his Coke bottles. "Is that how you talk about me when I'm not here?" He had a way of silencing rooms. "Just listen to the records," he told the reviewers. "Jubilee's problems aren't yours. There might be something on one of those records you might need to know."

"Jerry Blaine must be a good friend of yours!" joked a writer, referring to Jubilee's boss.

"No. I'm suing the son of a bitch," said Syd, flat as a pancake. We played the Jubilee releases, and sure enough, one song shone out— "White Silver Sands" by Don Rondo, which went on to become a hit.

When the session wrapped up, I got my chance to flap away like a seal. "Oh, my God, what an honor, Mr. Nathan. I've bought some of your records."

"Oh, yeah? Which ones?"

"Hank Ballard and James Brown, sir."

I obviously made an impression, because every time Syd dropped into *Billboard*, he'd always stop by Tom's office to say hello. One day, however, he began quizzing me with the look of a concerned father. Maybe he'd asked Paul Ackerman or Tom Noonan what I was doing hanging around, but whatever pathetic, orphaned figure I cut through his Coke bottles, the old man must have recognized something of himself decades earlier.

I wouldn't know his story until years later, but sometime around 1910, when Syd Nathan was only five, he'd been given his uncle's drum kit, which he whacked all through his unhappy childhood. It was probably what kept him sane, because he was so handicapped by his eyesight, he couldn't see the blackboard and failed every exam. His asthma was so chronic, he could barely run around the playground from the kids teasing him about his glasses. By the time he was fifteen, he could take no more. He followed his ears straight through the school gate and drummed his heart out in jazz clubs, weddings, and events around the Midwest. That's when Syd's life began.

His dream in the 1920s was to become a star drummer with his Forest Bradford Orchestra, but in those turbulent times when radio blew up and sent the phonograph industry crashing into a fifteen-year crisis, only the very best musicians could carve out a living. Poverty, recession, and disillusionment eventually pushed Syd onto the shadier side of life. He worked in a pawnshop. He got caught up in some political feud between Cincinnati clans. He bribed city workers to vote for some local kingpin in union elections, a "job experience" that almost put him in jail. Later, he ran a jewelry store that kept getting burgled, and he promoted wrestling matches and ran a shooting gallery that landed him in court for not paying prize winners. As a young man in the Great Depression, Syd Nathan had been what they call *a colorful character,* but once midlife hit, he returned to his passion. He began selling radios, phonographs, and secondhand records, until in 1943, he rolled all his life's experiences into King Records, the pioneer label that produced many of the seminal country and R&B hybrids that led to rock and roll.

By the time he laid his goggle eyes on me, Syd Nathan had done it all. He was wise enough, rich enough, don't-give-a-damn enough to spot a dropout who had no place in civilian society and point him to the nearest circus. "Kid," he said one afternoon in 1959, "I love *Billboard.* Paul Ackerman is the most honest man in the music business. I can tell him anything and know it'll be kept a secret.

But look, do you want to be in the game, or do you want to be a spectator? Because that's what *Billboard* is, a spectator. You'll be reporting what other people are doing. You'll be discovering records after someone else has signed them. And *maybe* you'll be participating in helping them become hits. But don't you want to do it *yourself*?"

"Yes, I do," I replied in what was to be the only marriage pledge I ever stuck to.

"Well, come to work with me." He smiled. "Come to Cincinnati."

I didn't know it then, but the single-biggest tragedy of the record-producing vocation is that the biological sons of label founders usually don't have the ears or gut force to carry on Daddy's adventure. The entire history of the record industry is littered with disaster sons who never should have been handed the keys to the castle. Syd was the oldest and the most successful of all the independent barons, but he didn't have any heirs, not even a spoiled brat to waste his hopes on. His only child, Nat, was what he always described as "almost spastic"—probably autistic, not that doctors even knew such terms in those days.

I was also too young to suspect that my real father might be hostile to this unexpected twist in the plot. When I brought home the amazing news about Syd Nathan's invitation to Cincinnati, Dad didn't look so happy and insisted on calling into *Billboard* to ask Paul Ackerman questions.

"Syd Nathan has a branch office in New York," Paul Ackerman told my father. "Why don't you meet him yourself?" To my horror, father telephoned King Records but had to wait months for Syd's next trip to New York. I was so embarrassed, I wouldn't talk to either of my parents for weeks.

When the big day came, my father and I arrived at King's New York branch on West Fifty-Fourth Street, where Syd was standing on the stoop. Syd must have seen my father tossing his cigar into the gutter or, considering his eyesight, only had to smell the cheapness. Syd pulled a fat Cuban from his pocket. "Here, have one of mine," he told my father, whose face lit up like a candle.

"I know you're a busy man just in from Cincinnati," began Father. "I don't want to take up much of your time. I have only two questions."

"Mr. Steinbigle," interrupted Syd. "*I* have only one question. Can I ask it first?"

"Yes, of course."

"How much money do you have?"

I almost shriveled into the nearest manhole, seeing my poor father's face turn beetroot. As if this whole meeting wasn't humiliating enough, Syd knew I was a poor kid. "I don't own a business," choked Father, trying to get the words off his parched tongue. "I work in the garment center. I've worked there all my life, and I've worked my way up. Seymour and his sister never wanted for anything . . . always went to summer camp."

"Mr. Steinbigle," interrupted Syd again, "all I wanted to know is if you have enough money to buy Seymour a newspaper route."

"A newspaper route?" My father was now totally confused. "But Seymour's never done anything like that."

"Listen, your son has shellac in his veins. All he wants to do is be is in the music business. I know him well enough by now to know that if he can't be in the music business, it's going to *ruin* his life. He'll wind up doing nothing and will have to deliver newspapers. But I can get him into the music business."

My dear father took a severe beating that day. Fortunately, he was a sensible, religious man who believed that his son's welfare must always come before his own pride. While he was looking out the window lost in thought, I was glowing like a Christmas tree on that train back to Brooklyn. I'd just been given the ultimate compliment from an old master; the legendary Syd Nathan thought I had the signs of a record man. Back on Dahill Road that evening, my parents began packing my bags to leave home at the end of June. Urgent behavior considering it was still only April.

2. SYD AND THE KID

It was summer, and I was fifteen and aching for adventure. I took the plane to Cincinnati, where Syd was waiting at arrivals. "Welcome to Kentucky!" He smiled, because the airport was in Covington, just over the state line.

Syd squeezed behind the wheel of his Buick and drove us down the highway, squinting ominously out of his porthole glasses. This I hadn't been expecting. A man this blind never should have been given a license, or knowing Syd, he'd probably bribed a cop to get one. I'd later learn that he'd had been in so many car wrecks, he was once sued by a friend. Whenever Syd drove, which he loved doing, it was best to look sideways at the scenery and focus on the radio.

Everything was green in Kentucky, and the air tasted different—warmer, stickier, filled with pollen and bugs. "This is WCKY," said the voice on the radio, "broadcasting from Covington, Kentucky, just six minutes over the L&N Bridge to Fountain Square, Cincinnati, Ohio, your Queen City." And just like the radioman described, we passed over the Ohio River, and there she was on the opposite bank, "Cincinnat*ah*" as Syd liked to pronounce his beloved hometown.

This was to be my first of two summer internships, working at King and staying at the Nathan house for about four weeks each. I soon sensed that Syd's wife, Zella, wasn't too keen on me being there, which I could understand, because I hated sleeping in the same room as Nat, who was just too weird for comfort. Nat was my age, hugely overweight, and he babbled like a child. He actually came from Syd's first marriage, and I knew he was being teased to death at school for being a "retard." Of course, Nat was hoping I'd be his best buddy and stuck to me like shit to a blanket.

Fortunately, King and the actual city of Cincinnati felt far more welcoming. Although Cincinnati was nearer the Canadian border than I'd ever been, there was something almost Huckleberry Finn about the riverfront. Old steamboats sailed to Louisville, and barges carrying heavy materials went down all the way down into the Mississippi. It made sense that King Records would be here, tapped into America's old river network where so much great music came from. Syd was just a few hours' drive to Nashville, Detroit, and Chicago, where King had been a major player since the war.

In the forties, King Records had started out as a country label and quickly built up an impressive catalog of country stars, such as Cowboy Copas, the Delmore Brothers, Grandpa Jones, the Stanley Brothers, Wayne Raney, Hawkshaw Hawkins, Hank Penny, Bonnie Lou, the duo Don Reno and Red Smiley, and Moon Mullican, a honky-tonk singer-songwriter who mixed up black and country music a few years before Bill Haley. Throughout the fifties, however, R&B began taking over as King's main specialty. Syd's newest star was James Brown, but he also had Hank Ballard, Little Willie John, Joe Tex, Bill Doggett, Bull Moose Jackson, Ivory Joe Hunter, Earl Bostic, Lonnie Johnson, Freddie King, Otis Williams and the Charms, and many others.

The whole operation was actually several interrelated companies spread out over a yard of neighboring buildings. Along an old train line at the back was the pressing plant called Royal Plastics, where Syd had first launched King in 1943. At the time, barely any record pressers or rural distributors had survived the Depression, so, from day one, Syd's crazy dream was to help rebuild the industry he'd loved so much as a young man. Talk about the blind leading the blind; the label's first-ever record was "Filipino Baby" by Cowboy Copas, and Syd stood by as the first turd of shellac glooped down onto the plate. An employee in a white coat lowered the presser but couldn't lift the thing back open. It was then they looked at each other and realized they'd forgotten to fit the machinery with pull-back springs. They grabbed a six-foot crowbar and managed to clunk the press back open. Syd then prized the disc off the plate with a pocketknife. Like a Catholic priest preparing Holy Communion, he held the charred and chipped mess aloft and declared to his staff "This . . . *record* . . . cost $65,000!" Thus began King Records.

As early as 1947, Syd announced to *Business Weekly* that his mission was to "create a market," which is exactly what he succeeded in doing. Around that factory, various offices, workshops, warehouses, and a recording studio were added. Everything was done in-house; recording, mastering, sleeve artwork, printing, pressing. Trucks arrived with chemicals and paper and then drove back out with neatly packaged boxes of records. He recruited a sales network and began opening wholesale distribution depots, city by city. He then diversified his first-party operations with sub-labels, Queen and Federal, bought out indies such as De Luxe, Bethlehem, and Four Star, and provided distribution and sometimes manufacturing services for a whole host of third-party labels, such as Bel-Tone, Willow, Miracle, Sensation, 4 Star, Fairlane, New Disc, Starday, Huron, and Cadence.

As volumes increased and stars were born, Syd quickly understood the importance of songwriting and set up several publishing companies, always run by proven songwriters. He had Lois Music, named after an old flame, but the most successful was Jay & Cee, created for King's talented A&R man, Henry Glover, a black songwriter. Giving Glover his big break as a producer as well, Syd promised, "I'm going to get you out of jail and put you in church," hence the company's initials. Henry Glover was one of the most talented music men I've ever met. Still to this day, I carry on the fight to get him inducted into the Rock and Roll Hall of Fame. As well as feeding King's own roster of R&B singers, Jay & Cee provided songs for competitors such as Ray Charles, Chubby Checker, and Aretha Franklin. Other A&R producers included Ralph Bass, Sonny Thompson, and most important of all, Henry Stone, who later went on to great success in Miami with TK Records.

In less than ten years, Syd Nathan created a diverse and bustling marketplace around a community of talented music fanatics. King was by far the biggest indie in America, directly employing about four hundred staffers, providing services for many hundreds of affiliates, and covering every genre under the sun: country, bluegrass, hot jazz, western swing, Delta blues, bebop, boogie, jive, polka, spirituals, kids' songs, even a few mambo and calypso records he picked up in Trinidad and Cuba. Curiously, Syd didn't do that much pop. He stuck to the edges—both musically and geographically. He did try, however unsuccessfully, with Guy Mitchell, Rosemary's sister, Betty Clooney, and finally Steve Lawrence.

Over two summers, I was moved around the company to learn every aspect of the record-making business. Syd was particularly proud of his pressing facility, a luxury he often described as "milling our own biscuits." One day, to my absolute horror, he ordered me into that back building, a stinking shithole of heavy machinery and barrels of acid, where a Nina Simone version of "I Loves You, Porgy" happened to be on the production line. A technician put me in front of a machine where a turd of melted vinyl slid down. My job was to firmly press the plate, lift it back open, and repeat the action all day. With my legendary butterfingers, I was terrified I'd weld a Nina Simone record onto my hand. I managed to press about ten copies and then ran out and begged Syd, "Please don't send me back to New York, but I really don't want to go the plating department again." He didn't fire me or even lose his temper, but whenever I hear that record, I always laugh at its line, "Don't let him handle me with his hot hands."

I was usually given various assignments, but some days Syd let me follow him around. As a boss, he spent a lot of time working his magic down telephone lines, fixing problems, and motivating the troops with his trademark brand of bullshit-intolerant humor. He always seemed happiest in the studio, either watching or producing, sometimes picking up the drumsticks to rattle out a rhythm. Occasionally, he wrote songs, usually the lyrics, because he had a sharp wit for catchy slogans and striking imagery. My favorite of his was "Signed, Sealed, and Delivered," a hit by Cowboy Copas. Syd was an entrepreneur, but you could see his love for music was the heartbeat of the enterprise.

His greatest strength, however, was distribution. By about 1952, even major companies didn't have the kind of regional operations Syd had—thirty-four branches coast to coast. In small cities like Birmingham, Alabama, just one staffer would cover an area from a store in a bad neighborhood. He'd take orders, pack boxes, and, once a week, fill his car with records and stop anywhere he saw an antenna by the side of the road. In bigger cities, there'd be two—an inside and an outside man. In New York, three. I don't doubt they all slipped payola into the pockets of disc jockeys, but it wouldn't have been big amounts. Most of these small-town jocks were music nuts living on scraps. In those days, nobody was doing it to get rich.

Even Syd was no Rockefeller. He owned his nice house in Cincinnati, he had a condo in Miami, and he'd bought most of the buildings that King operated from. He was careful with cash and always invested his winnings into real estate or affiliate companies run by people he believed in. I remember him explaining on one road trip that although he could easily afford a Cadillac, a top Buick had the same standard of engine but was almost half the price. He was always plainly dressed in old suits and didn't seem to care about gold watches, fancy restaurants, or any of the glittery trappings you'd associate with a record mogul.

The one thing he did love was traveling. As well as driving all over the Midwest and regularly visiting New York, he'd fly off on extended business trips to meet key partners, in particular his main man in London, L. G. Wood, the managing director of EMI, which handled King's overseas distribution. From London, Syd would usually travel onward to Paris, Hamburg, Milan, and elsewhere to meet his publishers. A popular destination was the Sanremo Music Festival in Italy, which was Europe's biggest music fair, albeit geared more toward publishers than record companies.

One of my favorite Sanremo stories involves my friend, Kuni Murai, who had a label I brought into Warner Music Japan that had, among other artists, Yellow Magic Orchestra. I had decided to go to Sanremo at the last minute, and asked Warner's to get me tickets. They told me that the tickets were sold out, but that if I didn't care about going the first day (which I didn't) they could give me Paul Simon's and Rod Stewart's passes, since they were performing the first night. I invited Kuni, and we were backstage having a ball, when one of the guards came up to me and said "Rod Stewart? You don't look like Rod Stewart." Without skipping a beat I said to him, "If you don't believe who I am, just ask my friend Paul Simon over here," and that was Kuni Murai. Syd taught me a lot about the importance of international and reinforced something I had believed as a young boy: that hits could come from anywhere. "Volare (Nel Blu Dipinto Di Blu)" was only one of many great worldwide hit songs to emerge from Sanremo. He was so good at making friends in all the right places, he somehow schmoozed his way into Cincinnati's WASP club, which was amazing considering how much the Midwest aristocracy was genetically allergic to loud Jews. Their private society was a grand old house on Garfield Street—the Cuvier Press Club—members only, wooden décor, big leather armchairs everywhere. Syd got Al Rogoff, his lawyer, to join, and puff away on Cuban cigars they mightily did as judges and city hall bigwigs sipped whiskies in nearby armchairs. Syd and Rogoff almost looked the part, except that when he first took me to the Cuvier Press Club, Zella roped him into taking Nat, who couldn't sit still or stop babbling. None of the old Dutch boys looked up from behind their newspapers at the Jewish riot in the corner, but you could smell two centuries of distilled racism in the air—not that Syd seemed to care.

The funny thing about Syd is that every side at some point or another accused him of bad manners. When neighbors realized who was behind much of the R&B (they called it "nigger music") on the radio, Syd's front windows got mysteriously smashed by unidentified flying bottles. When the government launched its anti-payola crusade, they picked on the white bosses behind R&B like Syd, whose offices were the first to be raided by the FBI. Although investigators found no incriminating evidence, Syd then pissed off his peers by publicly admitting that yes, payola was deejay extortion personally costing him $2,000 a month. After Syd was dead, music historians would accuse him and all his competitors of exploiting black musicians.

Who do you believe? I don't doubt that when it came to contracts, Syd took some advantage of black musicians, but you can bet he screwed the hillbillies just as hard. At least Syd actually signed contracts, issued royalty statements, and paid his artists what they were owed at a time when most of his competitors got away with doing none of the above. As one of his R&B competitors, the notorious Morris Levy, joked to one black artist who came in looking for royalties, "Royalties? If you want royalties, go to fucking England!"

Cheating one-hit wonders was a slob's business. Syd Nathan, on the other hand, had built a much larger company and was interested in careers; he *needed* long-term career artists to keep it all ticking over. He did everything in-house to keep costs to a minimum, knowing that most releases would lose money. If he didn't pay large advances, or just paid small advances as tokens, it was because the risk was all his. Most first-time recording artists were amateurs or touring musicians, happy to just make a record to show their friends and help get gigs. But make no mistake, when a record hit, even the most clueless rookies figured out damn quick how to move up the food chain. Syd was always standing by to mentor the cream of the crop to sustained success. He always looked after his best people and entered into new types of partnerships as their careers grew.

Take James Brown. When Syd heard the first record, "Please, Please, Please," he pulled one of his comical faces. "Son, do you really have to ask *please* one hundred times? Haven't you got nothing else to say for yourself?" James Brown was too young and too terrified to fire a smart answer back at the boss, but he'd eventually learn. To everyone's delight, that first record blew up and sold a million copies. Had the same jackpot fallen into the laps of one of the dirtier labels, James Brown might have been a one-hit blunder. Syd, however, took James Brown under his wing, got him touring, got songwriters writing and collaborating with him on hot new material. Syd made sure James Brown was earning and working on a career. James Brown was a country boy with little education, but he learned how to take care of business; years later, he was flying around in his own jet, performing at dictators' private parties for huge fees. And when James Brown was his own king, believe me, he was no saint to his own musicians, writers, or employees. It's a tough job, but someone's got to do it.

Syd enjoyed being crude and irreverent and was easily misunderstood. He was always teetering on the edge of rudeness and obscenity, but I think that's what talented people trusted about him. He'd be yapping away in his animated way when he'd suddenly call out, "Put that on a hard six!" and then rip a loud fart and continue on his spiel like nothing happened. It was mile-a-minute madness, but his extreme behavior had a way of sorting the men from the boys. The fainthearted couldn't handle Syd Nathan, and the true characters loved him and played him at his own game. And he was very witty. On one road trip, we stopped off at a public toilet where I heard a giant crack from inside Syd's stall. He was so fat, he'd snapped the toilet seat clean in two. He stepped out proudly holding up the two pieces. "I'm keeping these for my half-assed friends!"

The black and country musicians had all grown up on tour buses, but there was something about Syd's fearlessness that I think resonated with the serious intellectuals like Paul Ackerman. Syd cut straight through all the bullshit—the dumbness, the racism, the political correctness, the fear of failing, everything. Once, we were stopped at traffic lights in a poor neighborhood in Louisville when Nat suddenly shouted in full earshot of all the pedestrians, "Daddy, there sure are a lot of niggers here!"

Syd turned around to the back seat with his little grin. "Niggers? Nigg-*errs*? Son, are you trying to get us killed? This isn't Cincinnati where I can protect you. This is Dixie. You gotta call them *nigg-aaahz*." The lights turned green, and Syd hit the gas, which really wasn't wise, because on that very road trip, he nearly drove us straight into the Nashville train.

Oh, yes, Syd Nathan used the N-word as well as every other

profanity you'd expect from a former jazz drummer and wrestling promoter. Everything was fair game inside Syd's wild world, but he was not racist, unlike most people in border towns like Cincinnati or Baltimore, which were arguably worse than down South. In the Cuvier Press Club, I witnessed one revealing incident. The black opera singer Leontyne Price appeared on TV and a tableful of drunken men started throwing fruit at the screen. Syd turned around and shouted at them to crawl back into their cages at the zoo. It got him so angry he got up and left. I don't think Syd was politically committed to the cause of black people in the way that Paul Ackerman was. Talent was Syd's obsession. I just think he was too blind and too ugly to judge anyone on physical criteria. If you could sing, play, write, tell a good story, or even just engage with his humor, he didn't care what you looked like or where you came from. And the proof was King, half of which was black, not that I ever once heard him brag about being an equal opportunities employer for the socially disadvantaged.

I should know; I was bouncing around with all the multicolored oddballs he'd collected along the way, which is how I had my first-ever sexual experience. Syd had pressed up about a thousand special order records of old New Orleans King artists for two busy stores, one in the heart of New Orleans, the other at their airport. The guy they sent up to check the product was about my age and, like me, ate records for breakfast. Syd pulled a bill from his wallet and told me, "Why don't you take Monte out for a nice dinner tonight." He then jotted down an address and explained in his flat logic, "What I like about the Mills Cafeteria is that you see the food and you put it on your plate." I followed Syd's directions, but his beloved diner was one of those canteens where food sits around sweating all day. Instead, I found a Chinese restaurant nearby, which was what I missed most about Brooklyn.

Over the best meal I'd had in weeks, I began really feeling something with Monte, this handsome guy from New Orleans. He, of course, had a lilting Southern drawl that I found as exotic as he probably found my Brooklynese twang. By the time we were finishing our coffees, we both knew what was about to happen. We headed straight back to his hotel room.

"This is my first time," he said, "and I feel very strange about it."

"It's my first time, too."

We both knew what to do, but neither of us had a clue what to say afterward. Fortunately, Monte broke the stunned silence with a nice idea. "I think we should go see some burlesque. They have it in New Orleans, and they must have it here." It was late, but the receptionist pointed us to a club, where I sank into my seat and watched my first burlesque show, practically glowing in the dark. Now I knew what sex was like. I hadn't chickened out, and the way the guy's eyes were twinkling in the stage light, he didn't seem to be regretting it either.

My summers in Cincinnati confirmed what I always knew; I *belonged* in the music business. Aged seventeen and just out of high school, I enrolled on a journalism course at Long Island University, the plan being to improve my writing and editing skills and then stroll into a well-paid job at *Billboard*. Unfortunately, my internships at King had thrown up doubts. Having seen the excitement and wealth and satisfaction of Syd's life, I wasn't so sure anymore if I was cut out for journalism, and when term started, I didn't turn up for classes. As any young floater who's been in a similar position will tell you, my first September out of high school was frightening. I hadn't felt any pressure throughout summer, but it suddenly hit me that I needed to get my act together. Luckily, Tom Noonan took me back into *Billboard*'s chart department full-time for eighty dollars a week.

The sixties were dawning, and the charts were starting to really matter. Since the birth of the Hot 100, the phone was hopping with all kinds of sweet-talking label bosses and promotions men. Tom was too Catholic to countenance anyone accepting bribery, but he sometimes turned a blind eye to the rest of us enjoying other forms of human kindness.

Motown boss Berry Gordy, who hadn't scored a number one yet, called into the office regularly with his chief salesman, Barney Ales, and of course I was only too happy to talk music with them. One day, Gordy rang up from Detroit all excited. "I've got a number one!"

"Where? I didn't see it."

"It's not recorded yet. We've written it, and it's definitely gonna be a number one. The reason I'm calling you, Seymour, is because I'd like you to come up to Detroit when we record it."

"What? But why me?"

"Because you've got good ears."

"That's nice of you to think so, Berry, but listen, there's this promotions man you've got to meet. His name is Pete Bennett, and he works on Tenth Avenue in a distributor called Cambridge. I see all these guys, and he's absolutely the best."

"Both of you come up. Bring him with you. Talk to this guy and call me back."

When Pete Bennett and I got to Detroit, we were treated royally. The song in question turned out to be "Please Mr. Postman" by the Marvelettes, which Berry's people duly recorded as we hung around watching. We went home to New York feeling like number ones ourselves, but the record took surprisingly long to smash. It hung on the airwaves for six months, climbing ever steadily up the charts until it reached number one, Motown's first of many, the week before Christmas.

I'd love to tell you that it was me who twisted Tom Noonan's arm to give Berry Gordy his elusive number one, but I'm sure it was a legitimate winner, and anyway, I'd moved back down to Cincinnati by then. But you get the picture. You needed a great song to begin with, but everything else—airplay, press, TV, distribution, store visibility, jukeboxes, and, of course, net sales—the whole hit system ran on people making other people happy.

It was impossible not to love all the fun happening around *Billboard*, which had entered a golden age of influence. But I knew my prospects at *Billboard* would always be limited. The chart department was Tom's baby, and all he needed was one or two juniors. When it came to writing, I happily spent days poring over the liner notes of, say, a Champion Jack Dupree compilation that King released in 1961. If I had a few nights, I could spin a good yarn, but to make it as a music reporter, you had to bang out two thousand words every day and still find the time to ring scores of people for quotes, insights, and scoops. That just wasn't me. I knew I was more of a Syd Nathan than a Paul Ackerman, and I suspect both men discussed that very issue, because in October 1961, I got invited by Syd back down to Cincinnati to work as one of King's A&R and publicity trainees.

Syd and Paul even placed a bulletin in *Billboard* announcing that "Seymour Steinbigle, known as 'The Beagle' in the trade," would be working in King's A&R and publicity. What the fuck was this?

"St-ein-big-le?" He'd squirm like he'd bitten into a rotten apple. "You want people to associate you with *this . . . name*?"

"But, Syd, I'm the last male to carry it."

"What, you mean there are no others anywhere?"

"My father's two brothers changed their name to Steinberg."

"Your uncles were right. Look, kid, do yourself a favor and put *Steinbigle* out of its misery."

"But what about my father?"

"If you're serious about the music business, you need a name. We're all just names. Hello, I'm Syd Nathan, who are you?"

Syd was no bullshitter. The only place for misplaced sentimentalism was between the grooves of a tear-jerking hit record. When it came to the pursuit of happiness, you had to be ruthless. His own father had dispensed with the ancestral Galician name *Kriviansky* and adopted Nathan. It was a courageous choice considering the old man's first name was Nat. Nat Nathan—beat that for punchy. Syd, whose full name was Sydney, made name chopping a company ritual. Any time a hillbilly singer or a Jewish lawyer walked in the door with a mouthful of a name, Syd would take out his butcher's knife and chop away, whether they liked it or not.

I just ignored Syd's bitching until one afternoon he snapped. In the main office, there was a loudspeaker to page staffers who didn't have their own telephone. The operator announced "Seymour Steinbigle" eight or nine times, but when Syd could hear the word no more, his unmistakable voice wheezed over the same loudspeaker: "It's Stein or Beagle or back to New York!" You've heard of *baptism by fire*; this was my baptism by threat of being fired. Everyone in the office looked at me horrified as I sulked to the telephone. Humiliated and holding back my tears, I did what I was told. A beagle was a small English hound, which of course meant that anybody picking up a secretary's note with SEEMORE BEAGLE scrawled beside a number was going to assume I was a charity urging volunteers to walk impounded dogs. So, I picked the simplicity of Seymour Stein, and sure enough, I never had to spell my name out again.

After equipping me with my new persona, Syd sent me out on the road for ten days with James Brown. This wasn't the first time I'd met a star, but it was probably the first time I got to see what it takes to build a world-class legend. James Brown was an obsessive worker watching his rivals like a hawk. He had his favorite singers and songwriters, but when it came to stage performing, his number-one envy at the time was Jackie Wilson, a former boxer and by far the most athletic dancer on the R&B scene. James had his own little moves and electrifying stage presence, but he badly wanted to do the splits like Jackie Wilson. My God, I watched poor James Brown try so hard he almost tore himself a birth canal.

My main job at King was listening to tapes with the A&R staff and sending out records to Syd's promotions men, a nationwide network of radio pluggers who, along with the names I picked up at *Billboard*, laid the foundations of my rapidly growing address book. It was an education, but after two years in Cincinnati, my itchy feet became unbearable. I missed the big city and wasn't earning enough to live and eat comfortably. Syd's attitude to trainees was like that old African proverb: "I won't *give* you any of *my* fish, but I will teach you *how* to fish." I knew he wasn't going to crane-lift me into a managerial post; he had plenty of talent and experience to choose from. I didn't cost much, so he'd let me watch and help out until I was ready to make my own road. Syd had become my godfather, and I knew he'd always be a phone number away for advice, contacts, and interesting news. My success or failure was up to nobody but myself.

I also had long-overdue family business to clear up. Syd had set me up in a small apartment in Cincinnati, but my stuff was still back in Brooklyn. I sensed my folks were waiting for me to move out of Dahill Road so that they could prepare for their own retirement. Dad was sixty, and I knew he and my mother were already scouting around for a nicer apartment and thumbing through vacation brochures. They'd reached that vantage point toward the end of a long and arduous journey when they badly wanted to enjoy what time and health they had left. So, I left Cincinnati and moved into a place of my own on Ocean Parkway, which is where I got an unexpected call from Syd, this time about a job in New York.

It was a promotions job with Herb Abramson, the mad dentist

who had cofounded Atlantic Records with Ahmet Ertegun. It was common knowledge, just when Atlantic was taking off, that Herb had been drafted to West Germany to take care of Uncle Sam's teeth. There, he'd developed a taste for cocaine, which he was able to order on prescription, supposedly as a gum-numbing agent for dental work. Coked out his mind and filling GI cavities, Herb started screwing an American servicewoman even though his wife back in New York was Miriam, Atlantic's ballbuster manager who ran the whole back line—the accounts, the contracts, the office. Fortunately for Atlantic, Ahmet sought the advice of Paul Ackerman for a replacement, and he recommended his star reporter, Jerry Wexler, so things worked out fine.

Talk about the show business rule "Never stick your dick in the cash register," or in this instance, its sub-clause, "If you do, don't try anything stupid." When Herb returned to New York with his new sweetheart, Miriam filed for divorce and wouldn't let him into his own office. The other problem was that Ahmet Ertegun had turned into a nocturnal creature who'd go out to clubs almost every night in search of talent. Ahmet had left the whole nine-to-five running of the company to Miriam for so long, he couldn't fire her or even take sides without endangering the whole company. On Paul Ackerman's wise advice, Ahmet eventually set up a sister label for Herb. Called Atco, it was a neat compromise in theory; unfortunately, Herb was too fucked up by then. He lost faith and cashed out of Atlantic—a terrible mistake.

Syd felt sorry for Herb's predicament, however self-inflicted, and agreed to help him start a new production company plugged into King's distribution. As a favor back, Herb was going to offer me a job. I of course jumped down the telephone because it was in New York. "I'm not going to stop you," warned Syd. "You know I think of you as a son, but Seymour, you gotta know this man is crazy. He's a genius, but he's crazy. You'll be out of work in six months." Actually, I was out of work in three; Herb ran straight out of money. It all went up his nose.

I continued living frugally on my savings while calling around for jobs. I'd made an impression on a promotions man in Ohio, Dave Segel, who offered to throw my name around his network. Plugging was the music business rank above errand boy, and in this period of rapid growth, there were hundreds of tiny record labels in need of cheap, enthusiastic kids to push product down the throats of deejays and journalists. Not only did I personally know just about every writer in *Billboard*, I had access to some influential disc jockeys like Murray Kaufman and Jack Lacy. With the King and Hot 100 references, my résumé was pretty good for a twenty-one-year-old.

Dave Segel hooked me up with a character in Philadelphia by the name of Harold Robinson. He owned one of the world's biggest Chrysler and Plymouth dealerships, but his true passion was music. On WIBG, a major Philadelphia pop station, he bought his own show on which he somehow mixed his favorite R&B records with car selling. He'd also set up an imprint of his own, Newtown Records, through which he released a few singles from his big discovery, Patti LaBelle and the Bluebelles. I suggested he pitch a Patti LaBelle live album to Syd Nathan, because I knew *Live at the Apollo* by James Brown was one of King's best sellers. Without batting an eyelid, Harold paid for me to escort him down to Cincinnati accompanied by one of his loyal minions.

I left Syd a message to book two hotel rooms for me, Harold Robinson, and his assistant, Larry Riley, with details of when we were arriving. I was to stay at Syd's house. It was like old times. When Syd saw Harold Robinson and me with this black guy, he couldn't resist launching straight into one of his routines. "So, where's Larry Riley?"

"That's me, sir," replied Harold's driver.

"With a name like that, I thought you'd be Irish."

"I'm sorry if that disappoints you, sir," mumbled poor Larry.

"Of course not, Larry. You're more than welcome in my home. Hank Ballard stays there regularly," said Syd, trying to put my road companion at ease. Syd's problem, however, was that he couldn't stay serious for too long. He then pulled out his pocketknife and twirled it around. "Don't worry, Larry, we'll make a Jew out of you in no time!"

"I'm already circumcised," said Larry, dead serious. "And I'm a proud and devoted Christian." Jesus Christ, I wanted to crawl into whatever hole Larry was digging for himself.

"Already circumcised?" said Syd, whose smile could seem menacing if you weren't used to the freaky goggles. "Well, then, the next cut will have to be your nuts!"

Larry Riley had failed Syd's personality test in two sentences flat. He looked relieved to be dropped off at his hotel while Syd made no excuses about driving me and Harold onward to the Nathan house for dinner. It was the only time I ever saw Syd snub a black man, but it wasn't his color; Syd had no patience for humorless bores—it didn't matter if they were black, Jewish, or Martian. It all worked out fine, of course. Syd and his staff agreed to pick up the Patti LaBelle live album, which sat snugly in King's catalog beside the James Brown classic. Needless to say, Harold Robinson was, excuse the pun, *happy as Larry* to secure his group such a perfect deal. Although I'd only earned a plugger's fee, it was technically my first scalp, complete with a trip, hotel, and expenses. I remember thinking, *You could get used to a life like this.*

That live album, *Live at the Apollo*, contained a Top 40 hit, "Down the Aisle (The Wedding Song)," which broke Patti LaBelle and the Bluebelles nationally. Unfortunately, by then I was back in New York for another rough few months. I ended up having to do some extraordinary record promotions, sending records to a rack jobber named Danny Gittleman, of U.S. Records, in Fall River, Massachusetts. I'd known him from my *Billboard* days, because his sales reports were high among the samples used for the charts. I struck a relationship with Danny to report on my clients' records, which of course improved their chart position. I'm not very proud of this lost period, but I was young, unemployed, and needed to make a living.

Luckily, I'd befriended Teddy Troob, a young guy whose father, Warren, was a lawyer for various top music business players like the Chess brothers, disc jockey Alan Freed, and record producer George Goldner, who I had met several times while working at *Billboard*. Teddy knew my situation and got word of a new label being set up by the songwriting duo Jerry Leiber and Mike Stoller. They'd just hired George Goldner to run the show, so Teddy's father secured me an interview with George, who instantly hired me as his assistant.

Their new label was called Red Bird, and this time, I got seriously lucky. Working out of the eighth floor of the Brill Building, our very first release in May 1964 was "Chapel of Love" by the Dixie Cups. Just weeks after the Beatles invaded, the record took off like a Sputnik on steroids and hit number one in June, eventually selling over a million copies. Home runs this spectacular do not happen often, but this was to be my education in major-league pop promotion under the watchful eye of a champ slugger.

The legendary George Goldner had been around since the forties, when he made his name breaking Tito Puente, Joe Loco, Machito, and other Latin stars. Although he'd always be synonymous with Cuban rhythm, George possessed a golden ear for any genre and scored a string of doo-wop hits throughout the fifties, including "Gee" by the Crows, widely considered as the first rock-and-roll hit. The man was both an incredible dancer and an A&R

genius who could have picked a winning tune out of ten-ton dump of demos. I don't know if his talent was an ear for melody, an eye for lyrics, a feel for rhythm, or some kind of extrasensory smell for success. Whatever *it* was, George Goldner had the thing.

He lived fast and worked me hard. My job was to deliver records to stations, call program directors, organize business trips, and do whatever it took to get our records into the right channels. We enjoyed more hits with the Dixie Cups, like "People Say" and "Iko, Iko" as well as one other global smash hit number one, "Leader of the Pack" by the Shangri-Las. From the word *go*, Red Bird was a bona fide hit factory, meaning George had to go to London and around Europe to set up license deals, hire local promoters, and get balls rolling in all directions. But because he was pathologically terrified of planes, he'd take ships and trains and send me on ahead to set up his meetings, book hotels, deliver records, and take care of whatever groundwork had to be done. Talk about doing more than I was *un*qualified to do, aged twenty-two, I had to go to the Sanremo Music Festival in Italy or walk into London's major labels like Pye and Decca and not fuck up until George's ship docked.

I can't overemphasize the privilege it was for a kid like me to get sent to Europe. Transatlantic flights cost the equivalent of about three grand in today's money; it was a luxury reserved for rich men. Beatlemania was in full swing, which made London's music business feel like the center of the world, but it wasn't just their pop music; from the moment I first stepped off the plane at Heathrow, everything about England grabbed me by the senses. Since the late fifties, I'd been prepped and converted by Paul Ackerman, who loved reminding *Billboard* writers that our former masters, the British, hadn't colonized the globe with ships and muskets alone. There was something about their schools and attitude to public life that bred such high standards in writing, music, theater, and broadcasting. If you wrote reviews for *Billboard*, you were not allowed to dismiss England's quirky fashions without incurring the wrath of the editor.

As I explored the streets of London for the first time, I thought a lot about Paul Ackerman. Although I didn't know my way around, I could sense what he'd always promised. This was no ordinary city or island nation.

The "special relationship" between Britain and America had taken on a musical dimension, making *New York–London* a busy route for music business characters, including a growing number of people my age, like two English guys who dropped into Red Bird one afternoon looking for songs. The taller one introduced himself as Andrew Oldham, the manager of the Rolling Stones. I'd heard the name, but at that point, the Stones were only stirring in England and were still so underripe they'd barely written any material of their own. The second guy was Keith Richards, no more than twenty-one, very shy and letting Andrew do the talking. I picked them out a stack of Red Bird releases containing one tune they'd later cover, "Down Home Girl," performed by Alvin Robinson. We chatted for a while, and Andrew and I exchanged numbers and promised to stay in touch. To get ahead, you had to pick up phones, knock on people's doors, and get yourself around, but the important part was making friends and keeping them.

The Brill Building was a great place for meeting people, and believe it or not, I clocked up a total of three girlfriends in those Red Bird years in the midsixties, a personal record. One was Roberta Goldstein, Neil Sedaka's cousin by marriage, and a rich kid whose grandmother owned Esther Manor, a hotel in the Catskills, where Neil Sedaka played and was first discovered. I always felt that Roberta was envious of her famous cousin and threw herself at the music business as an act of inter-cousin rivalry. She wasn't particularly skilled at anything except hosting great parties where there always seemed to be grass and other substances. At one of her parties, Bob Dylan showed up and plopped himself next to me on a crowded sofa. He wasn't a star yet, but he was well on his way and already hard currency among people like us. I don't know if he was spaced out or bored senseless, but as the evening wore on, he started burning a houseplant with his cigarette end. *Not very nice*, I thought. I guess true genius has a way of being truly weird.

My innocent father somehow detected Roberta's wild streak and put it to me bluntly. "Please don't think of ever marrying that girl." Even though Roberta was Jewish, Dad much preferred the third young lady in my Red Bird trilogy, Sarah Smithers, a knockout beauty. "Now, Seymour," said my father this time, "we won't be upset at all if you were to marry this girl, even if she's a gentile." Sarah's mother, DoJean Sayman, was an heiress to one of the great St. Louis families, and Sarah's father, Sir Peter Otway Smithers, was a British ambassador, lawyer, horticulturist, photographer, and all-round adventurer. He'd been a spy during the war, taking orders from Ian Fleming, who apparently based aspects of the James Bond character—the good looks and multiple talents, on his former boss, Peter Smithers. Coming from a family like this, Sarah was quite the princess who had class to match her traffic-stopping looks. I really did love her.

It was a period of late-night parties and long-playing albums. We were licensing Red Bird product to Pye Records in the UK, so we received advance copies of all their releases for consideration. One little gem I took home in early 1965 was the album *What's Bin Did and What's Bin Hid*, which had Donovan's debut single, "Catch the Wind." He was obviously listening to Bob Dylan, but he had some finely written songs that evoked their own style of English folk. I played it to George Goldner, who allowed me make inquiries with our usual contacts in Pye. Alas, Donovan's North

American rights had already been grabbed by Hickory Records, but the speed and closeness of Donovan's success marked a point on my own personal learning curve. "Catch the Wind" became a U.S. top-twenty hit that summer, and within a year, Donovan topped the Hot 100 with "Sunshine Superman." It was like seeing a prize salmon swim right under my nose.

Musically, I still preferred King's gutsy rhythm and blues to the girl pop we fired out at Red Bird, but the excitement of scoring global hits in the center of New York City more than made up the difference. The Brill Building was a cross between a casino and a summer camp for grown men. You didn't even need to be enrolled or have money; the door was wide open to any player, big or small. There were stars in the elevators, future hits being whistled in the toilet stalls, funny characters bumping around from floor to floor hustling their dreck—like Johnny, a singing, suntanned body-builder who was introduced to us by Ellie Greenwich, the female songwriter behind "Be My Baby" and "Da Doo Ron Ron." Johnny kept dropping into Red Bird to play his latest creations and must have seen in my eyes that I was gay. He began calling me privately until I eventually offered to show him my new apartment overlooking the river on the Lower East Side. He was my second gay experience.

It was actually George Goldner who talked me into buying that apartment. He needed a safe house for a rendezvous with his latest flame, and he put $3,000 toward the purchase, although I paid the rest, which was not very much more, and did the furnishing. George took the nicer room and would call ahead to warn when-ever he'd be coming with company. I was to stay in my room, hear no evil, and above all, play dumb if his crazy wife ever cornered me. With his first two wives, George had already fathered six kids that he knew of, but at the office, we received photos of a smiling child sent by a lady in Cuba claiming George was the padre. He obviously had a penchant for Spanish beauties, especially the hot-blooded diva types, like his stunning wife, Susan. She knew his corrupt ways and watched him like a detective.

George Goldner was a serial lady-killer. Lethally handsome and always sharply dressed, he radiated a charm that made women melt, even when he wasn't trying. He accepted a few invitations from my parents to join us for Shabbat supper in Brooklyn, and I could even see my aging mother getting all hot and flustered as she served him. George wasn't religious, but he loved her chicken soup and homemade latkes. "He's *so* handsome," she once whispered to me in the kitchen like it physically hurt. Coming to my folks' place was probably George's way of staying out of trouble on Friday evenings—or who knows? Maybe he was feasting up before his real night of excess began. You never could tell what George Goldner was up to. He wasn't a heavy drinker or a coke fiend, but his private life had more dark secrets than a rabbit's warren.

His most dangerous vice of all was gambling at the racetrack. I'd heard rumors, but I didn't take them too seriously until I bumped into him at Hazel Park in Detroit. I was still working for Red Bird but happened to be in Detroit helping Andrew Oldham's partner in Immediate Records to meet people in Motown. I offered to play matchmaker and, through a series of mishaps, wound up spending an afternoon with a black beauty named Joanne Bratton, whose sweetheart was the numbers king of Detroit, Ed Wingate. Joanne dragged me to Hazel Park and told me to put two-dollar bets on this and that horse, which, to my delight, kept winning or coming second. That's when I spotted George Goldner in the crowd with the city's top promotions man, Sammy Kaplan. I ran over and raved about my inside source, but when George turned and saw Joanne Bratton, he laughed in my face. "I'm not taking advice from no woman!" Famous last words. I kept winning all day as George squandered hundreds of dollars on his own supposedly hot tips.

George Goldner should have stuck to records. For a guy who could spot winning songs with such pinpoint accuracy and, in essence, pull money out of thin air, his passion for horses was a curse. As we'd all soon learn, Red Bird was probably George's last chance of a clean slate. Although Jerry Leiber and Mike Stoller had heard the jokes about George's bad habits, they'd walked in innocently thinking that if they owned their own label, they'd net eleven cents a hit, not just two as songwriters. Getting an old pro like George Goldner seemed like such a dream team, and in fairness, it was in the first year. Unfortunately, they had no idea how much deep shit George had gambled himself into. Nobody really did, except for one man watching from the shadows.

I'll never forget walking into 1650 Broadway one morning, when two goons appeared on the sidewalk. "Morris Levy wants to talk," said one. I had no idea who they were or why they'd picked on me. All I could feel were my legs going weak.

"You've got the wrong guy," I told them. "My name is Seymour Stein."

"Yeah, you're the guy he wants. C'mon."

"But I don't know Morris Levy."

"Tell him yourself. You're coming with us."

They escorted me to Roulette Records where its boss, the notorious Morris Levy, was on the phone. I'd never seen him in person, but the face fit the reputation. He had that Mussolini jaw and piercing eyes that fit every mug shot and Wanted poster you'd ever seen. He even had the husky Crooklynese voice. I'd been told by George Goldner that Morris Levy had started out in the fifties with Birdland and acquired other clubs like the Roulette Room, the Roundtable Lounge, and the Peppermint Lounge. His brother, Zachariah, was shot and killed in Birdland, mistaken for him. Officially, he owned various labels and a chain of record stores called Strawberries, but Morris Levy's main business was money laundering.

Nobody knew the full reach of Morris Levy, but it eventually transpired that he'd been a childhood friend of Genovese don Vincent "the Chin" Gigante, otherwise known as "Demented Don" or "the Odd Father" for the way he feigned mental illness when questioned by the law.

I sat there with my guts in a shivering knot until Levy placed the receiver on its cradle and turned to me. "Relax," he said, unaware that I was one small relax away from crapping all over his lovely chair.

"Mr. Levy, there must be a misunderstanding," I whimpered.

"Hang on," he said. Then, through an adjoining office door, in walked a character whose psychopathic eyes made Levy look like a choirboy in comparison. "This is Dominic," announced Levy. If there was any last faint glimmer of hope my invitation to Roulette Records wasn't about Mafia business, the mystery Italian peered straight into the back of my skull and asked me a distinctly non-musical question. "What date is it today?"

It had been my twenty-third birthday two days previously, so even though I was terrified, I knew the answer. "April 20!"

"Yeah, so what wuz five days ago?"

"The fifteenth?"

"Right. The day you wuz meant to help me pay my income taxes."

"Income taxes? I dunno know what you mean."

"George Goldner said you'd gimme ten grand to help me pay my income taxes."

"What? I don't have that kind of money." This wasn't exactly true, because I'd been such a good little piggy banker since long before my bar mitzvah. But George didn't know that. "There must be some mistake," I pleaded. "George never mentioned any of this to me, I swear."

"Wait a minute," interrupted Morris Levy. "Something ain't

right here." He then swiveled his phone around toward me. "I want you to call George and tell him you're here." Levy then picked up an ear extension so that he could listen in but gestured with his fat finger to not let George know. Like a good boy, I dialed Red Bird. Under the circumstances, I would have shot George in the face had Morris Levy ordered me to.

"George, it's me, Seymour."

"Where the fuck are you? I got a lot of stuff for you to do. We're going on the road."

"I'm over at Morris Levy's."

"What! Get the fuck out of there! Right now!"

Levy grabbed the phone and barked at George, "I'm sending him back over, but *you* better get here, right now."

Back at Red Bird, I continued shaking like a leaf all day, and when George arrived back from Levy's, he wasn't looking too rosy either.

"I hope nothing bad happened?" I asked.

"Nah, nuthin'. Forget about it," was all George ever said about the entire incident. Over the next days, however, I could see the crippling pressure in his behavior. George Goldner was a hard pusher by nature, now he needed to sell records like never before, and sadly, the atmosphere in the office would never be the same. It was like that old saying, "When poverty knocks at the door, love flies out the window." Or, in George's case, when Dominic knocks at the door, poverty *jumps* out the window.

It wasn't the last I ever heard from Morris Levy about George's spiraling debts. Several months later, I got an unexpected call. "Hey, Seymour, it's Morris Levy. I'd like you come over to my office right away."

"Mr. Levy, I don't understand. I hope there hasn't been another misunderstanding."

"No. I just wanna show you that I'm really a nice guy. I've got something for you. And there's someone here I want you to meet."

"Not Dominic, I hope?"

"No, a fella your age."

You never said no to Morris Levy, especially when he was being friendly. When I got to Roulette Records, I saw a vaguely familiar face looking terrified in the same seat I'd almost shat in.

"This is Micky, who's a program director at a New York station," said Levy. "Micky, why don't you tell Seymour your little story about George Goldner."

The overweight young man, actually wobbling with fear, proceeded to unload this story about our latest release, "The Boy from New York City" by the Ad Libs. The saga started innocently a few weeks previously when our main R&B promotions man, Johnny Brantly, presented the record. The program director didn't really like it, so George telephoned personally. "Hey, Micky, Johnny tells me you don't like the record."

"Well, it's okay," replied Micky, a bit caught off guard. "But we've got so much stuff at the moment."

"Listen to it again," pleaded George. "It's gonna be a hit."

Micky gave it another spin and phoned George. "Okay, I'll try to add it next week." When the song didn't air, George called back. "Sorry, still no room," apologized Micky. "Hopefully next week."

This routine repeated as the record began breaking in other parts of the country. Eventually, Micky felt so bad about not keeping his promise, he called George, which was earlier that day. "George, I'm sorry, but we've just got in the new Marvin Gaye record and we have to add it. I'm doing what I can, but there's no room for yours this week."

This time, however, George's voice turned to ice.

"Micky, do you work out front, or do you have your own office?"

"I have my own office. It's small, but I need my own privacy. Why?"

"Does it have a window?"

"Yeah, a little one."

"I hope you have a nice view."

"What do you mean?"

"I want you to stand at the window, Micky. And look out. Take in everything you can."

"Uh, all right."

"Now, tell me what you see."

"I see a building, a parking lot. Not much. Why?"

"Because it's the last thing you'll ever fucking see, Micky. Dominic is coming over to your office right now. And he's gonna pull your eyeballs out of your head."

Levy and I both knew George couldn't get Dominic to clip anyone's toenails. The only connection George had to the Mafia was owing them money. He was just so desperate, he was turning his own hell on other people.

"Micky, why'd ya come to *me*?" asked Levy, keeping a straight face.

"Because everybody knows you're *connected*!" exploded Micky in tears. "I need your protection, Mr. Levy. Please help me!"

Holding in his smirk like a true pro, Levy then turned to me. "See what George is capable of? I hope you're paying attention, Seymour." He then turned back to Micky. "Let's listen to this record and see what got George so mad."

Micky had brought along a copy of "The Boy from New York City," which Levy placed on a turntable beside his desk. After the first chorus, Levy shouted, "What d'ya think?"

"Loved it the first time I heard it," I began to explain.

"Shut up!" interrupted Levy with a stingray glare. "Let *him* speak."

"I just don't like it that much," said Micky, turning to me for support.

"Okay, well, let's keep listening," said Levy, putting the needle back to the start. "Are you starting to like it now?"

"Yeah, it's growing on me," said Micky, getting the message.

"See? George does know a hit. So, just add it, Micky. And I'll tell George to mind his manners, okay? Everything will be fine; just play the record and forget about it. We're all friends."

"Thank you, Mr. Levy," said Micky, taking back the record and looking a whole lot better.

"And this is for you, Seymour," said Levy, handing me a card. It was an invitation to the United Jewish Appeal, an annual music business gala. "I just want you to know that I've got heart," said Levy in his best puppy dawg voice.

As I'd later learn, every year Morris Levy would buy a stack of invitations for this dinner and order people to buy them any way he could. It was his sin-absolving ritual, his own personal equivalent of Yom Kippur, except with food, liquor, and jokes. Its official purpose was to raise money for charity, but what all the big Jews couldn't miss were the hilarious comedy speeches. Every year without fail, at least one Mafia gag was fired at Levy from the stage, and like a good sport, he'd laugh out loud in front of everyone. This was his way of telling the business, "I ain't so bad, fellas. Look, you can mock me. I'm wunna yooz." For sure, Morris Levy wasn't like anyone else in the room, and everyone knew it, but we all had to stay on his good side, half thinking we might need a favor one day.

Two Jews who wouldn't be laughing at any Morris Levy jokes that year were Jerry Leiber and Mike Stoller. Red Bird had scored a string of hits in just eighteen months, but poor Jerry and Mike were getting very concerned about all these Dominic characters hanging around the office. In the bitter end, the only way out was to "sell" Red Bird to George for a symbolic dollar and for George to clear his debts by signing everything over to Morris Levy, who miraculously made the bookie debts disappear.

We all should have seen it coming. Since the late fifties, George had watched his entire life's work get appropriated by the same people, chapter after chapter after chapter, until *it* and not the music became George Goldner's legacy. In total, Morris Levy wolfed down all seven labels George had ever been involved with: Tico, Rama, Gee, Roulette, Gone, End, and Red Bird—fifteen juicy years of hit records, artist contracts, and publishing deals. You couldn't have made it up. Every time a polo-necked beatnik bought a copy of "Oye Como Va" by Tito Puente, another dollar rolled into Levy's piggy bank; the same with "Why Do Fools Fall in Love" by the Teenagers and "Gee" by the Crows. Airplay, store sales, international licenses, covers, every spin-off imaginable on scores of Latin and doo-wop standards. Hundreds of thousands of dollars kept pouring out of George Goldner's past straight into Morris Levy's paws.

People said George Goldner was his own worst enemy, which he was, but I always felt sorry for him. Morris Levy and his bookie pals preyed on George's weakness like a pimp uses drugs to enslave a woman. It was a tragedy that slowly condemned George to an early grave. He'd survive all the dagger-wielding Latinas, he'd retain his golden ears and movie-star looks, but George Goldner would die of a broken heart. There's only so many times a man can fuck up so much winning. By the time he was forty-nine, George was broken inside.

As for me, I was twenty-four and out of work, but ever since my ice cream days on Coney Island, I'd managed to keep adding to my stash with every job I'd ever done. I was the guy who really did have the first dollar he'd ever earned. I'd built up a pot of about fifty grand, an absolute fortune for a young man in 1966. For me, the Cyclone ride of life was only just cranking its way up to the top.

The music business was at a major crossroads, and it wasn't just all the psychedelic music pouring out of London and California. Now, young people everywhere were trying their luck as managers, promoters, and independents. Some of them, like Phil Spector and Andrew Oldham, were already driving around in limousines, building million-dollar empires. I was sick of hustling for jobs and getting very curious about the alternatives. It was time to just do it myself.

3. SIRE FOR HIRE

Before our Red Bird got stuffed and caged inside Morris Levy's filing cabinet, I kept bumping into a character who worked from an office on the tenth floor of the Brill Building. His name was Richard Gottehrer, one of the *G*s in the FGG songwriting and producing trio alongside Bob Feldman and Jerry Goldstein.

Richard was just two years older than I was, but in professional terms, he was playing in a league above. His gang had written some major hits like "My Boyfriend's Back," a number one for the Angels, and "Sorrow," a UK hit for the Merseys, which David Bowie would immortalize seven years later. They'd produced the colossal smash "Hang On Sloopy" by the McCoys and were now calling themselves the Strangeloves, three mop-topped Jews pretending to be a family of Australian sheep breeders.

When I met Richard, his group had just appeared on TV banging on zebra-skinned bongos to their latest hit, "I Want Candy." He was something of a pop star, but what interested me were his all-round talents: musician, songwriter, producer, he'd even done a year of law school, so he was smarter than the average musician.

Above all, Richard Gottehrer had that special something I trusted most in creative people; he was a *fan* who followed music business events and listened to other people's records with appetite, zeal, and affection.

His gang was drifting separate ways, so, with the help of Tom Noonan—who had left *Billboard* and was running a Columbia imprint called Date—we decided to set up a production company. Richard would be the producer, I'd be the A&R and promoter, and together we'd combine our contacts as a hustling duo. All we needed was a name. Mixing up initials to create label logos was something of a tradition. Phil Spector and Lester Sill had Philles Records. A cleverer example was Bang Records, set up in 1965 by Burt Burns, Ahmet Ertegun, Nesuhi Ertegun, and Jerry Wexler, whose real name was Gerald, hence the word *bang*. We quickly hit upon Sire by mixing up the first two letters of *Seymour* and *Richard*. In this era of frilly shirts and British accents, what I loved about the word *Sire* was that it was a theatrical, British-sounding variation of *King*.

Tom Noonan secured us $50,000 from Columbia as operating capital, a serious investment considering we were so young. The plan was to provide Columbia with some real-deal soul, a genre they were trying to break into. We needed an office, and luckily, Syd Nathan offered to rent us King's old New York brownstone office at 146 West Fifty-Fourth Street on the parlor floor. For the bargain of $235 a month, it was in an old brownstone with four spacious rooms, each with a fireplace. Richard turned one of the back rooms into a studio, and for $150 a month, we sublet the biggest room to two brothers, Roy and Julie Rifkind. Roy Rifkind ran a talent agency, and his brother Julie had previously been Vice President at Bang Records and had just started his own label, Boom. So, from its very birth, Sire stepped straight into one of King's old shoes on a street between Seventh and Sixth Avenue, around the corner from the Brill Building. Opposite us was Al & Dick's, a popular steak house among showbiz wheelers and dealers, and a bit further down the street was La Scala, probably the most popular Italian restaurant in the music business at the time.

Our first record as Sire Productions was a cover version of the soul thumper "That's How Strong My Love Is" by Mattie Moultrie, which Richard produced beautifully. I still think it's a great recording, but to our disappointment, it got lost in Columbia's dense release schedule. We kept batting away with other acts, such as a young group called Chain Reaction introduced to us by my old friend Pete Bennett. "I've got this great band for you," he said. "They're from Yonkers, and the singer, Steven Tallarico, is actually my best friend's son."

We said, "Yeah, sure, bring 'em down." So, these kids filed in and performed a song they'd written called "The Sun," which Richard also produced.

We couldn't get anyone in Columbia's New York or London offices interested; the only takers were CBS in Italy, probably on account of Steven Tallarico's name. When the band realized their debut single was only being given a push in Italy, the singer's father stormed in demanding that we rip up the contract. "What, are you kidding me?" I protested. Then he pulled out a gun. Richard had experienced situations like this at Bang Records and calmly fished out the contract. "Life's too short." He sighed, handing the agreement to me. I wasn't happy about ripping up a deal at gunpoint, but we got a laugh out of it years later when Steven Tallarico became Steven Tyler of Aerosmith.

These and other false starts lost us our Columbia deal within a year. The whole experience, however, taught us a vital lesson. Just delivering masters to a major company as big as Columbia was like throwing darts at a board from fifty feet away. We knew we'd get far better results by promoting our records ourselves, which meant running a proper independent label. So, in 1967, we changed our name from Sire Productions to Sire Records, and with the help of my old friend from Massachusetts, Danny Gittleman, we got a distribution deal with Pickwick, a budget label owned by his friend Cy Leslie. It was the wrong fit, so very quickly Danny helped us secure a more lucrative distribution deal with London Records, which was British Decca's operation in New York.

There was just one snag. Danny Gittleman's wife was convinced a thirty-four-year-old Broadway actress and singer named Phyllis Newman had the makings of a pop star. For all of Danny's invaluable help, she and Danny guilt-tripped us into making an album with Phyllis, the idea being to give her a younger, radio-friendly sound. Phyllis was married to the lyricist and playwright Adolph Green, and together they introduced us to classical music giants like Leonard Bernstein, Isaac Stern, and others. Phyllis was a lovely woman, but the musical and generational chasm was pretty ludicrous considering that Richard and I were twentysomething rock and rollers. Richard accepted the uphill challenge even though we both knew the casting was all wrong.

To find talent we could sell, we were going to have to look a lot harder than just around the Brill Building, so while Richard was working on Phyllis Newman's album, I ventured off in search of bands, foreign licenses, loose connections, *anything* that could broaden our horizons. Thanks to our low rent and all the savings I'd stashed away while working for George Goldner, I was able to attend the Sanremo Music Festival in Italy as well as the second Midem trade fair on the French Riviera. It was expensive traveling around, even staying in cheap hotels, but I was showing up in different places, collecting contacts, records, and news as I went.

On the way home from Cannes in early February 1967, I stopped off in Paris, where I stayed the night with an old friend from New York, Barbara Baker. She was living there with her husband, Mickey "Guitar" Baker, cowriter of "Love Is Strange." He was black, she was Italian, and together they believed their biracial kid would have an easier childhood in Paris, which was more racially integrated than New York. Barbara had found a job with a hot Parisian record company, Disc'Az, and Mickey was getting session work all over Europe. When I arrived, Mickey was packing a bag for London, where he had a recording date with a producer he rated highly. That's how I first heard about Mike Vernon, the producer and owner of Britain's purist blues label, Blue Horizon.

It all smelled too intriguing to not investigate, so I changed my flights and tagged along to London with Mickey. When we walked into the session in Decca's studios, there was a situation brewing. The singer Champion Jack Dupree wasn't going to sing a note unless Mike Vernon paid him up front. Because Mike Vernon didn't have enough money on him, I reached into my pocket and offered to buy the publishing rights of whatever was about to be recorded. Dupree accepted my £50, and the session continued.

After the session, Mike Vernon introduced me to his kid brother, Richard, who was his partner in Blue Horizon. Mike was a lovely guy with an impressive knowledge of American blues and spoke openly about how tough it was to keep his label running. To fund the label, both Vernon brothers were doing freelance producing. For Decca and its Deram imprint, Mike in particular was making his money by producing the debut albums of David Bowie, Ten Years After, Savoy Brown, John Mayall, and Eric Clapton.

I hung around London and called up a contact my ex-girlfriend Roberta Goldstein told me I absolutely had to meet. Her name was

Linda Keith, something of a London starlet, who at the time was dating Keith Richards. Linda took me to a club called Middle Earth, where an American friend of hers named Jimi Hendrix was playing. After about an hour of earsplitting blues, the fucker started smashing his guitar up. Unfortunately, I was standing beside Linda, who practically went through the roof herself. Turns out it was one of Keith Richards's guitars that she'd loaned to Hendrix for the evening. I have to say that under the circumstances, it was hard for me to appreciate the theatrical value. I later learned that Linda had broken Hendrix's heart, but even still, a Fender Stratocaster in those days cost about $200, more than Hendrix was probably getting paid to perform. Apparently, that guitar marked the end of her romance with Keith Richards.

London's electric blues scene was scorching hot but so small. The audiences of one hundred or so people were mostly comprised of other musicians and their girlfriends. There were already a few managers lurking in the shadows, but nobody had a clue how big the whole thing was about to blow up. I mean, who'd o' thunk; a bunch of white English guys selling the blues back to America? Still, I must have smelled something cooking because when I got back to New York, Richard Gottehrer and I put on the Blue Horizon records I'd taken home and marveled at the smoky atmospheres.

Very quickly, London's blues scene began to bubble over, and in the space of just weeks, familiar names started showing up around America. In May 1967, Cream recorded their second album *Disraeli Gears* in Atlantic Studios in New York, which marked their turning point into big business rock. In June, Jimi Hendrix took the Monterey Pop Festival by storm, even though there wouldn't be an American release of Hendrix's debut album *Are You Experienced?* until August, and the now-legendary Monterey film wouldn't come out until a year later. In New York, Jimi Hendrix was still just a fast-spreading English rumor who packed out Café au Go Go on Bleecker Street that July, and in fact, Eric Clapton joined him onstage for a number. By late summer, however, the race was on. American majors were all over the West Coast hippies like a rash, while the more clued-in American labels began sniffing around this new electric blues scene in London.

That fall, the original Fleetwood Mac—fronted by Peter Green and formed from John Mayall's old group—recorded their self-titled debut album on Blue Horizon. Produced by Mike Vernon, it was mix of blues covers and original material that shot to number four on the British charts. Hugely impressed he'd scored a major hit on his own little label, I sent Mike a congratulations telegram. Just three months later, he scored another; *Forty Blue Fingers, Freshly Packed and Ready to Serve*, by Chicken Shack, featuring a then unmarried Christine McVie of future Fleetwood Mac fame. So, I duly telegrammed a second congratulations note. It was then that *Record World* published a spotlight on Blue Horizon in which Mike Vernon mentioned both Sire and me in praiseworthy terms. I was so astounded, I had to phone up and personally thank him. During that call, he told me that aside from all the chart success, he was having difficulty running the label and was fighting with his brother. He wondered if we wanted to buy half the company. I told him we would love nothing more, but given his rising stature, there was no way we could afford it. "I really want you involved," Mike said, "and I'll make it easy for you. Our father lent us £15,000 to start the company. If you would just return that money to him, Sire could become half owners of Blue Horizon." In what turned out to be our first serious business discussion, I sat down with Richard Gottehrer and laid out a case. "We can't license any of Mike Vernon's records, because Blue Horizon already has a worldwide deal with Columbia. But what if we buy into Blue

Horizon, the label? Mike urgently needs money to keep going and we need inside connections." Although we'd have to gamble a huge chunk of cash that we couldn't really afford, Richard liked the idea. We got the money together and became full partners in the company.

Richard Gottehrer and I still needed to find our own artists for Sire and knew that London remained our best bet. For the price of a plane ticket, nobodies like us could pick up the American rights for wacky English albums that our big-money competitors hadn't noticed. You just had to get there, dig, and move fast. That's how we found what I consider as Sire's first proper album, *Ptooff!* by the Deviants, one of London's cult psychedelic albums of 1968. It wasn't even in English record stores; only a few thousand copies were available by mail order through London's underground press. We found the two producers, Peter Shertser and Ian Sippen, who were happy to grant the American rights to anyone. Richard and I knew *Ptooff!* wouldn't sell many copies in the States, but we loved its attitude.

In that first year of scouting, Richard and I were really only fumbling through the dark. Richard's reference at the time was Elektra, probably *the* bohemian label moving into all kinds of psychedelic areas with acts like Love, the Doors, and Tim Buckley. Because I hadn't indulged in much drugging, I wasn't all that blown away by psychedelia. My model still remained R&B and country. Don't forget, I was arriving into work every morning through the very doorway where Syd Nathan had told my father that only the music business could save me from a life as a newspaper boy. Can you imagine the effect that must have had on me psychologically?

The irony wasn't lost on me either that the birth of Sire coincided with Syd's slow death. I was still in regular touch to pay our rent and chat about business, and we'd meet up whenever we could, but it was getting harder. Syd was sixty-three but looked about ninety. Pumping out of time between his wheezing lungs was a diseased heart that was about to blow out at any second. He was getting the best possible treatment in Miami Beach, where his brother, David, was a respected cardiac specialist in the Mount Sinai Heart Institute. My parents often took vacations in Florida, and sometimes I'd join them. Whenever we could, we'd meet up with Syd for a drink or a meal. Considering how they first met, I was pleasantly surprised to see that my father and Syd actually got quite close in the end.

Poor Syd, who'd always been a big eater, had been forced onto a strict health diet. Dreaming of greasy cheeseburgers and other forbidden indulgences, he was always trying to drag me off around the causeway near the Harbor Island Spa. It wasn't easy denying this dying man some last moments of happiness, but I, like everyone else who visited him, talked Syd out of temptation. We all knew Syd was on his last legs, as did Syd himself. By then, King had been downsized, trust funds had been set up for his family, and various new companies swarmed around James Brown, who had become Syd's main concern.

When he finally died in March 1968, it was Paul Ackerman who telephoned me with the news. I immediately called up Syd's lawyer, Jack Pearl, to get details about the funeral and asked him straight out, "Why didn't you call me?"

"I'm only just getting around to you; I'm working through Syd's address book alphabetically. Paul Ackerman's an *A*, so he was among the very first." I don't doubt that Jack Pearl had hundreds of people to call; Syd had been a boss, friend, and godfather to so many. "I'll pay for your ticket to come to the funeral," offered Jack. "I'm sure Syd would have wanted that. But you have to escort my wife, Fanny, because I've got to rush off to Cincinnati to clear up some matters before the funeral." I can only guess what those *matters* were. If there was any skullduggery going on around King, Jack Pearl and James Brown's manager, Ben Bart, would have been the chief suspects. They were brothers-in-law; Ben Bart's sister was Fanny Pearl.

I think only my parents understood how much Syd's death affected me. He'd been my guardian angel over the previous decade, and to this day, I still can't see where my life might have ended up without him. I took the plane to Cincinnati with Fanny Pearl and was proud to be one of the pallbearers, alongside James Brown, Hank Ballard, and Henry Glover, who I think in their own ways all realized that afternoon just how much their lives had been changed by the old man. It was nice to hear Syd's relatives and friends say how much he was proud of the road I'd taken; some even said I was the son he'd never had. I'd spend the rest of my life learning how this vocation runs on mentors and adopted sons. A dying record man has to leave his assets to his blood family, of course, but it's usually some outsider apprentice who'll inherit the trade secrets. Around the grave of every successful record boss, there'll always be two families looking at each other jealously.

Syd's death was my first professional heartbreak, but I had to walk away from that cemetery. So much was happening around Sire; all the seeds we'd planted over the previous year were beginning to sprout. Every few weeks, we kept opening these killer records from Mike Vernon. His first Fleetwood Mac knockout was "Black Magic Woman," followed by "Need Your Love So Bad," which happened to be a cover of the Little Willie John classic that first came out on King in 1955. Then came the classic instrumental "Albatross," which climbed to number one in the UK and went top five in countries all over the continent, a European smash.

Unfortunately, early Fleetwood Mac was too bluesy for American radio. Although their song "Albatross" managed to get onto *Bill-board*'s "Bubbling Under the Hot 100" Chart for several weeks, it nonetheless failed to make much of a commercial impact. The problem was that Columbia's HQ in New York didn't consider Fleetwood Mac as anything special. Fleetwood Mac's situation in America was much like our own frustrating experience with the same company just two years before. Columbia was North America's biggest major, releasing so many titles every week, the third-party licenses tended to slip through the cracks. There was also a generational problem. Even in the late sixties, the record business was still very middle aged and old-fashioned, but at least the smaller majors were so hungry, they had to take risks. The problem with Columbia was that they could afford to be lazy. They didn't get Fleetwood Mac because they didn't really have to.

It still feels like a terrible injustice that America seemed to ignore such an important band. To my ears, Peter Green had more soul, magic, and creativity than any of the other English bluesmen he's compared to. As a business investment, however, at least Richard Gottehrer and I were shareholders in Blue Horizon, the mother company that was enjoying all this European success. There was no doubt about the spin-off image value, too. I made sure that Fleetwood Mac's winning streak in Europe was reported in *Billboard* bulletins about Sire, which gave us some extra credibility in American music business circles, even though we had nothing to do with the band. A little bit of bullshit won't kill anyone—especially if it's half-true.

In August 1968, Mike Vernon invited me to the Windsor Jazz and Blues Festival in Richmond, a flowery suburb on the banks of the Thames, just outside London. We were there to check out bands and cheer on Fleetwood Mac, who were topping the bill alongside Cream. Also performing was Blue Horizon's new group, Chicken

Shack, featuring a young Christine Perfect, who later became Christine McVie of latter-day Fleetwood Mac.

At one point, I was sitting between Mike and his sound engineer, Gus Dudgeon, when this unknown band called Jethro Tull stepped onstage. They were managed by Chris Wright and Terry Ellis, who managed Ten Years After and Savoy Brown, two bands Mike was still producing for Decca. "Hey, this band is great!" I said to Mike after the first few numbers. "We should sign them to Blue Horizon immediately."

"Seymour, I don't want any bands with *flautists* in them," replied Mike.

Flautists? What the fuck were *flautists*? Maybe it was the contempt in Mike's voice and the way the guy onstage was standing on one leg like a Shakespearean jester, but I just presumed Mike knew something I didn't. In Brooklyn, a fella who plays the flute is called a flute player, right? A *flautist* sounded like some kind of English pervert who liked to get whipped. Instead of looking dumb, I just shut up.

But after the show, I turned to Gus. "What's Mike talking about? That was a great band."

"I thought they were terrible," said Gus just as dismissively. Whatever dumbfounded face I was wearing, Gus then looked into me. "Can I ask you something, Seymour?"

"Yeah, sure."

"Do you play a musical instrument?"

"What on earth has that got do with this band?"

"Because if you played an instrument, you'd have heard all the bum notes. God, they were awful."

Being condescended to by real-deal producers should have plunged my already shaky self-confidence into nuclear meltdown. Until that very moment, I would have given my left testicle to go back in time, learn the guitar, and become a studio producer like Mike Vernon, Gus Dudgeon, or Richard Gottehrer. For years, I'd suffered from a musical chip on my shoulder. Ironically, all that was about to be cured. I guess you have to take hard knocks to learn where your true strengths lie. This and other incidents were teaching me the virtues of musical illiteracy, or to put it another way, I was waking up to the dangers of technical virtuosity. Sometimes it's better to be a dumb fuck just like all the other dumb fucks in the audience. In fact, it's usually better not to know the disgusting secrets of how the sausage got made.

Fuck it, I thought. *I'm going to go after Jethro Tull myself.* I sent an offer for the North American rights to the band's managers, Terry Ellis and Chris Wright. Alas, Terry Ellis replied by typewritten letter a few weeks later. "We are, in fact, in the final stages of deciding between two companies, although it will probably be Reprise." I was gutted, but them's the rules. "We have been most impressed by the complimentary things we have heard about your company," he signed off diplomatically. "We are most hopeful that we will be doing business in the future." Probably untrue but never mind. Terry Ellis and Chris Wright would go on to great success as both artist managers and label bosses of their very own Chrysalis imprint. In the meantime, I'd have to look enviously at Jethro Tull's rise to American stardom, much like I'd watched Donovan's. This time, however, I was half smiling to myself. Yes, just like a prancing English *flautist*, there was a pleasurable relief in this particular whipping.

Although Sire was gradually becoming an Anglophile label, we did sign some Americans in the late sixties. We released *Silver Currents*, a dreamy folk album by David Santo. On Broadway, we spotted Martha Veléz, a gutsy singer from the musical *Hair*. We sent her to Mike Vernon in London where they made *Fiends and*

Angels, a romping R&B album we were very proud of. We weren't scoring hits, but we were having fun, getting by, and there was every reason to be hopeful. Our audience was tuning in to a whole new network of new FM stations whose deejays and program directors were mostly our own age. It was like the previous fifty years of mono records and AM stations were becoming obsolete as demand for hip, stereo-produced rock albums was lifting the tide for so many young independents. A new generation of labels like Island, A&M, Immediate, Virgin, and Chrysalis were becoming big players on the psychedelic rock scene. All we had to do was keep shooting; our lucky strike would come.

Even still, survival as a hand-to-mouth indie wasn't easy. There were always barren financial periods between checks, and, of course, dipping into my savings was no way to run a business. Luckily, I'd picked up magic tricks from the likes of George Goldner and his promoter sharks. Looking at the stacks of unused promotional records being returned from our distributor, I salvaged an old iron from my mother. By heating the sleeve gently, Richard and I would take turns carefully peeling the Not for Sale—Promotion Only stickers without leaving any traces. When we had a freshly ironed pile, we'd call up a one-stop supplier and sell the fuckers for cash. It was more hassle than it was worth—we'd only get $100 or $200—but it paid the rent in those empty-cupboard months.

Looking back, Richard Gottehrer and I made a funny team. I'd always been a hustler since my first jobs on Coney Island; Richard was more of a college kid who read books about Eastern philosophy and health food. He got me schlepping down to Souen, a macrobiotic restaurant just below Houston Street, which became our standard dinner through the hippie years. As for Sire's circular *S* logo, it was an adaptation of the yin-yang symbol, which I think subconsciously befitted its two founders. I was the money guy, the ducker and diver; Richard was the artist in Cuban heels and Swiss watches. On our trips to Italy, I'd follow him to the flagship Brioni store on Via Barberini in Rome, where we both had Brioni suits made to measure, complete from scratch, for the ridiculously low prices of between $200 and $300.

Teaching each other various tricks of the trade and giving each other our different viewpoints on life made us great partners. At the time, I thought I was the responsible one. Truth is, I was lugging around a ball of terror in my gut. I kept hearing Syd Nathan's words to my father: "Your son has shellac in his veins . . . if he can't be in the music business, it's going to *ruin* his life." For me, Sire's success was a matter of life or death.

About nine months after Syd's funeral, I heard a bizarre story through the grapevine about Nat getting arrested. This didn't make any sense to me, because I knew Nat couldn't ever steal or hurt anyone, so I telephoned Cincinnati to find out.

"What happened?" I asked Nat.

"Well, I went to see the Reds play, and I had a lot of money with me," explained Nat, who, like his late father, was a huge fan of the Cincinnati Reds. "We were winning, so I wanted to buy everyone in the stadium a hot dog."

"And that's why you were arrested?"

"Yeah. They thought I was crazy. But, Seymour, you know I'm not crazy. It was a Wednesday afternoon game, there were only about a thousand people in the stadium. If I really was crazy, I would have bought everyone a hot dog at a *weekend* game."

What could I say except "That was nice of you, Nat"? He'd just inherited a ton of money and would have given it all away for the only thing he ever wanted: friendship. Syd had taken Nat from his natural mother when he was a teenager, I think when Syd realized he was sick and didn't have much time left. Syd wanted to set up his only son with some kind of future. Unfortunately, he was so busy running King that Nat had felt neglected, which I'm sure he was—both medically and emotionally. To get his father's attention, Nat used to run away or get into trouble until Syd put him in military school, hoping it might teach the boy some self-discipline. Nat just kept getting into trouble or swindled.

I dunno, maybe I was finally starting to grow up, but in those months after Syd's funeral, I made some big decisions. I invested $19,000 of my stash on a two-bedroom place at 75 Central Park West. It didn't quite have a park view, but almost. It was facing Sixty-Seventh Street, just on the corner. With the dubious help of an interior designer who Tom Noonan recommended, I got an aquarium fitted into a wall and redid one bathroom in marble, complete with a sauna. I got ripped off on those refurbishments, a beginner's mistake I'd never repeat. Still, it was an ambitious project which, when finished, enabled me to put up my London gang, who also put me up when I was in London. Mike Vernon was among the first to stay over with his girlfriend. He almost creamed in his pants seeing my collection of *Billboard* magazines, which he studied backward into the fifties like the hungry blues researcher that he was.

I was coming up in the world, but I remember sitting on the subway heading out to Brooklyn to see my folks, thinking long and hard about the bleak prospect of never having children. I was twenty-six, and all I had for a private life were a few old secrets that still made me uncomfortable. It's not that I felt lonely, I loved what I was doing, but the niggling thought of your family looking at you like a tragic loner will make you wonder. I'm sure my family *was* talking about me behind my back, because one day, innocent as a dove, my little niece Robin called me at the office, overjoyed with what she thought was a major scoop. "Oh, I just love my teacher. She's so cool. You know what she did in class today? She asked us if we had older brothers or uncles that were single and looking to go out. So, I told her about you."

"What?"

"Seymour, I know you'd like Miss Adler."

"Are you serious?"

"I really think you should call her."

Whoever Miss Adler was, she could have been fired. Even in 1969, it was *not* kosher for third-grade teachers to hustle schoolyards for stray uncles. Unfortunately, I admired Miss Adler's balls and dialed the number like a man under hypnosis. This loud, extra-large personality came thundering down the telephone line; Linda, a Riverdale Jewess who was obviously a bit crazy. When we met up, she was even more intense in real life. She was five-foot zilch and buxom with thick brunette hair, all eyes and mouth, raving about all the rock stars she loved, all the places she'd traveled, all the things she wanted to do. It was like standing in the main street of a small town looking at an approaching tornado. I was so put off, I took a while to call her up again, and by then, she'd disappeared. My niece said she'd taken a leave of absence and moved to France to learn French.

Miss Adler had definitely made a big first impression, but not a very good one. Never mind, I was too busy to give the whole incident much thought, because our first business crisis erupted in London. Fleetwood Mac's new manager, Clifford Davis, had just stabbed Mike Vernon in the back. In the middle of recording "Man of the World," Davis suddenly announced the band had left the label on a contractual technicality. Mike's brother Richard, who was in charge of Blue Horizon's paperwork, hadn't noticed the option to renew their contract had expired, which allowed Davis to negotiate a bigger deal elsewhere. To make matters even messier, the label in question was Immediate, owned by my old friends Andrew Oldham and Tony Calder.

I jumped on a plane to London with Richard Gottehrer, even though we didn't have a legal leg to stand on. Blue Horizon's contract for Fleetwood Mac was a one-page document signed only by Peter Green for a one-year period, with an option for two further years that hadn't been re-signed on time. In an effort to work around the hardball manager, we met up with Mick Fleetwood in an Indian restaurant. He was mortified, but there was nothing he or the band could do. The contract with Immediate had already been signed.

In a crunch meeting with Clifford Davis, we agreed to accept £5,000 as a sort of thank-you-but-fuck-off gesture. He also promised to let Mike finish "Man of the World," which Blue Horizon could release as a last single. Imagine how Mike felt when Clifford Davis gave the finished master to Immediate. "Man of the World" was another smash-hit single, reaching number two on the UK charts and top ten all over Europe. Mike had invested all the hard work, but from here on in, others would harvest the biggest rewards. He was devastated, we all were, but Fleetwood Mac were his friends and proudest creation that he'd supported since the Bluesbreakers days. It wasn't just business for Mike; it was the best years of his life.

Further complicating Mike's nightmare, Clifford Davis insisted Immediate put Mike's name on the single's sleeve notes as some kind of half-assed guilt-redemption gesture. That little credit landed Mike into hot water with Columbia, who, of course, were steaming with rage about losing such a great band. After various legal threats, Columbia didn't sue Mike, but the whole episode left a very sour taste in everyone's mouth, compounded by the fact the band told Mike in private that the only reason they didn't stop their manager pulling such a nasty stunt was because Columbia weren't breaking them in the States. It was time to blame the Yanks, even though that Columbia deal had nothing to do with me and Richard Gottehrer.

To cap everything off, Immediate Records went into receivership soon after and couldn't pay the advance. Talk about a disaster. In the States, however, Reprise got Fleetwood Mac's North American rights and, to be fair, had better success than Columbia ever did, but only marginally. Even with TV appearances, Peter Green's Fleetwood Mac never really broke America like they deserved to, and I'd bet the whole door-slamming mess was one of the reasons for Peter Green's disillusionment over the subsequent eighteen months. Mick Fleetwood and John McVie say it was a damaging LSD trip in West Germany that cracked Peter Green's mind and drove him into reclusion. I don't doubt it, but I wonder how Peter Green might have rolled with the punches if he'd avoided so much bad business and just stuck with the original gang. Put it this way: if you had to pick a song that marked a turning point in Peter Green's downward spiral, it would have to be "Man of the World." Between its lines, you can hear something breaking. And that's exactly when Clifford Davis was bullying him into screwing a friend to get famous.

The very definition of regret is wishing you'd done things differently. I know that Richard Vernon still kicks himself for not having taken more care with the paperwork. I still kick myself for not having kicked both Vernon brothers into hiring a lawyer the minute "Albatross" hit number one. From that moment, it was only a matter of days before bigger labels came crawling out of the woodwork waving their checkbooks. What were we expecting? Sadly, such are the pointless gremlins that will haunt your sleep for years after a major crash. At the end of the day, we were all in our midtwenties and making it up as we went along. This was London in the late sixties, a time when music came before business. The troublemaker was the manager, an old-school shark. Managers are supposed to prey on mistakes and make money for their bands, but he should have been more open and let Blue Horizon make a counteroffer.

For this and many other shenanigans, the remaining members of Fleetwood Mac ended up suing Clifford Davis a few years later. As they say, *Oh, well.*

In the end, what actually launched Sire turned out to be a contact Syd introduced me to when I was still a teenager. The jovial L. G. Wood, or Len as everyone called him, was managing director of EMI, Britain's biggest major, which had licensed the entire King catalog all over Europe. Len had worked his way up through EMI's sales ranks since the Depression, a long career interrupted only by his service in World War II as a flying control officer for the Royal Air Force. In the early fifties, however, EMI was dealt a body blow when both RCA and Columbia refused to renew their matrix exchange agreement, depriving EMI of surefire American hits. This existential crisis for EMI explains why, in 1952, they spent nine million buying Capitol, one of America's big four. In London, however, EMI had to take bigger A&R risks and gave more signing power to their in-house producers such as Norrie Paramor and George Martin, who in large part sowed the seeds of Britain's golden age in the sixties. As Len Wood told *Billboard*: "Looking back, these setbacks were the best thing that could have happened to us. They put EMI on its mettle and forced us to re-think our policies fundamentally. We have been much better for the experience, although I must be quite honest and say it did not seem so at the time."

Throughout EMI's soul-searching years, Syd had been one of Len's chief American confidants, and they became such close friends, the Englishman usually visited Cincinnati on his annual American trips. I think Len never forgot Syd's loyalty, especially when the tables turned. In the first six months of 1964, EMI artists held America's number-one spot for a record sixteen weeks, thanks mainly to the Beatles. Funnily enough, it was actually Len who had to fix the absurd situation of Capitol refusing to release the Beatles' first singles in America.

When I met Len again around 1965, he was on top of the business, but to his credit, he was just as friendly as the first time I'd met him. He told me to contact him once I had my own label, which, at the time, I was still about eighteen months from doing. People make empty promises all the time, but even after Syd was dead, Len kept his word and gave me a red-carpet welcome into EMI's engine room. In many ways, he breathed life into Sire's future when we urgently needed it. Without Len, I don't think we could have survived as a Broadway indie for more than five years. In that period of English dominance, American indies who didn't have any special connections to London generally got left behind and went bust.

In urgent need of hot product, I was picked up at Heathrow Airport by a young EMI staffer named John Reid, whose Scottish accent was so strange to my untrained Brooklyn ears, he may as well have been speaking medieval Viking. Pushing my trolley through the arrivals hall, I asked him if he was driving us to EMI. He replied, "Ham on-lee tse-venteen, aye kayne d*rrr*yfe," which I eventually translated as "I'm only seventeen, I cannot drive." I won't spoil the surprise of who this virtual child later became. At this point, he was just the office junior who got sent to airports to meet small fries like me. Never mind, we took a cab to EMI, which gave me time to attune my ears to the wild cadences of Scotland. John Reid was from Paisley, one of the poorest parts of Glasgow, and he'd arrived in London about a week earlier. Even through his rough Scottish accent, what struck me were his feminine traits. I later learned that he was the lover of a Scottish TV boss who'd just been moved down to London. It was through London's gay networks that John had landed his new job.

At EMI, Len Wood introduced me to the managers of his inter-

national division, the in-house lawyers and clerks who issued foreign territory licenses for EMI product. Our arrangement was dead
simple: for little or no advance, I could sign North American rights
for EMI records that hadn't been picked up by Capitol or anyone
else. It meant rummaging through their trash cans for leftovers,
which didn't put me off me because I knew that Capitol and other
American majors were constantly turning their noses up at good
English records.

Len Wood was so eager to set me up for the long haul, he would
arrange for additional sub-publishing deals on top of the records,
which was generous considering I wasn't really a publisher yet. To
make my trips to London easier, LG also made a few calls so that I
could borrow a desk and office at EMI publishing, Ardmore &
Beechwood, which was on the second floor of the original HMV
record store on Oxford Street. I could even use their telephone. So,
thanks to the wonderful Len Wood and the simplicity of international licensing, Sire found a regular source of hot product that
Richard and I didn't have to spend much money on. For $1,000 or
$2,000 in manufacturing costs that we could get our distributor,
London Records, to advance and deduct from our sales reports,
we could take relatively safe bets on lesser-known British rock. Like
transatlantic phone operators, it was as simple as plugging the right
cables into the right channels. The first of many EMI licenses was
the self-titled *Barclay James Harvest*, from a psychedelic rock band
from Oldham, a northern town just outside Manchester.

As my hunting trips to London became more frequent, I stumbled on an effective calling card—Turf cheesecakes, the tastiest in
New York City. I'd first discovered them at the Turf restaurant and
Jack Dempsey's, both on the lobby floor of the Brill Building. I
found the bakery uptown, which of course was the cheapest place
to buy them in bulk. When Richard and I began arriving at record
companies around London carrying boxes of top-class cheesecake

straight from New York, we were welcomed with open mouths. For some reason, cheesecake was a rarity in London, so there wasn't a boss, junior staffer, or secretary that wouldn't wolf down every last chunk like they were biting into the Big Apple itself. Sire hadn't yet exported a single record, but that cheesecake was our first American hit in England. The more we delivered, the easier it was to walk out with bargains, such as our second big EMI license, the Climax Blues Band, a group of electric bluesmen from a country town called Stafford in the British Midlands. We only had to pay £1,000, a sale price tag compared to what we'd make back.

And the cheesecake kept opening doors. From Polydor's London office, I picked up a psychedelic singer-songwriter named Twink, whose wacky *Think Pink* album featured some of the Deviants. That record later evolved into one of London's great cult groups of the seventies, the Pink Fairies. From Spark, an indie on Denmark Street, we also picked up an electric blues band named Killing Floor. It was at EMI, however, that my name was spreading through the grapevine. I started getting contacted by EMI's European affiliates, who'd obviously heard I was a sucker for obscure records. Suddenly, they all wanted me to release their French, Italian, and German shlock in the States. I knew I'd be poking around for a needle in a haystack. It takes a something special to scale the Berlin Wall of foreign language, but strange surprises do occasionally happen, so I kept my ears and office door open until I eventually found something.

EMI's Dutch company, Bovema, had a hot little imprint called Imperial that had released an instrumental album called *Talent for Sale* by a guitarist named Jan Akkerman. When I heard the amazing guitar playing and a stand-out track named "Ode to Billy Joe," I telegrammed Amsterdam. "I don't have much money," I explained, "but I'm interested in putting out Jan Akkerman's record in the United States."

"You can take it for free," Theo Russ replied. "Just pay us a royalty. However, we can't include any option, because he's just left us. We hear he's returned to his old Focus bandmates."

To find out what was going on, I jumped on a plane to Amsterdam and found Jan Akkerman and the rest of Focus earning a living by playing in the Dutch production of *Hair*; the problem, however, was that they'd already signed a publishing deal with Radio Tele Music, a Benelux publishing company owned by Radio Luxembourg. Part of that deal was that the publisher had a say over which label got the recording rights. So, I called its main man, Hubert Terheggen, who knew he couldn't do much for Focus in a country the size of a shoe box.

"Do you go to Midem?" he asked me.

"Yes, of course."

"Well, let's do this deal in Cannes."

I took the train down to Paris and telephoned my French connection, Lucien Morisse. Not only was Lucien a presenter on Europe 1, France's most popular pop radio station, he ran the record label Disc'Az, which my old friend Barbara Baker still worked for. I'd been introduced to Lucien by Barbara, so whenever I was in Paris, I'd call into their fabulous office overlooking the Arc de Triomphe. Lucien was a real-deal record man who'd married French pop star Dalida and discovered an important French singer-songwriter named Michel Polnareff. He was Jewish, and one of our little traditions was to eat at his favorite kosher restaurant on Île Saint-Louis.

When I played him the album, he offered me $10,000 for Focus's French rights, and when I met Hubert Terheggen in Cannes, he asked for only $5,000 to grant me the worldwide rights, excluding the Benelux. So, just by running around between Amsterdam, Paris, and Cannes, I flew home to New York with Focus's rights and a profit of five grand before we'd sold a single copy. And that's how

Sire got Focus, a deal that would eventually change our fortunes and put us on the map.

The logistics of licensing finished European records into the United States were pretty simple. We'd either take the masters on the plane back to New York or receive them by special courier. We'd adapt the sleeve artwork and send everything to our distributor, who'd press and ship to stores. I make it sound so easy, but try carrying a stack of cakes all the way to Europe in economy class, then spend days sifting through shitloads of major company dreck. Do this twenty times and I swear you'll deserve your one-hit wonder.

There was one afternoon in EMI's head office, I was so jet-lagged, I must have fallen asleep on a desk. I woke up to find the whole building dark, deserted, and locked. It was still early enough to telephone my main contact John Reid, but unfortunately, he didn't have a key. He had to call a senior boss named Ken East, who later dropped in accompanied by his wife, Dolly, with John Reid in tow. They found my situation so hilariously pitiful, they took me out for a late-night dinner.

Ken and Dolly East were a well-known socialite couple, especially among gay show business characters whose company and wit they seemed to love. There were rumors about Ken, because he'd once turned up to an EMI party in drag, but I don't think he was gay or bisexual. He was just a dandy who enjoyed speaking the gay slang they had in London. It was a century-old jargon called Polari that had evolved between gay men to avoid being understood by eavesdroppers at a time when homosexuality was illegal. According to the most plausible theory, it was first begun by Punch and Judy puppet masters, who were mostly Italian travelers. From there, it spread into the navy and theatrical circuits and continued evolving and growing. To my American ears, it sounded as incomprehensible as the slang in *A Clockwork Orange*, but I was nonetheless fascinated. It's certainly an indication of how strong the gay subculture was in Britain.

The more I was accepted into the EMI gang, the more I couldn't believe how many characters in the British music business were gay. In New York's music business, it was always "Did you know he's Jewish?" whereas in London, it was "Did you know he's queer?" Nearly all the managers behind the British Invasion were gay. The Beatles had Brian Epstein, the Who had Kit Lambert, the Yardbirds had Simon Napier-Bell, the Bee Gees and Cream had Rob Stigwood—who, although Australian, worked out of London. The Stones had Andrew Oldham (known as being very flamboyant even if he wasn't gay). Ever wondered where the sixties' fashion of long hair originally started? Yep, blame gay managers, especially Brian Epstein, who was both gay *and* Jewish. The tradition went even back even further. In the fifties, a guy called Larry Parnes was a hugely successful gay impresario behind most of Britain's rock-and-roll stars, such as Tommy Steele, Billy Fury, and Marty Wilde. There was also Joe Meek, the mad-genius producer behind the Tornadoes 1962 smash, "Telstar," the first-ever British number one on the *Billboard* Hot 100.

Even the almighty chairman of EMI, Sir Joseph Lockwood, was gay. Since the fifties, Sir Joe, as everyone called him, was the banker and strategist behind Britain's incredible rise as a pop superpower. It was Sir Joe who bought Capitol in 1952 and also Sir Joe who promoted a working-class prodigy named George Martin to revive EMI's ailing Parlophone imprint. With all the Beatles money that kept pouring back from America throughout the sixties, Sir Joe then invested heavily in TV production, which changed the BBC forever after. The British should erect a monument to the man.

Sir Joe always seemed like an upright British gentleman, and I wonder if there's any truth in the rumors that he liked a bit of rough stuff with some of the impresarios he helped. Probably scurrilous gossip, but you get my point; in London, it was no big deal to be gay, because so many important players were. And it wasn't just the record business; it was the same in the BBC, which had plenty of hugely talented gay actors, producers, and radio deejays. The West End theatrical scene was the gayest community of all—that's where the culture originated. In fact, both Larry Parnes and Robert Stigwood were theatrical agents before they moved into pop music.

Even my new Scottish buddy John Reid had gotten his job at EMI through these networks. His superior was a friendly guy named Phil Greenop, who was also a fixture of that Ken and Dolly East social set. I guess John Reid sensed I was gay and invited me out to meet his new lover, a young musician named Reg Dwight, who was performing under the stage name Elton John. Needless to say, when I first met him, I didn't immediately see Elton John's lucky star flashing across the restaurant table. That all changed when I heard "Your Song." His career as a recording artist had barely begun, and we were just a bunch of guys hanging out after work. Amazingly, the independent label that had just signed him, DJM, was owned by the same Dick James who built the publishing company behind the Beatles, Northern Songs. Back in 1962, Dick James had pointed a desperate and demoralized Brian Epstein to George Martin and was later rewarded with their publishing. Beat that for a lucky streak; the year before the Beatles broke up, Dick James signed Elton John for both publishing *and* recordings. For some people, the good times don't stop rolling.

What immediately struck me about Elton John was his deep knowledge of music, not just songs and artists but the whole family tree of labels and genres. There was a touch of the musicologist about him, and I'm sure it's why John Reid introduced us: he knew we'd talk the same language. Before Reg became Elton, he'd served customers for years in Musicland Records on Berwick Street, one of London's very best record stores. I can only presume all his research and record collecting earned him high standards as a listener, which he eventually put to the service of his own music. It's a side of Elton John he keeps to his private life, but he's always been a true *fanatic* who spends hours every day listening to other people's records and keeping up with new artists and releases and industry business.

Life is partly what we make it and partly made by the friends we choose. I was only twenty-seven, but through trial, error, and plenty of lucky mishaps, I was building up an international network of young and old players whose talent and ambition fired me up and kept me believing in myself. You can't succeed on your own; we all need a circle of like-minded crusaders to stay fired up and relish the daily battle. Although we hadn't scored any major hits yet, I felt I was part of a community, and that sense of support and belonging made me feel secure about Sire's future.

The time had come for Richard and me to our move office and stand tall in our own building. The small amount of rent we were paying for King's former New York office became an issue once we were dealing with Syd's estate. Jack Pearl didn't throw us out, but the feeling of overstaying our welcome got me thinking about how Syd had tied up his money in real estate, usually cheap, run-down buildings that he'd turn into business outposts. It made perfect sense. By owning the building, you stopped wasting profits on rent, and you could even pay wages and cover office costs by renting out the space you didn't need. And unless the Russians nuked Manhattan, the building would go up in value.

Considering Sire had become so synonymous with international rock, the whole Broadway district didn't matter to us anymore. We bought a pretty brownstone at 165 West Seventy-Fourth Street on the Upper West Side and named it Blue Horizon House, confident that the slightly run-down neighborhood was too near the prettiest parts of uptown Manhattan to not go up in value. It was one of the smartest moves Richard and I ever made.

Our international connections began throwing up surprises. On one of my London trips in 1970, Ken and Dolly East introduced me to an Australian producer named David Mackay, who was behind one of Britain's and Australia's pop hits of 1970. For months, no Englishman or Aussie could escape this novelty song that was all over the airwaves like a jellyfish epidemic. Called "The Push Bike Song," it was Mungo Jerry–styled bubblegum, written and performed by an Australian group called the Mixtures. It was a bit goofy but fiendishly catchy, so I gobbled up the American rights, and hey, presto, flew home Sire's first little pop hit on the Hot 100. It peaked at forty-four—not bad at all.

What Sire needed a lot more than lucky singles were long-term album artists, so we reinvested the profits into our main acts, including Jan Akkerman's group, Focus. Their first record in 1969, *In and Out of Focus*, had a dreamy, psychedelic sound, but it lacked punch. Knowing the band had gone through personnel changes and were hungry for bigger things, I called Mike Vernon and asked him to go to Holland to check them out. Mike tracked the band down to a giant hangar in the Dutch middle of nowhere and called me back from a phone booth, saying he liked what he heard and wanted to produce their next album. This was my revenge for Jethro Tull, because the organist and singer in Focus, Thijs van Leer, also played the flute. "This time," I joked, "like it or not, you're gonna produce a *flautist* and you're gonna enjoy it!"

With all this traveling and office moving, I'd forgotten about the third-grade schoolteacher, but in early 1971, my niece Robin telephoned the new office. "Miss Adler is back from France, and she asked about you!" So, I called Linda, and lo and behold, she'd changed completely. We caught up with each other's adventures over the previous year and suddenly got along just dandy. Whether France had changed her, I don't know, but the first night we went out on a date, I slept with her.

What surprised me was that I had no problems screwing a woman. In fact, I was rather proud of myself that I could keep doing the business whenever Linda wrestled me into bed. Very quickly, she started dropping whopper hints about marriage. This of course threw me, but, I *was* flattered. Linda saw a winner in me, and whatever about my own sexual confusion—my self-confidence was doing somersaults. I guess I'd bottled up my true desires for so many years, all I consciously cared about was success, which, for me, didn't mean money. My vision of success was a type of wide-screen, Technicolor lifestyle, and I could see that Linda hungered for the same. She wanted to know about every rock star and kingpin I'd met. She'd sit there, eyes on fire, hanging on every name and detail like her life depended on it. She wasn't just listening politely like my mother did; Linda was studying, asking all the right questions, remembering names, following the news like a reporter, and often offering smart tactical advice.

Our dating was getting serious, but I now understand why an aging father will advise his twenty-eight-year-old son to take a good look at his girlfriend's mother. I didn't need Sigmund Freud to figure out where Linda picked up her commando traits. Her mother, Mabel, was an iron lady even by the standards of Bronx matriarchs. It's a pity nobody told me that Mabel's own mother had died young; I might have better understood the Adler glitch. Deprived of a mom, Mabel hadn't had it easy as a kid and grew up tough as nails. All I noticed was how Linda's henpecked father, a lovely man named Ira, seemed to protect his girls from the mother's forked tongue. Considering how gentle my own mother had been, I just found Mabel terrifying. Once, my phone rang in the middle of the night as Linda lay asleep beside me. I fumbled for the receiver and croaked, "Huh-low," half-unconscious but thinking it was London.

"Sorry to interrupt you, but I know you're fucking my daughter!" was Mabel's 3:00 A.M. greeting. As wake-up calls go, it was like Sandy Koufax throwing a wet cloth at your sleeping face.

At first, I didn't agonize over the glaring question marks of our impossible relationship, but as soon as I bought us tickets for a vacation to Bermuda, I was suddenly overcome by fear and guilt. I knew I had to tell Linda the truth about myself before she stepped on that plane. I kept putting it off, but on the morning of our flight—a little late, I admit—I stood before Linda in the hallway of the Adler home. Her suitcase was packed and waiting, all the Adlers were out, and right there, I told Linda the truth. I was attracted to men; I'd slept with men, not just once or twice but several times. I'll never forget the scene. She fell into silent shock for about ten minutes like the Bronx sky was draining into a sinkhole that had collapsed inside her. Then she erupted into wails of "No! No! No!" while punching her own head with two clenched fists. Her whole life was spinning down the existential toilet bowl. Shock, shame, hatred of me, self-hatred, everything, all at once. Cool Miss Adler, the third-grade teacher, thought she'd met her Mr. Rock and Roll. It was all so perfect. Now this.

Witnessing Linda's complete meltdown, I hadn't expected my own reaction. I suddenly felt even guiltier than before. And terrified of losing her. All my life, I'd wrestled with the same riddle. Maybe if I gave it a chance, I'd learn to desire women? Maybe my attraction to men was just something I could fix? I still didn't know, because I hadn't tried. Dear reader, I know what you're thinking, but please try to understand. Just because I may have been gay didn't mean I wasn't Jewish. There's a saying in the Talmud that you are not born by your mother or father but by your children. Even for nonreligious Jews, even for show business Jews, our culture is all about passing the flame to the next generation. We're meant to have families. It's engraved into our dreams. "The show must go on!"

Something profound happened that morning. Two egotistical misfits realized they held the missing piece of each other's obsession. "I can change," I promised her, and I truly meant it. I didn't want to be gay; I wanted to have a family and make my parents proud like all Jewish sons and daughters want to. "I'm glad you told me," Linda eventually said. My secret had knocked the living shit out of her, but if there's one thing Linda understood, it was the frustration of being trapped in the wrong body. She was twenty-six, she'd been through college, she'd traveled the world and danced till dawn in a thousand dives. But behind her loud mouth, Linda felt ugly, overweight, inferior to other women. She had her faults and weaknesses, but fear was not one of them. In fact, Linda was probably attracted to danger.

Like two punch-drunk zombies, we loaded our cases into the cab and drove silently to the airport. Getting away to where nobody knew us was probably the only thing to do. We needed to swim in the ocean, stare at the sun, and ease the pain away. Any other odd couple would have known this was a bridge too far, but there's something about planes, flying above the clouds, and looking down on life. Knotted up in the tragedy of our situation, sobbing, clinging to each other's hands for dear life somewhere over the Bermuda Triangle, a powerful magnetism was holding us together. Call it trust, sympathy, destiny, love, or just the liberated spirit of the times, but whatever the "it" was, *it* was there. We had to get married. I just couldn't go through life without having a family, and Linda was so desperate to join me in the circus, I think she was able to accept that it was now going to be crazier than planned.

4. SURFING IN KANSAS

The actual wedding was the easy part—Linda's father was a kosher caterer. A date was set for October 23, 1971, but as the big day approached, my father started asking the Adlers too many religious questions and incurred the wrath of Mabel. She clearly didn't think much of us Steinbigles and was so appalled at my mommy's-boy airs, she once called me a mocky. With all the cross-family tension, Linda and I had a monumental row on the Tuesday before the Saturday wedding, nothing unusual for us, except that this time, Linda locked herself inside her bedroom in public protest.

It didn't take long for Mabel to hunt me down by telephone. "Seymour, I know you and Linda had a big fight. Now look, Ira's working very hard on all this food. We've had cancellations before, usually due to a death in the family or something horrible. But here's the deal—Ira can freeze just about everything: the roast beef, the lamb, the chicken, the soup, the vegetables, even those sweet breads you love so much. The one thing he can't freeze is the Viennese table." She was referring to the platter of dairy-free desserts that decorated Jewish banquets, usually kosher, nondairy variations of ice cream and custard pastries. "Now, Seymour, Ira makes the best Viennese table, but if there's no wedding, he can't freeze it. So, tell me, are you going to marry this girl?"

I never could tell if Mabel was a winder-upper or really as bad as she sounded. Like a good little son-in-law, I wasn't taking any chances and asked my future mother-in-law to coax my future wife out of her bedroom. Linda unlocked her door and came to the phone, peace broke out, and the Viennese table was saved from who knows what fate.

When the big day came, my father, Richard, and I donned our matching suits and top hats, and with my parents, we drove up to the Conservative Jewish Center in Riverdale, where Ira's crew handled the day's events like a Swiss railway network. Although I sensed that not everyone on my side of the hall was entirely sure about Linda's domineering personality, all the elders sang and wished us well. My folks had stopped trying to understand me years earlier, and now that I was officially terminating their contract as parents, even I was starting to not worry about what they thought.

Linda's family were just as unsure about me. Our fights were already a secret all over the block, we'd once been seen exchanging slaps on a Riverdale sidewalk, Linda had even hinted to her kid sister, Arlene, about my sexual deviance. The Adlers, however, knew what Linda was like and accepted that she was marrying into rock and roll, the only place where she probably belonged. I think they were even a little impressed themselves. I was twenty-nine, I had a successful record company, and I owned a two-bedroom apartment on Central Park. Linda could have done worse.

I knew Linda was marrying into wealth and show business, but what nobody else realized was that she was the first person I'd properly come out to. Her admiration and belief in me was sincere, and yes, I felt a stirring male pride to get her out of the classroom and into a high life she'd long dreamed of. Okay, so our fairy-tale castle was maybe built on sand, but I somehow knew we'd make a rock-and-roll king-and-queen combo anyway—even if the roles were a little confused.

With all those eyeballs staring at us, the wedding was an exhausting experience, and I woke up the next morning with a burning urge to travel. Fortunately, Linda was busy with school, so I waited a while and then ran off on my own personal honeymoon with a story about doing business in India and Australia. I needed to be away from everyone—Linda, Richard, Sire, my parents, Mabel, and the whole nonfreezable Viennese table of my life.

There really is nothing quite like travel to get your soul back in tune. I'd grown up on forties and fifties movies in which plane journeys into the Orient were always geographically illustrated by a red line advancing slowly across an old map. Flying from Europe over Arabia and Persia down toward India was a sensation like no other flight I'd previously taken. I was venturing into the East, and who knows what I might find—maybe the next George Harrison or Ravi Shankar standing on one leg under a tree. Failing that, my ulterior motive was to experience real Indian food. There were plenty of Indian restaurants in London, but the only good one that I knew of in New York was the Ceylon India Inn on Forty-Ninth Street. Surely, I thought, there'd be nowhere to eat Indian cooking like India itself.

I was picked up at the airport in Bombay by a Polydor staffer who kindly drove me to the Taj Palace Hotel, where my room was booked. While chatting during the ride into town, I asked if Bombay had a Jewish community. The guy's face lit up because, as he explained, his daughter happened to attend a private school run by an influential Jewish family. "Today's Friday," he beamed. "I'm sure they'd love to show you the synagogue!" So, as I checked into my hotel, my friendly Indian guide returned to his office and began making arrangements for me to meet this family at the local synagogue.

Unfortunately, with the killer journey and ten-hour time difference, I was so starving and disoriented, I sneaked out to a nearby restaurant called the Delhi Darbar, where I stuffed myself with delicious curry. When I turned up at the synagogue afterward, the family whisked me off to their palatial home, where I was then presented with a tableful of gourmet oriental dishes. It wasn't typical Indian food, nor was it anything like Ashkenazi cooking. Indian Jews ate a spicy variety of kosher that reminded me of what I'd already tasted in Syrian or Sephardic restaurants. I continued eating like a pig, of course, and spent the whole next day groaning in bed.

I would have gladly spent a month eating my way across India all the way up slopes of the Himalayas, but having met with Polydor India and experienced the insane chaos of Bombay, I had to continue on my trip southward to Australia where I hooked up more music business contacts in Sydney and Melbourne.

I eventually returned to New York three or four weeks later via Los Angeles, my first circumnavigation of the globe. I'd found new overseas partners along the way who'd either sell our records or send us their releases. I'd technically done business, meaning Linda couldn't eat my face off for having done a Houdini act straight after our wedding.

My apartment was now *our* apartment, and within months of being married, Linda was pregnant. When I broke the news to my parents, my father took me aside and advised that because mothers always did the hardest work, I should make a point of asking Linda to choose the name of the child. As he explained, it would create a stronger bond between mother and child and improve all-round family harmony. Linda adored her father, so, as a tribute to Ira's deceased parents, Linda chose the name Samantha Lee for our first daughter, based on the Hebrew name Sara Leia. My father's theory seemed strange at first, but it made a lot of practical sense.

It was a happy period when Elton John and John Reid were coming through New York all the time, regularly checking in to our guest bedroom. Thanks to global smash hits like "Your Song" and "Rocket Man," Elton was getting recognized on the streets of New York. John Reid was both his lover and manager, and together they could easily afford the best hotels in town, which of course they sometimes stayed at, depending on their reasons for being in New York. But for whatever reason, they liked hanging out with us, even after our screaming newborn arrived. We loved having them over and always provided a great spread of food, grass, and entertainment.

Elton was in the eye of a storm, and I think he enjoyed being in a real home around friends who were sincerely happy for his success. That's the thing about becoming famous; you don't change— everyone else does. It's natural for a famous person to crave the company of old friends. Unfortunately, it's easy for old friends to feel inadequate or even jealous. For all our faults, Linda and I were the opposite of all that. We loved hearing their stories of conquering the world, and we were behind them all the way. Plus, of course, we were the last couple on earth who'd judge them for sharing a bed. If anything, they were more normal than Linda and I.

Professionally, I wasn't in Elton John's league at all, but by Sire's own indie standards, we were selling healthy numbers of records from our main acts, the Climax Blues Band and Renaissance. I was getting so good at delivering cheesecake to London and walking back out with bargains, I even managed to leave EMI's head office in 1972 with the American rights to "Power to All Our Friends," a single by Cliff Richard, England's answer to Elvis. Another steal was Stackridge, an English rock group produced by George Martin. However, it was our Dutch group Focus who started to take off throughout 1972 and eclipse everything else we had on sale.

For this their second album, *Moving Waves*, Mike Vernon had given them a ballsy, electric sound that took their playing to a whole new level. When we received the master, Richard and I felt we had a potential winner on our hands, but lo and behold, our new distributor, Polydor, passed. I couldn't get a clear answer why, so I knocked on the boss's door. "Okay, I'll tell you why," said Jerry Schoenbaum, who ran what was the American branch of the German-owned conglomerate, Deutsche Grammophon. "There's this asshole over in Holland, Freddie Haayen, who runs Polydor, and he's got this fucking horrible Dutch band called Golden Earring that he keeps pushing me to release. Listen, I don't mind Focus, but I really don't want to release Golden Earring. So sorry, I just can't take anything Dutch right now."

"But, Jerry, Golden Earring are great. You're missing out on something here."

"Oh, puh-leeze, Seymour. You sound like him."

Jerry Schoenbaum was an old-school folkie who had good ears in the genres he liked. He'd been the right choice for distributing Blue Horizon's catalog in the States, but he just couldn't stomach all the glitter and pomp of glam and progressive rock. In the States, we had our own Frank Zappas, Captain Beefhearts, and Dr. Johns, but Britain and continental Europe were leading the left field and getting more experimental by the year. Some acts like Jethro Tull and Yes had shown that just about anything could be imported into America, and that audience was ours to chase. If we were serious about breaking Focus in the United States, then we had to find the appropriate distributor. After a bit of shopping around, we managed to bullshit ourselves an incredibly high percentage with no advance from Tony Martell at Famous Music, a division of Gulf and Western, who, in their own way, were desperately in search of success. They were our fifth distributor in six years, and this was probably rock bottom, but never underestimate the determination of underdogs.

I'll never forget our first Paramount gala in honor of the boss's late son, T. J. Martell. In T. J.'s dying months, Richard and I had taken him to an Elton John show and brought him backstage to meet the artist. We knew how much the poor guy's subsequent death had affected his father, who was our new distributor, so Richard and I showed up to the charity dinner in our matching wedding suits. The master of ceremonies was the entertaining Warner vice president, Joe Smith, who often performed the comical speeches at the United Jewish Appeal. As Smith introduced the ballroom's many guests, he turned to us. "Next, we have Seymour Stein and Richard Gottehrer from Sire Records. What, you've never heard of them? Sire is as important to the music business as surfing is to the state of Kansas."

We gritted our teeth and smiled as a wave of chuckles rolled around the ballroom. But *ouch*, that one hurt. Luckily, the gods of music watching overhead also had a sense of humor. In the madhouse of music, all it takes is three minutes for the proverbial state of Kansas to run out and buy surfboards. Yes, in 1973, Sire suddenly and unexpectedly hit the big time thanks to a Focus single. To be exact, three minutes and forty-two seconds of hard rock interrupted by a Dutch *flautist* yodeling operatic scales. I'm serious. Add some drum breaks like Animal from the Muppets and you get the idea of "Hocus Pocus" by Focus, probably the only ever perfectly rhyming number-one title and artist.

One million singles and five hundred thousand copies of the

accompanying album unleashed this six-month monsoon of dollar bills all over our laughing faces. It was glorious. We even had the export rights to the world except Holland, which meant nearly every sale on planet Earth came through our bank account. We'd made it. All those years lugging cheesecake through the desert suddenly felt like a passage to the promised land.

Did everything change? After the initial shock, no, not really. If anyone has ever accused me of being cheap, here is the proof. I was thirty-two, rich, and should reasonably have invested in a gold-plated bowl of coke and matching bedside table. However, I just kept doing what I'd always done. The only thing I splashed out on was a bigger apartment, because Linda was pregnant with our second child. For $110,000, we found a three-bedroom apartment in an elegant French-style building at 151 Central Park West, or the Kenilworth, as the building is called. At the time, Richard was living in a nice ground-floor space on West Seventy-Sixth Street looking at the planetarium and the American Museum of Natural History, but I nagged him to buy a bigger place of his own. As the old proverb goes, make hay while the sun shines.

Getting a majestic view over Central Park was a big step up the social ladder for the expanding Stein clan, but I'm glad Richard and I didn't go *too* insane with all that "Hocus Pocus" money, because the comedown was faster and harder than we saw coming. Like all record labels who score their first smash hit, we thought success would get easier, so we hired some new staffers and pushed the roster in different directions. The office was suddenly buzzing with activity; we had an art guy, radio pluggers, a tape copy boy, secretaries, and a constant stream of managers and agents dropping by.

As well as putting out a batch of new releases from our main acts, I began compilations and reissues like *Nuggets*, *The History of British Rock*, *The History of British Blues*, and offsets by early Duane Eddy, the Turtles, Paul Anka, and others. I couldn't produce original music like Richard could, so carefully researched compilations were my way of telling musical stories, complete with elaborate liner notes. At least digging up old stuff and negotiating nonexclusive licenses was cheap. The expensive bit was producing new albums that sold seventy-two copies. We threw a load of fresh shit at the wall that didn't stick—stuff like Chilliwack and Nucleus. What, never heard of them? Yeah, I know.

There was one third-party investment that came out of that period. The Focus connection led to a strange encounter at a David Bowie concert around 1972. I was lining up to take a piss when this young guy tapped me on the shoulder and said, "Focus?" I thought he was on drugs for criticizing my aim, but then he said, "Thijs van Leer?" He introduced himself as Marty Scott, one of the owners of a New Jersey import company called Jem Records, who I knew had imported copies of Focus's first record directly from Europe—not something I was too happy about. The guy then explained that a year previously, I'd talked at a music business seminar that he'd attended, and that's how he recognized me. He seemed friendly, and I was definitely curious about whatever he was getting up to in New Jersey, so I told him to drop by the office.

When he called in, he told me his full story about how he and his two best friends had started selling imported records in the three different colleges they had attended. Their importing started as a student hobby that grew so successful so quickly, they rented out a warehouse in Plainfield, New Jersey. What got my ears standing to attention, however, were his references to obscure artists and record labels in Britain and Europe that only a pro could possibly know. These guys were sniffing down the same dark alleys as I was. We began hanging out, Marty met Richard, Linda, and some of my friends, and over the next months, Sire invested some "Hocus Pocus" profits into a joint venture called Passport Records, Jem's very own label that Sire half owned. Passport signed experimental and kraut-rock acts like Nektar, Tucky Buzzard, Lucifer's Friend, and other obscurities, as well as Synergy, actually a solo artist, Larry Fast.

The thing about pop music is that no matter how hard you work the land, you'll always be at the mercy of the weather. The mainstream scene just wasn't that great around 1974 and 1975. Like Linda and me, millions of young adults had gotten married and were having kids. For this increasingly domesticated hippie audience, American majors kept churning out blockbuster albums from established names, generally aging stars from the sixties who were also juggling babies and careers. In England, glam and progressive rock had grown along the edges, but apart from Elton John, David Bowie, Jethro Tull, and a few others, not much new English stuff was gaining traction in the States. It had been a decade since the Beatles first landed, when virtually anything with a British accent would sell. Since then, American companies had been quietly opening offices around London, which meant it was harder for small fries like Sire to compete. Up against CBS, Atlantic, Warners, A&M, MCA, EMI, Decca, Island, and the big continentals like Polydor, Phonogram, and Ariola, our one-hit wonder with Focus meant nothing. We'd have been laughed out of any bidding war.

As soon as I started moaning about business, Linda started nagging me about Richard. "He's not putting in the effort you are," she'd say.

Richard was my brother in arms, the guy I'd always idolized, so her accusations hit a very raw nerve. "You don't know anything about our business!" I'd yell.

"Yeah, well, I don't see him running around the world like you!"

"But I'm the business guy; he's the producer."

"Why's he not produced any hits lately? *You're* finding stuff. What the fuck's *he* doing when you're off in London or wherever?"

I never knew if Linda's problem was really Richard or actually about my constant traveling. Or if it also had something to do with Richard's wife, Judy, who did not even pretend to like Linda. In fact, Linda was capable of such paranoid jealousy, she actually suspected something going on between me and Richard, which was just absurd. Whatever it was, when Linda got a bone between her teeth, she'd snarl and chomp and slobber and grind. There'd be no letting go until the thing had been picked to death and buried in some unmarked grave.

I ignored her bitching for months, but eventually, I had to admit to myself that Richard's heart maybe wasn't in it too much anymore. He was the best friend I'd ever had, I'd learned so much from the guy, but neither of us were twenty-five and single. I had a family, and Richard had plenty of shit on his own plate. For our own sanity, we needed to stop blaming each other for the way Sire was bumping along. It was hard to actually sit down and confess to each other that we maybe had personal problems, too. Your mid-thirties are a funny age: old enough to know your best years are mostly over but still young enough to keep fucking up and never ask yourself why. I think Richard felt my distance and began taking breaks, including one extended stay in New Orleans. Eventually, he moved his studio out to his own premises. When it was clear he wanted out for good, we struck a deal so that I could buy his stock.

After months of avoiding embarrassing questions, the split was surprisingly cordial; he even seemed relieved. But for me, the months thereafter were Sire's absolute low point. When Richard was gone, the building was empty. I had enough back catalog ticking over to pay the bills and take something home at the end of the month, but there was nothing happening on the horizon. Like steering a ghost ship through the fog, I was trapped in the music business until death do us part.

To everyone's surprise, Richard got divorced from Judy shortly afterward. That's how far we'd grown apart; I knew he had problems at home, but I didn't know they were *that* serious. We'd all noticed Judy's overprotective streak—it was impossible not to. She was actually worse than Linda. Judy was basically a small-town girl from southern Illinois and would impose all these clingy house rules on Richard, like him coming home at 6:00 P.M., or stopping him from traveling at the weekends. Her insecurity was holding Richard back and probably putting huge mental pressure on him, not that I ever dared to tell Richard what I really thought, partly because I knew he had his own opinions about what Linda was doing to me.

I guess we were both experiencing the record man's equivalent of a midlife crisis. As anyone who's lived a full life in music will tell you, it isn't easy to adapt to middle age when you've enjoyed such a wild, carefree youth. Most experience some kind of wobble when suddenly your body starts changing and everything in your professional and personal life feels like a failure. Most don't make it through to the other side. Thankfully, Richard and I both did in the end, but this was our career equivalent of "the difficult third album." We each had to reassess, dig deep, and start anew.

I was in no position to judge Richard's problems, nor anyone else's, because my own home was turning into a war zone. Linda didn't hold me back professionally; her father had worked in a competitive, labor-intensive business that required total dedication. For Linda, working eighteen-hour Sundays was how you got ahead in New York City. But we had plenty of other things to fight about, and the domestic tension intensified once Linda was pregnant again while Samantha was a tiny toddler charging around. We loved Samantha with all the passion in our hearts, but the pressures of parenthood seemed to turn up the volume on all our problems as a couple. For me, it was always simple; career took precedence over everything, including fatherhood. All I wanted to do to was keep running around, which I did, to London or Cannes or Los Angeles or wherever I had fresh meat to chase. I felt immense affection watching Samantha playing with her toys, and I felt pride and accomplishment to see Linda's pregnant belly. But in practical terms, I was the world's most absent father, incapable of much except providing money.

I'd see all the hippie fathers in Central Park, rolling around on the grass with their kids. My own father had spent most of his life either at the garment center or in the synagogue, and I don't remember him *ever* getting down on his hands and knees to *vroom vroom* my toy cars. I think I would have called the psychiatric hospital myself. All I wanted was to continue his orthodox model in my own rock-and-roll manner, which might have been possible had Linda been as motherly as Dora Steinbigle. Sure, Linda could hold the fort if she had to. Linda *did* hold the fort; she was a natural organizer. But the ambitious, fun-loving freewheeler I'd married hadn't traded my niece's classroom for a life of washing machines and diapers.

To put it mildly, being motherly didn't come naturally to Linda. When I was a boy, my doting mother used to creep into my bedroom every winter morning and hang my clothes on the radiator so that little Seymour would go out to school nice and toasty. Mabel didn't exactly shove Linda's clothes in the refrigerator, but she did force Linda onto diet pills because "You're fat!" Linda had been dragged screaming through the School of Hard Knocks and left home with mixed feelings about the whole institution of motherhood. And once she got a taste of show business, she liked its effect so much, she couldn't get enough. To put it bluntly, Linda wasn't interested in being like anyone's mother; she wanted to be like *me*. This became ever clearer once we hired nannies. Even though Linda had time to herself, her screaming continued.

Linda's frustration about being stuck at home became so unbearable, she'd yell at me in pregnant or postnatal fits that I'm sure
frightened the neighbors. "You're ruining my life!" was the scream,
regularly accompanied by flying objects. With two pregnancies in
four years, she'd put on a lot of weight, which of course gnawed
straight into her deepest wound. She felt disfigured and ugly with
the extra problem that she'd lost her career as well. For Linda, it
was simple; if I wasn't going to give her the life she wanted, she'd
just take it herself. She'd thumb through my address books. "Look
who's in here?" she'd beam. "We're gonna have a party!" She didn't
mind that I didn't really know a lot of these celebrities whose numbers I collected. She'd schmooze, call people up, charm them into
a dinner, party, or club date. I'd cringe watching her working so
much strategy into jet-setters and pop stars she hardly knew, but on
the night, she'd be fabulous, and I'd have great fun.

One party led to another, until next thing I know, Iggy Pop is
rolling a joint on the living room carpet and all these faces from the
Andy Warhol crowd are lining up to do blow in the bathroom. On
Thanksgiving 1974, we had Elton John and his band over for tur-
key and pumpkin pie. Linda actually hired her father to do the ca-
tering for that unforgettable banquet. We watched the parade from
our balcony and the musicians ate up before they played Madison
Square Garden that night. John Lennon, who was set to join Elton
onstage, even dropped by for dessert. This was during his lost
period, separated from Yoko Ono and partying like never before
with his new girlfriend, May Pang. Imagine everyone's reaction when
he called for silence and handed Elton John a present. Elton un-
wrapped the little box and produced a gleaming cock ring.

We certainly had the space to entertain. We'd done up this nice
old library room where we watched TV or hosted late-night parties. If guests were too whacked to get a cab, they were welcome to

pull out the sofa and crash, which they didn't mind doing, because it was so comfortable. Elton John slept on that bed so many times, we eventually bought him a piano. In the middle of all this madness, there were toys on the floor and milk bottles in the kitchen sink. Nobody seemed to mind. This was the midseventies when it was both normal and cool to mix kids with rock and roll.

Our second daughter, Mandy, was born in January 1975, shortly after Linda's mother died. Although I hadn't been Mabel's greatest admirer, I took my father's wise advice and looked for a similar-sounding name as a show of respect to Linda's family. I chose Mandy because I loved the old Irving Berlin song of the same name. By coincidence, Barry Manilow had a hit at the time called "Mandy," which I hadn't paid much attention to until I received a congratulations message from Clive Davis, the boss of Arista. "Thank you for naming your daughter after my hit," said Clive, who was of course Barry Manilow's Svengali, and, I hope, just winding me up.

There's an old joke that when you have a kid, your whole life changes, and when you have two kids, you don't have a life anymore. Linda's solution was to hire more help. Teresa was our reliable full-time nanny from Barbados who, I think it's fair to say, basically raised Samantha and Mandy over the subsequent roller-coaster years. At one point, we had a total of three women working different shifts, which allowed Linda to become the major-league socialite she wanted so badly to become. Don't get me wrong, it wasn't all selfishness and ambition. When I met Linda, she was already a hard-core partier who lived to meet people, dance, booze, toke, and feel her head spinning in the bright lights. Fast, hard living was Linda's true nature, and this was New York at arguably its wildest ever period in history. Focus had put me on the map and bulged my wallet; Linda had no intention of missing out on all the fun.

I know that some of my old friends were sickened by Linda's habit of off-loading Samantha and Mandy onto nannies, baby-sitters, grandparents, aunts, and friends. I was, too, and we had many screaming matches about the dysfunctional family we were becoming. But who was I to lecture? "Why don't you ever spend any time with your children?" was a line Linda screamed at me at least five hundred times, possibly more. At the end of the day, I have to be honest with myself: Linda was putting me on the celebrity radar. My desire for success trumped whatever father instincts I possessed. As a team, we were doing what we'd set out to do: conquer New York and live life to the limit.

Our eldest daughter, Samantha, was a galloping toddler, and as kids do, she found our little Mickey Mouse mirror and matching coke grinder yet somehow knew this particular toy was for adults only. Fortunately, no powder was lying around, not that it would have been a big deal in those days. Cocaine was like toothpaste or gum—you didn't go anywhere without some in your pocket. I'm sure it sounds strange, but I discovered at the tender age of thirty-three that drugs actually suited me, especially blow because pot wasn't my kind of buzz. What had I been missing? I still don't know if drugs relieved stress or blew things nicely out of proportion, but they sure took Linda's mind games to a whole new level. When Linda got stoned, and she really did smoke a lot of grass, she'd stare into me with this mischievous, goofy, horny grin.

It took me years to figure out Linda's king-sized personality, but I think she just wanted to be loved, as if by hanging out with all the beautiful people from New York's gossip columns, her low self-esteem would be cured. Her drinking and drugging was the same; it made her feel good about herself. She came alive when she was partying. She also had this curious habit of taking lost characters under her wing, generally gay men, because she was easily jealous of pretty women. Her favorite of all was Danny Fields, a gay rocker you'd always find sniffing around at every dogfight. I already knew him; sometimes he was a journalist, sometimes he was publicist for record labels, but most of the time he was being Danny Fields. In late 1974, he tracked down Linda while trying to get photos of Elton John for *16*, a teenager magazine where he was editor.

For Linda, it was platonic love at first sight. Danny was a Harvard grad, he was Jewish, razor sharp, funny, charming, interesting, he knew everyone worth knowing, he got her black humor, and just like Linda, he was a closet sentimental, genuinely interested in people. Danny was the Oscar Wilde of New York's rock underground who should have been included among the characters in Lou Reed's "Walk on the Wild Side." In the sixties, he'd been one of the Velvet Underground's friends at the Factory. He then worked for Elektra, where he did PR for the Doors and personally found both MC5 and the Stooges—major A&R scoops, which alone made him a legend. Being so openly gay probably didn't do his career prospects much good in the relatively homophobic music business, but I knew he had great taste. Linda, however, was his number-one fan. She saw unsung genius in Danny that she wanted to help and feed off.

In restaurants, Linda started asking for doggie bags. "Danny's probably starving," she'd tell me, and then ask the cab driver to swing by his place. Danny was such a night creature, he'd usually fall into bed at dawn and wake up late afternoon to an empty refrigerator. I'm sure he found it hilarious in his anarchic way that, *ding dong*, Linda would appear with these nicely wrapped half-eaten steaks for his evening breakfast. The pair of them were like the fawning Jewish mother and her naughty son who could do no wrong. I'm grateful to say, however, that this bond led to some life-changing surprises for all of us.

One evening in the summer of 1975, Linda got an excited call from Danny insisting that she drag me down to the Bowery. There was a band called the Ramones I absolutely *had* to hear! I'd already heard the buzz and had been meaning to check them out. The problem was, I'd just returned from London and was dying with a flu. When it came to seeing bands or battling jet lag, I was a soldier by nature, but this time, I was truly wounded. I'd been to CBGB several times before and knew it would be best to be in top physical form to venture down into the Bowery, Manhattan's very own Turkish toilet—definitely not a place to be stranded after dark, praying for a cab. This was the bankrupt, scum-encrusted downtown underworld of Martin Scorsese's *Taxi Driver,* a merciless jungle for injured animals.

Linda went down on her own, met up with Danny, and came home raving. They were so determined to hook me, I booked a studio the next day to see the boys rehearse. When I walked in, I was knocked sideways by the energy. It wasn't that it was so electric or that they were squeezed into tight jeans doing all these funny moves; I'd sort of expected something heavy from the moment I walked in and saw them standing around in biker jackets. What left-hooked me were their quirky songs, which only lasted about one minute, like the Beach Boys driven through a meat mincer.

I was standing there not sure whether to laugh. What the fuck was this? A hard-rock parody of early-sixties bubblegum? Whatever sick joke these guys were playing, they really meant it, and it was new and original. I loved it. The character on stage left, wearing his guitar like a pair of low-hanging balls, looked about as mean as a Nazi accelerating into Russia. Even his hair was a perfect cross between a Monkees mop top and a Wehrmacht helmet. But hang on, did I just hear the skinny malink singer actually say, "Second verse, same as the first verse"? On stage right, the bass player looked like a long story who really had sniffed glue and strangled girl-friends. The tiny drummer at the back played like Moe Tucker, and like his incessant whacking, the Ramones just kept banging out these miniature songs in battle formation—every one a chorus with some wacky slogan. The Ramones were pushing all extremes out as far as Johnny Ramone could stretch his legs.

In about twenty minutes flat, they emptied all their artillery in my face, probably about eighteen songs, which gave us forty minutes of prepaid studio time to talk shit. I didn't know what to say, except, "Wow, guys!" Their special something was hard to pin down, and I noticed that even Danny, our Harvard man of letters, couldn't explain why they felt so good. This was the filthiest sugar and the sugariest filth either of us had ever tasted, a clear-cut case of "sign now, make sense of it later."

The contract was signed in about two days, and when I ventured down to CBGB to watch them play to a crowd, the energy in the air was overwhelming. Among that performance-art scene on the Lower East Side, the Ramones were already well on their way to being the hippest show in town. Arty people just got it instantly. Photographers like Roberta Bayley and Bob Gruen were down there photographing them. In the underground press, they already had believers, such as Lisa Robinson, who first alerted Danny. Danny in turn wrote about them as did others in magazines like *Rock Scene* and *Circus*. And let's not forget the owner of CBGB, the lovely Hilly Kristal, who gave the Ramones their first break. If anyone deserves special credit, he does.

Talk about right place, right time. I later learned that Richard had almost signed the Ramones to Sire on a singles deal a few months before he left, while he and his trainee producer, Craig Leon, were working on a CBGB group called City Lights, one of those Sire releases that sold about eleven copies. The Ramones turned *them* down. I also learned much later that they'd failed a big test in Connecticut for an Epic sub-label called Blue Sky. Luckily for me, the crowd had come to see the headliner Johnny Winter and started throwing bottles at the Ramones, which of course was curtains for any record deal. They'd taken some knocks along the way, but by late 1975, the Ramones were fully formed yet nicely underripe.

But here's the thing: Danny was insisting that Linda co-manage the group with him, which of course she wanted more than anything. He had great contacts in the music press, his name was magic, but he wasn't a businessman and felt Linda would make things happen the way she organized her star-studded parties. The fact Linda could squeeze dough out of me and frighten Sire staffers was a bonus, but that wasn't Danny's Machiavellian master plan. There was a feeling between Danny and Linda that they'd complement each other, and to be fair to them, they genuinely did. They probably wouldn't have pulled it off without each other.

Was I worried about this managerial alliance? No. I was relieved that Linda was being cast by a respected figure like Danny Fields into a role I'd never thought of. Co-manager for the loudest band in New York? This was so much better than me giving Linda some token job in Sire, something I never wanted to do. As for Danny, he was back crusading for a band he believed in—which was good for the investment, because people trusted his opinion. Even Craig Leon, who'd stayed on at Sire after Richard's departure, was already trusted by the Ramones for having flagged them so early on. So, he was put in charge of producing the debut album. Everyone clicked effortlessly into place like everything was meant to happen.

Linda co-managing the Ramones had benefits and disadvantages. The band knew my every move, so one day I received a call from Johnny Ramone only fifteen minutes after I walked into my flat dead tired from one of my English trips. "We've got some new songs," he announced. "We really want you to hear them."

"Johnny," I begged, as if he didn't already know, "I've just walked in the door after ten days in London. Give me a day or two, and then come in and play them for me."

Then he called me back with a gig date. "Look, we know you're not doing anything on that night, so we booked ourselves into CBGB. We want you to hear them live."

On the appointed evening, I went down to hear their new stuff. The opening act was meant to be one of Hilly's bands that I had heard several times before and had no interest in signing. To avoid running into Hilly, I stood outside. It was mid-November, but yet a warm night. I was chatting to Lenny Kaye when all of a sudden I heard the warm-up band playing a strangely hypnotic air that I later found out was called "Love Goes to Building on Fire." It was like nothing else I'd ever heard, and my heart started pounding with excitement.

"This isn't Hilly's band," I said to Lenny

"No, of course not. This is Talking Heads."

As I was listening, I was being sucked in through the door, like a snake being charmed by an Arabian flute.

The front man was this handsome short-haired figure with piercing eyes, singing something cryptic about love on fire. I had no idea what he meant, but the melody had hit qualities. Behind him was just a drummer and a girl bass player. The whole thing was dead simple yet so intense.

After the set, I tried to help the girl down with her instruments.

"Hello," I said, stopping them. "I'm Seymour Stein from Sire Records. You guys are amazing!"

They looked flattered, but unlike most young bands, they didn't click into salesman mode.

That's when David Byrne spoke up. "We know who you are,"

said the singer, who seemed a lot shier offstage than he'd appeared during his performance. His speaking voice, however, had the same lilting cadences I'd been struck by when he sang. "Why don't you come down to our loft tomorrow?" he suggested, then scribbled down an address beside a phone number.

It's funny how the greatest moments in your life take years to sink in. Although I didn't know it right there, this was one of the most important encounters of my entire career. I met up with the three musicians the following day on Allen Street, but once again, they didn't engage in the way that bands generally do. They weren't aloof; they were just young and unsure of what they wanted for their future, especially David. They'd only recently moved into New York and still had ties up in Rhode Island, where'd they'd been to art college and formed their group. I didn't force the issue and just kept on their tail, going down to CBGB to hear them, always inviting them for a proper record company meeting that never seemed to happen. It wasn't that they were playing hard to get; they just didn't feel ready, and as I'd later discover, they were telling each other, "If we make a record with this guy, it'll tank, and we'll never get a second chance with anyone else." Luckily, I didn't know their exact reasoning and kept telephoning, saying hello, sniffing around after them like a stray Bowery dog.

At the time, I had several other pots bubbling on the fire. In England—or, to be exact, in the Oxfordshire countryside—Mike Vernon was busy producing the Climax Blues Band's seventh album in his very own Chipping Norton studio. He'd telephoned to warn there was a possible hit in the pipeline. Meanwhile, Linda was crawling up the walls about the Ramones' debut album. During that period, Danny Fields was certainly the dominant co-manager, doing wonders for their self-confidence, but there's no doubt Tommy Ramone was the natural leader. Joey was the sweet one, Johnny had the gang attitude that rubbed off on all of them, and Dee Dee was the wild one out on the edge. But Tommy had been the original manager and the main conceptualist who'd previously worked as a studio engineer. He held a special inside-outside position in the group, which probably gave the whole package such a cutting edge.

The heart of the enterprise was a flashing metronome, which Tommy placed above his kit to stay in time, because he wasn't really a drummer. That pulsating light created the hypnotic, almost disco feel behind Tommy's drumming and Dee Dee's thumping bass lines. It's subliminal, but it's a big part of what made the Ramones sound so modern. The other trick they used on their debut album was Beatles-style hard panning. Guitars were stacked up in one speaker, bass in the other, vocals in the center—like a sonic representation of their stage formation. Everything was designed to be extremist pop art. And again, that was Tommy talking in conceptual language with Craig Leon, who came from contemporary music and understood what Tommy wanted.

Just six grand bought me twenty-nine minutes of electrifying rock and roll—the likes of which hadn't been heard in years. The hard part was getting the public to like it. And let me tell you, in early 1976, way before the idea of "punk" was even invented, radio stations wouldn't touch the Ramones with a toilet brush.

In the middle of all of this, Paramount shut down, with its assets sold off to ABC. Gulf and Western had enough of the music business and wanted out. My new distributors were ABC, Sire's sixth. We could have gone elsewhere, but we stuck with ABC mainly because I respected their boss. Jay Lasker, a veteran who started at Decca's Chicago branch in the 1940s, was Mo Ostin's partner during the Sinatra days of Reprise, then at Vee-Jay and Dunhill, and came along after ABC bought Dunhill. He'd hired some talented characters like Charlie Minor, one of the greatest promotion men ever, and chief marketing man Dennis Lavinthal, who went on to cofound *Hits* magazine with Lenny Beer, and producer Steve Barri. Knowing the Ramones needed to be explained, I flew out to ABC's head office in Los Angeles and presented this high-voltage rock that I knew wouldn't make much sense to anyone outside of that Lower East Side art scene. I think ABC only took the record because in that same batch of releases, I was also giving them a potential hit album from the Climax Blues Band.

When *Ramones* was officially released in April 1976, the record was physically delivered to record stores in tiny dribbles of two or three copies, and of course, nobody cared or even noticed. If anyone was capable of pulling off a miracle for the Ramones, it was Charlie Minor, who I begged for special help. According to legend, the previous year he'd been plugging a record called "Love Hurts" by English rock group Nazareth. On his rounds, he'd called a radio programmer who sounded unusually depressed. "What's up?" asked Charlie, who was then given a grim story about the guy's ex-girlfriend being killed in a plane crash. After some words of sympathy, Charlie couldn't resist, "You see, it's true, *love hurts*. That's why you've got to play this song!"

The guy was a scream, so I played the Ramones to him, thinking if there was one plugger crazy enough to sell this record, it was Charlie Minor. "Look," he said, scratching his head, "I really don't get these guys, but I get what you're doing at Sire. If this is the band you want me to go after, I will." Even for the legendary Charlie Minor, plugging that first Ramones record to hippie jocks was like head-butting a brick wall. He did, however, convince a few mavericks to spin "Blitzkrieg Bop," which was a start.

The only instant reaction was negativity from people inside the business. The worst was Miles Copeland, the manager of the Climax

Blues Band and Renaissance. He was so appalled by the Ramones, he threatened to take his acts off Sire in protest. Pretty rich considering I'd given him the Climax Blues Band. Clive Davis was another. Lots of music business players thought the Ramones were an insult to musicianship and just could not see the charm. In the long run, I have to say, although unpleasant at first, all this hostility succeeded in rallying my troops.

To sell the Ramones, we were going to have to tour them. We knew that most people became believers when they witnessed the band live. This meant hiring an in-house booker and playing a whole new game of gigs and underground press—working city by city. There was CBGB and Max's Kansas City in New York, there was also the Rat in Boston, but apart from these three clubs, there weren't that many obvious clubs. In fact, it's a telling indicator of how the music business had changed by the midseventies; there were big theaters for established rock bands and a growing number of dance-floor discotheques where records were played. But small-capacity clubs for emerging rock groups? There really weren't that many options, and of those that were small enough, not many would stomach the Ramones.

In the beginning, the boys played wherever Linda and Danny could find them an audience. They'd squeeze into cars, sleep three to a hotel room, play colleges, basements, anything, anywhere. Colleges were the most inventive with turning spaces into makeshift venues, but none of these road adventures would have been possible had the Ramones been precious artistes. No matter how shitty the shitholes were, they took every show seriously and always stuck around afterward to sell and give away their merchandise to any stragglers who'd been bitten by the bug. One of the few things we spent money on were pins, T-shirt, and miniature Ramones base-ball bats. The bats were a reference to the chorus "Beat on the brat with a baseball bat." They were also cute little mementos that summed up the joke: the old-school American dream that slugged you in the face.

The one city where Linda and I managed to pull off a promotional heist was in London, but even that was a ramshackle accident where the headline was another of my bands, the Flamin' Groovies. The just-formed Stranglers would open as the first warm-up before the Ramones took to the stage on this triple bill. I don't know how it came together so perfectly, but you really couldn't have made it up. It was July 4, 1976, the bicentenary of American Independence, and we somehow managed to sell out the Roundhouse: two thousand tickets by word of mouth. The crowd was way bigger than anything the Ramones had played to in the States, but like all great acts, they rose to the occasion once fate presented itself. They blew away the Stranglers, the Flamin' Groovies, and the two thousand people watching, many of whom were musicians and tastemakers, including our label manager at our UK licensee, Nigel Grainge at Phonogram, and his thirteen-year-old brother, Lucian Grainge, current chairman of Universal and recently knighted. Lucian and his brother have both told me it was seeing the Ramones and Talking Heads that made him want to be in the music business.

The following night, the Ramones headlined Dingwalls, a smaller venue where, once again, they sold out and brought the house down. I was there watching this momentous occasion, and so was every punk wannabe in the kingdom. Johnny Rotten, the Clash, the Damned, the Stranglers, Billy Idol, Pete Shelley of the Buzzcocks, Keith Levene of Public Image Limited—a whole generation of future punk stars got hypnotized by this new high-energy art rock from New York. Talk about a bolt of lightning hitting the primordial soup; the Brits are still recovering from that weekend.

So much has been written about this "birth of punk." The joke is, as it was happening, it took months to notice any effect. The Ramones didn't have time to hang around London. They had to get back to more shithole gigs in American towns you'd happily drive through without stopping. By August, however, they got a glowing review in *Rolling Stone*, their first major-league plug. Even still, Linda and Danny had to keep calling and begging promoters and colleges to keep the boys on the road. That's where Linda's skills really shone. Danny's name opened doors in the big cities, but Linda's brass neck proved vital in breaking them out of the usual circuits. Thankfully, the Ramones were so motivated and so electrifying, the promoters got their money's worth, the crowds got thicker, the fees got better, and everyone at Sire started wanting a second album. Let's not exaggerate here; the Ramones were barely paying for themselves, but the band was determined to conquer the world, as were Linda and Danny. Meanwhile, I was getting itchy fingers about all these other acts in CBGB.

It's amazing how the old feeds the new. Sire had already released six albums by the Climax Blues Band since 1969, but their seventh, in 1976, produced the hit single "Couldn't Get It Right"— number three on the Hot 100, ensuring massive orders for the album. I have to be honest, however, that for this hit, I solicited "the help" of *Billboard* charts man Bill Wardlow. As a former *Billboard* vet, I had access to Bill who, as everyone knew, was taking the charts into a shadier era than the age of innocence I'd known under Tom Noonan. My other secret weapon was ABC's promotion man Charlie Minor, who was busy treating the gatekeepers of radio to all kinds of recreational enticements. Don't blame me; that's how it worked in the midseventies, folks. So, just as the Ramones were starting to smoke, I hit the jackpot with the Climax Blues Band, which gave me the cash and the lucky feeling to take several rolls on a handful of CBGB acts.

I wasn't the only one sniffing around the Bowery. Richard Gottehrer had been to CBGB before I had, and along with Craig Leon, they were producing a group called Blondie, who he had just been hawking around town. No big labels had been interested, so Richard ended up signing them to Larry Uttal's Private Stock label—not a great home, but that's how underground the CBGB scene was in 1976. That little deal turned out to be a huge mistake that just about everyone regretted. Except Larry Uttal, of course. Blondie's first album sold only eighteen thousand copies, but everything changed when my old friend Terry Ellis stepped in. Onlookers thought he was crazy, but farsighted Terry fell so head over heels in love with Blondie, he forked out a million bucks to buy the contract off Larry Uttal. Thus began Blondie's lucky run on Chrysalis.

I'm embarrassed to say that like so many others who saw Blondie perform in the very early days, I just didn't see any star of Bethlehem twinkling over the stage. I *saw* that Debbie Harry was a beauty, and I knew she was a friendly lady who had a great voice of her own. I definitely saw *some* potential, but the songs being written by Chris Stein in the early days were nowhere near the level he'd reach about two years later when Blondie began scoring hit after hit. I guess Chris Stein hadn't fully tapped into his own imagination yet. As the very best songwriters all seem to say, you generally have to write forty songs before you stumble on a killer. It's a craft even the very best have to earn.

For me, of all the unsigned CBGB regulars, Talking Heads were top of my shopping list. From day one, they had some knockout tunes like "Psycho Killer" and my personal favorite of their early stuff, "Love Goes to Building on Fire." I *had* to sign Talking Heads.

It took me almost a year. In all that time, I still can't believe that nobody came along and gave them an offer they couldn't refuse, like dangling David Byrne from a top-floor window. When you're chasing a band, it's natural to address the main man, but David

Byrne was a tough nut to crack. For a guy capable of such fearless performances, offstage he seemed to want to be left alone. I don't know if you've ever seen a five-year-old kid get handed a telephone by his mother. "Hey, Billy. It's Grandpa. Say hello." Well, trying to cozy up to David Byrne made you feel like poor old Grandpa, asking dumb questions and filling up the silence, saying *anything* to feel some love back, but only getting *yes* and *no*, all the while knowing Billy can't wait to hang up and get back to his playing. I thought David Byrne was a genius, and I'm sure he felt my awe. But I think extreme talent just doesn't want to be disturbed or distracted; it's constantly busy and enjoying its own company. You could see his mind working nonstop, and I guess he just wasn't interested in hanging around at the bar, talking business with a record guy like me.

Talking Heads drummer Chris Frantz was the friendly one. He was a happy, smiling, unpretentious Kentucky kid who'd known David Byrne since college. They were best friends. The bass player, Tina Weymouth, was Chris's girlfriend, who the guys had talked into joining the group. She was a classy young lady, half-French and always polite, but maybe because she was only just learning her instrument, she hung back slightly, too. When you spoke to the three of them, they seemed to let Chris Frantz give the appropriate reply, which he always did without ever being bossy. Chris and Tina knew all eyes were on their singer, and I think understood David's bizarre genius needed constant support—both on- and offstage. Tina even cut her hair short to look as plain as possible. She didn't want audiences to look at her instead of David. I hadn't yet figured out the complex chemistry between the three of them, and I doubt I ever fully did.

Luckily, the Ramones started offering them support slots, so "the Heads," as they quickly become known in our circle, were being gently pulled into the Sire orbit by everyone else who revolved around me. By winter 1976, the Ramones were recording their second album, and there was this amazing energy carrying them to cult status, which started to rub off on the Heads when they played together. I guess David Byrne got thinking, *If Sire can give the Ramones a serious break, maybe this Stein character can do something for me.*

One night after playing a show together, Chris Frantz cornered Danny Fields. "How is it dealing with Seymour?" he asked.

"Well, Seymour has always done right by the Ramones," replied Danny.

After months of chasing, that one little endorsement from Danny must have clinched it. Talking Heads knew Sire was nothing special, but by then, they knew they were too special for any major. What they needed was a hip indie who understood what they were about; the rest was down to themselves.

"Okay, we're ready to record something," Chris Frantz told me on behalf of his bandmates. This fabulous news deserved a celebration, so I took them to Patrissy's in Little Italy. Over the best pasta in New York, I finally got a laugh out of David Byrne when I sang some of his songs in what he'd describe as my "drunken sort of way." He'd always looked at me suspiciously, like I was a shark from the sewers of Crooklyn, but he'd probably never heard anyone sing his songs before.

We agreed to start with a single, and I thought "Love Goes to Building on Fire" had the best chance of airplay. I was wrong. It didn't chart and didn't get much action beyond college radio, but never mind—it was a happy anthem that launched the adventure on the right note. Above all, it got both the band and Sire staff hungry for a full album. To expand their sound, they recruited a second guitarist, Jerry Harrison, a former member of the Modern Lovers who had already jammed with Talking Heads on a few occasions.

My other mistake was to have suggested Tony Bongiovi as producer without giving enough thought to the delicate team chemistry. It was the last time I'd ever get involved in a producer casting for Talking Heads. They got the work done; however, Tony didn't know how to handle David Byrne, who insisted on doing simple things funny ways, like evacuating the control room when he sang his vocals. David was so shy, he didn't want anyone gawping at him through a window.

Midway through the album in April 1977, all four Talking Heads flew off with Danny, Linda, and the Ramones to Europe to play six weeks of one-nighters, including some prestigious venues like the Bataclan in Paris and the Rock Garden in London. At the London show, Brian Eno appeared backstage with John Cale and introduced himself to David Byrne. Linda saw the twinkling eyes and organized a brunch for Eno and the Heads the following day in a pub called the Spotted Pig. That's when they first discussed working together in the future. As Linda told me over the phone, Brian Eno and David Byrne spoke the same conceptual language. Eno was the man for their next album.

I would have loved to have been there, but Sire was at a critical juncture. The lucky combination of the Climax Blues Band scoring a mainstream hit while punk began making headlines in England got Sire bleeping on major corporation radars. I urgently needed a better distributor than the mess ABC was becoming. I loved working with Charlie Minor, but the company was going through a senseless shake-up. The owners kicked out Jay Lasker because he dressed badly or some such ridiculous reason. In his place, they put in a guy with the unlikely name of I. Martin Pompadur, a total stranger to music, to run ABC's parent company, and Jerry Rubinstein who was a relative, but slick, novice. Neither of them knew much about music and they began steering ABC straight into a ditch. Our distribution deal was set to expire in August 1977, and I had four high-risk albums in the pipeline: *Talking Heads: 77, Rocket to Russia* by the Ramones, *Young Loud and Snotty* by the Dead Boys, and *Blank Generation* by Richard Hell & the Voidoids—all excit-ing CBGB art rock that could either take off if given a real push or stiff in total embarrassment if mishandled.

I sent out signals, and hey, presto, I got offers from the two big-gest companies in the business, Warner and CBS, both of which I knew were interested mostly in the Climax Blues Band. I talked with a friend at CBS, Ron Alexenburg, about what their third-party distribution wing could do for us. My natural instincts, however, leaned toward Warner, who owned most of my favorite imprints: Atlantic, Elektra, Asylum, Reprise, and the flagship label, Warner Bros. Records. CBS and the Warner group were about as huge as each other, but Warner was the younger, fresher, more audacious group that had a reputation in the business as the friendly super-power.

Getting into bed with Warner meant sitting at the same break-fast table as the Atlantic brothers, Ahmet and Nesuhi Ertegun, two old-schoolers I really looked up to. There was also Joe "Surfing in Kansas" Smith, who'd just taken over the Elektra-Asylum wing from the recently departed David Geffen. But it was Mo Ostin, the mogul behind the biggest label in the group, Warner Bros. Rec-ords, that I'd be dealing with directly. Warner Bros. Records—or WBR, as the trade called it—was based in Burbank, California, right next the Warner Bros. movie studios. All these labels operated and promoted separately but funneled their records into WEA, their collective distribution network. WEA was a global monster, carry-ing the likes of Led Zeppelin, the Rolling Stones, Fleetwood Mac, the Eagles, Neil Young, Van Morrison, Aretha Franklin, Tom Waits, AC/DC, Chic, and hundreds of fabulous acts, both new and old.

Before signing up with Warner's, we all still had to wait a few weeks for our existing deal with ABC to expire, but while the sun was shining, it was time to make hay. In midsummer of 1977, before *Talking Heads: 77* even came out, Chris Frantz and Tina Weymouth decided to get married in Chris's hometown. Linda and I flew to Cincinnati, rented a car, and spent a day visiting, accompanied by Sire's new label manager, Ken Kushnick. I paid a long-overdue visit to Syd's grave, then wandered around all the old places where King used to reign supreme. The next morning, we drove down along the Ohio River to a little white church in Mount Washington, Kentucky. Throughout the whole trip, I couldn't stop thinking about Syd, who'd been dead nine years.

That Kentucky wedding seemed very midwestern for a trio of Noo Yawk Jews like us. Not only was everyone Christian, the bride's and groom's fathers were both military figures. Tina's father, Ralph, was a retired U.S. Navy admiral, while Chris's father, Robert, was a West Point and Harvard Law graduate who had served in the army as a general and at one point worked for the Pentagon. I'm sure Linda, Ken, and I stood out like three sore thumbs. No other music people from New York had come down. It was all family, except us and David Byrne, looking dapper in his seersucker suit. I have to say, however, that Kentucky church scene has stayed with me ever since. The drummer kissed the bass player, and although nobody could have known that day, Chris and Tina would become the most enduring and loving husband-and-wife rhythm section in rock and roll.

Both Linda and I had high hopes for the guy we'd taken down, Ken Kushnick. I'd just brought him in from the live and management side of the business to provide operational assistance to all the punk bands I was signing. Talking Heads were our big new hope, but they still didn't have a manager—and to me, a good manager was an absolute necessity. Artists need to focus on their music, and all the touring and administration of a hardworking band needs to be handled by a pro. Both jobs, if they're being done right, are full-time. Managers would always haggle with the label for more money and from time to time be pains in the ass, but if you chose them yourself, they tended to be cooperative. I wanted Ken Kushnick to manage Talking Heads and offered to lend him $20,000 to go out on his own. He toyed with the idea while acting as their temporary confidant. In the end, he decided not to go backward from where he'd just moved. I think he was relieved to have found a good post at Sire.

He introduced Talking Heads to Gary Kurfirst, who, as a young man in the sixties, had started out running gigs in the Village Theater on Second Avenue for the likes of the Who, Hendrix, Cream, Janis Joplin, and others. Unfortunately for Gary, San Francisco promoter Bill Graham bought the lease from out under him and created the Fillmore East. So, Gary turned his hand to management with hard-rock group Mountain and later, their post-split offshoot, West, Bruce & Laing. He branched into reggae, managing Peter Tosh, Toots and the Maytals, and the Mighty Diamonds. By 1977, however, he'd been out of action for a few months with thyroid problems and was in need of something new. Ken Kushnick had no better candidates around, so lucky Gary Kurfirst was handed the Heads on a silver platter.

I was disappointed in Ken Kushnick's decision to not manage them himself. The upside, however, was that Gary Kurfirst knew all the promoters. Meanwhile, Ken remained personally attached to Talking Heads, which definitely helped their cause in other ways. It was Ken who went out to Burbank to present Sire's upcoming releases to all the Warner marketing and radio pluggers. With all his impassioned, youthful zeal, he explained punk to a roomful of Warner staffers who sat back and listened politely. They were probably hoping for a hit album from the Climax Blues Band and asked him to choose one band out of the Ramones, Talking Heads, Richard Hell, and the Dead Boys. Ken of course hadn't expected such a blunt question and blanked.

"Listen, we're only making 18 percent on the distribution," they explained, "so we can't push all four of them. Choose the best one, and we'll give that band a push."

"B-but they're all important," stuttered Ken. "This is an entire scene."

"Well, then," they explained flatly, "maybe we should be talking about a joint venture rather than a distribution deal?"

Ken Kushnick returned to New York convinced that we didn't have a choice: we had to enter into discussions. The numbers weren't hard to understand. What hit me, however, was the game-changing madness of it all: Warner Bros. Records, the world's hottest major, was dropping hints to buy into my little company. I left the door wide open, as the distribution deal began in a spirit of camaraderie and growing curiosity. I think it's fair to single out the artist development people in Burbank, characters such as Bob Regehr and Carl Scott, who were the very first to sense that Sire was tapping into something big. This boded well for the long term, because they were key string-pullers in the day-to-day machinery who'd send publicists on the road with our acts to handle local press and radio or organize in-store retail visits.

Knowing that key corporals on the battlefield were sincerely on your side for *musical* reasons made the new partnership feel like it was meant to happen. Plus, of course, the financial power of the Warner group mattered to me also. I knew they'd pay on time and weren't going to suddenly go bust. I'd been in the game long enough to know that distribution is about size, financial clout, and the promotional people involved. It's a nonstop job of telephone calls and relationships. If the guys at HQ sending out the messages to the ground soldiers genuinely valued your records, they'd all go the extra mile to get results.

In September 1977, *Talking Heads: 77* was our very first record to come out through WEA, and boy, we noticed the difference.

Fireworks didn't exactly burst over Manhattan, but Warner had a well-oiled distribution machine with a magical aura that made our records shine. Before Christmas, "Psycho Killer" charted at ninety-something on the Hot 100 and broke into the top twenty in a few countries around Europe, thanks partly to the French lines in the song. Also that fall, we released our two new CBGB acts, the Dead Boys and Richard Hell, which weren't as easy to sell outside the big cities, but the cool factor was definitely noticed. The Ramones third album, *Rocket to Russia*, wasn't a massive hit either, but it made noise and was the biggest seller they'd enjoyed until then. Sire was suddenly so hip, it felt like a Hula-Hoop was swinging around Blue Horizon House.

And that's when the WBR boss, Mo Ostin, entered the picture. The fast-evolving case of Sire Records had been moved up to the desk of one of the world's most powerful record moguls. Unfortunately, I just couldn't believe my luck, which is the wrong signal to give off if you're walking into a life-changing negotiation. If ever there was a time when I needed the ghost of Syd Nathan wheezing "load of crap" into my ear, the imminent lunch was it. All Mo Ostin had to do was dangle a million-dollar carrot in my face, and I'd be too busy drooling all over myself to notice the accompanying stick I'd eventually beat myself with for the rest of my life. The truth is, I wasn't really looking critically under the hood. I didn't even seek legal advice about the type of deal I should even want. This was the late seventies, Sire was a small independent, and I had no idea what was up ahead.

At that moment, my blinding obsession was David Byrne, simply because I knew not only were Talking Heads totally unique and incredible but that David Byrne was someone Mo Ostin would want to get to know better. Mo became a sycophant of David's. Although to me, it was always Talking Heads, and Chris and Tina were every bit as important as David. In fact, it was Chris who was the glue that held the band together. I knew that Warner would greenlight the necessary promotional support to break Talking Heads, and they were possibly the only major daring enough to do so. It was like I didn't have a choice. A new day was dawning for Sire, and I could feel it coming.

5. ROCKET TO RUSSIA

Before sitting down with Mo Ostin, one of the wise old men I called for advice was Jerry Wexler, who'd just quit Atlantic on bad terms. Atlantic was the *A* in WEA, Warner's distribution company; I knew I'd get an informed opinion from straight-talking Jerry, who'd helped build the whole consortium.

I got along with Jerry, who, like me, always leaned more on the side of the music than on the business. He was a *Billboard* alumni, probably Paul Ackerman's number-one protégé, so although I was a lot younger, there was a tribal connection. As I expected, Jerry confirmed much of what I already knew: Warner would be great for the types of left-field bands I was signing. However, he warned me about the vicious corporate politics between the various arms of the group, and he slipped in a cryptic comment about Mo Ostin that took years to compute. "Mo likes to create the impression Warner is *The Waltons*, when it's really *The Brothers Karamazov.*"

I'd seen the TV show, but I hadn't read the Russian novel. Unfortunately, the full thrust of Wexler's warning had to be personally experienced. Mo seemed like a nice guy on the phone.

I'd first bumped into Mo Ostin at a Focus gig in about 1973. He was backstage talking to the band, which of course gave me heart palpitations. "Mr. Ostin," I said as politely as possible, "my name is Seymour Stein, and I'm afraid Focus are under contract to my label, Sire Records."

"Oh, I know," he replied, shaking my hand with a big smile. "Pleased to meet you, Seymour. I just loved the show and wanted to tell the guys." I had no relationship with Mo, but I did telephone him shortly afterward, asking to be distributed. He was very friendly, but he turned me down.

By the fall of 1977, all that was long-forgotten prehistory. Sire was hot, and Mo was obviously interested. He flew to New York, and we met up in Fine & Shapiro, a lovely kosher deli just two blocks around the corner from Sire. Sitting there in a neatly ironed Hawaiian shirt, he looked more like a tax inspector on vacation than a major company mogul. He must have been no more than five foot five and wore huge glasses. How this unassuming little smiler got to be the one of the most powerful players in the record industry was a mystery to me. You'd have expected the chairman of a giant like Warner Bros. Records to descend into West Seventy-Second Street from a black chopper with a briefcase handcuffed to his wrist. No, little Mo was just seated in the corner, thumbing through the menu, wondering if he wanted pickles on his pastrami or onion relish.

The term *soft power* didn't exist in the seventies, but it was already evolving inside Californian pioneers like Mo Ostin. He never gave interviews and barely even talked about himself to music business vets. "The artist should be in the foreground," was how he'd fob off snooping reporters. Artists and their managers loved reading this stuff. Truth was, Mo was secretive by design. In a trade that trudged around balls deep in its own self-aggrandizing bullshit, he understood that beige sweaters and humility were how you ran circles around the competition, which in his case meant everyone.

You see, unlike most of the moguls in the Warner group, Mo had never been an owner, nor did he have vinyl in his veins—two missing ingredients in this otherwise genius diplomat and strategist. People always thought he was a lawyer or an accountant, which is exactly what he almost became. What he really was, however, was a natural-born politician who I'm sure could have succeeded in any other field. Not many knew the finer details of his rise to power, but he eventually told me how he got his lucky breaks. "I owe my career to Ricky Nelson" was his line. This part was partly true. The rest of his story, however, I'd have to piece together from a long trail of abandoned and wounded comrades that he'd left along the highway.

Mo's full name was Morris Otrovsky, and he was born in 1927. This made him fifteen years older than I was, basically a generation above. His long and winding ascent to the Warner throne began way back in 1954 while studying law at UCLA. His wife, Evelyn, got pregnant, which threw his academic plans in to crisis. Luckily, one of his friends was the brother of Norman Granz, the man behind the jazz label Verve, so Morris dropped out of college and became Verve's "controller," a nuts-and-bolts man handling royalties, contracts, and company management for the likes of Duke Ellington and Charlie Parker. Verve provided the perfect all-round schooling, and it was there that Morris Otrovsky changed his name to the hipper-sounding Mo Ostin.

Manning the machines down in Verve's engine room was where Mo's destiny shifted tracks thanks to a TV show he had nothing to do with. *The Adventures of Ozzie and Harriet* was a fifties blockbuster, starring a real-life family: Ozzie Nelson, a big band leader from the thirties, his wife, Harriet, a jazz singer, and their two sons, David and Ricky. One night in 1957, young Ricky Nelson sang a teeny version of Fats Domino's "I'm Walkin'" and became a pop sensation overnight.

Through Ozzie Nelson's old jazz connections, Verve was handed the rights to Ricky's single and sold a million copies. With Ricky Nelson fever spreading, Verve then released the B side, "A Teenager's Romance," and bingo, they sold another million copies of the exact same record except flipped with new packaging. It doesn't often get this wonderful, and of course, Ozzie was very happy with himself. "Look what I did for you!" he kept telling Ricky, who, being a typical teenager, threw it back in his father's face. "I didn't wanna be on a jazz label. I wanna be on Imperial, the same label as Fats Domino." This racket bounced back and forth until the old man cracked. Ozzie knocked on Norman Granz's door and announced, "Ricky doesn't want to be on a jazz label!"

"That's not my problem," said Granz. A lengthy argument ensued.

"I wanted us to settle this as friends," said the father, "but if that's how you want it, fuck you. Ricky's only seventeen. The contract's not worth the paper it's written on!"

Granz hit the roof, Ozzie slammed the door, and guess who was quaking down the corridor? "Ostin!" yelled Granz. "Get me the meanest fucking lawyer in Hollywood!" This could only mean Frank Sinatra's attorney and chief confidant, Mickey Rudin. Mo got Rudin on the line, but it was "Ricky who?" and "Who gave you my number?" Knowing his job was on the chopping block, Mo kept schmoozing away in desperation until Mickey Rudin gave in. "Okay, okay, pay me a retainer, but I don't want to hear from you people more than twice a year."

When Mo met Mickey Rudin for lunch, it went swimmingly. They discovered that both their fathers were commies in the thirties—a big deal if you're into that kind of thing. Mo's genius dropped some idea into Rudin's soup that afternoon, because two years later, Rudin set up a record label for Frank Sinatra, called Reprise. Frank, who was getting on, could keep his masters, get a bigger cut as an artist, sign his Rat Pack buddies, and even claim expenses as "Chairman of the Board." In theory, Reprise made perfect business sense. Unfortunately, Mickey Rudin knew what Sinatra was like—big ego, slight drinking problem, incapable of managing a business. What the plan needed was a reliable little mechanic, a master fixer in a butler's mask to keep the books straight and deal with Sinatra. And that's when Mo Ostin got his big break, cleaning up for the big boys.

With Mo running the new office, Reprise released modest hits from Sinatra, Dean Martin, and Sammy Davis Jr., but within two years, the company began losing serious amounts of dough. As well as Reprise, Frank Sinatra had invested in other business ventures, like a radio station. Luckily, Mickey Rudin was thrown a joker once the movie *Ocean's 11*, starring Frank Sinatra and his Rat Pack buddies, became a Warner Bros. blockbuster. Jack Warner wanted to sign Sinatra for a three-movie contract, and buying Reprise was a small price to pay for Sinatra's signature. It was rumored that Jack Warner was willing to pay big money for the label, and he eventually did. Mickey Rudin's stroke of genius was to keep a straight face, refuse the fabulous offer, and suggest a convoluted stock transfer whereby Reprise would be merged into the existing Warner Bros. Records, which was already operating beside the film studios and releasing some successful pop acts like the Everly Brothers. And because all Jack Warner really cared about was the movie deal, he agreed to let Sinatra's two-thirds stock in Reprise become one-third of the combined labels. It seemed like a costless reorganization, but in the end, Frank Sinatra swapped a liability for an asset and, years later, made a killing.

Once again, Mo Ostin's bleak prospects had been turned around by a genius negotiator, except that by the time the ink was dry,

Frank Sinatra had lost all interest in record labels. Not only did he *hate* rock and roll and early-sixties pop, Reprise's problems had become personally embarrassing. Sinatra and his crew simply retreated further into the movie business. Apart from getting his daughter Nancy into the charts and picking up his checks as a minority shareholder, Frank became an absentee landlord and left Mo to his own fate.

It was probably a blessing in disguise. For a nuts-and-bolts guy with no ears, Mo had no choice but to find product himself. Simply by negotiating a few licensing deals with the French indie Disques Vogue and Pye Records in London, Mo landed Reprise the American rights for a string of British pop hits from Petula Clark and the Kinks. Thanks to smash hits like "Downtown" and "You Really Got Me," Mo pulled in more than enough cash to keep Reprise evolving profitably through the midsixties.

To be fair to Mo, what he didn't naturally possess in musical culture he made up for in intelligence. He understood how the business operated, and by watching London like a hawk, he scooped his next game changer in Jimi Hendrix *before* he took the Monterey Pop Festival by storm. When Hendrix stepped onto the Monterey stage and eventually set fire to his guitar, I imagine Mo sitting in the crowd, thinking, *What's Frank gonna say about this guy?* Fortunately, within a year, Hendrix had the biggest-selling album in America, and of course Frank was very happy picking up his checks.

From there, Mo's career went from big to bigger, thanks to two key people. The first was his new A&R man, Andy Wickham, an Englishman and former employee of Andrew Oldham's, who pointed Mo to a slew of great acts, including Jethro Tull, Van Morrison, Joni Mitchell, and many more. But the person who really changed Mo's destiny was Steve Ross, a devilishly astute New York tycoon from the car park and funeral home business. If anyone was possibly cuter than Mickey Rudin, it had to be Steve Ross, who, in 1969, bought up Warner Bros., Atlantic, and Elektra and reorganized the whole smorgasbord of film studios and record labels into an entertainment superpower. Ross renamed the mother company Warner Communications and began pumping money into its many tentacles.

By that stage, Mo was a black belt politician who helped Steve Ross buy out Frank Sinatra's remaining stock and, over time, even managed to turn Steve Ross against Ahmet Ertegun, the very person who'd helped Mo get a big promotion to run WBR. Mo suddenly found himself standing at the confluence of Wall Street finance and Californian flower power, running the Burbank HQ alongside the talented Joe Smith, whose subsequent fate you can guess. Seizing the day, Mo read *The Greening of America* by Charles A. Reich and went about transforming Burbank into what Andy Wickham eloquently described as a "college campus." The WBR staffers were mostly young, hip, and focused on intelligent singer-songwriters, especially that whole Laurel Canyon scene. It was adios to the old school of jukebox jobbers and Brill Building cheesecake, and it was "Hey, man" to the new world of what Mo called "creative services," basically quirky, high-brow advertising aimed at underground magazines and college radio. A liner notes writer named Stan Cornyn became the mastermind of all these clever slogans and alternative techniques that in many ways gave not only WBR but the entire Warner Music Group a serious edge in hippie marketing. Stan Cornyn was a genius.

I sometimes wondered whether to stay in control, Mo liked to hire people with drinking, drug, or sexual problems and then play the daddy figure. I should know. Let's just say that over corned beef sandwiches in the warm bosom of Fine & Shapiro, the term *joint venture* sounded dandy. I mean, doesn't it still *sound* lovely? It's team-y, it's adventurous, it's a deal you can roll up and smoke. And it sounds so equal. Especially when your half looks miraculously bigger than theirs. As Mo explained, WBR would pay me a million bucks for half of Sire's stock so that his heavyweight marketing division, working in concert with the equally powerful distribution company WEA, could do all sorts of promotional tricks for my records. It was like all my birthdays had come at once.

Did I have a choice? I probably did. Then again, I was thirty-five years old, right at that midlife showdown where the past, present, and future are looking at each other like the final scene in *The Good, the Bad, and the Ugly.* I'd been in the game for twenty years and had seen plenty of tragedy. It was bad enough that Syd died in his sixties; the decline of King was a lasting reminder of how fast things can change. But even King's fate was pretty compared to George Goldner's, who died in 1970, stone broke at the age of fifty-two. Or what about my man in Paris, Lucien Morisse, who committed suicide the same year—driven to despair by loneliness, overwork, and bitterness about his father being gassed by the Nazis? Even right there in the late fall of 1977, my old mentor Paul Ackerman was dying in reclusion, surrounded by his beloved cats and pigeons. He died on New Year's Eve, by which stage the biggest star of my generation, Elvis, was already pushing up daisies in a king-sized box. There were innumerable ways of becoming a casualty. The game I'd chosen was a gladiator sport.

I'd nonetheless survived long enough to understand the tidal forces that wise old Paul Ackerman was the first to predict ten years previously. "The trend toward bigness, mergers, and corporate maneuvers" was how he described it. The shock sale of Atlantic Records in October 1967 had prompted Paul, who was almost sixty at the time, to write a milestone piece for the front page of *Billboard.* "The great era of the indie," he lamented, "was the late 1940s and 1950s. Toward the end of the 1950s, it became the fashion for the once-pure indie to be tied with an umbilical cord to a film company, a broadcaster, or even a non–show business corporation looking for new money-making outlets . . . The pure indie was evaporating. He could no longer take it. He was even preyed upon by his indie distributors, many of whom were derelict in their payments and would pay only when the indie produced another hit . . . The indie distributor developed the habit of running with a hit single while leaving his established lines dormant on the warehouse floor."

Tell me about it. After wearing out six distributors in the ten years since Paul's grim prediction was published, I was truly sick and tired of forking out money without ever knowing our records would get properly promoted or even released. And it's not like I didn't understand why. The United States wasn't like little old England with its entire media and distribution circuits centered around one city. We were a sprawling continent of fifty states with hundreds of radio stations and newspapers. Even if you could get jocks in Nebraska or New Mexico to spin your records, there was no telling if interested listeners could actually find them in local stores. The odds were cruelly stacked against independents and getting slimmer as the majors kept growing.

The fact that Warner was the slickest outfit on the field made my choice a no-brainer. Plus, Mo Ostin's valuation of Sire at upward of $2 million represented more than just a resounding personal endorsement; it was a huge amount of cash in 1977. I knew that if I invested my million wisely and got in tight with Warner's top brass, we Steins would be secure for many years ahead. Here was my chance to ensure I could have a lifelong career running Sire. So, I took that giant leap of faith knowing Warner needed skin in the game to get behind us and keep spending.

At Sire, everyone was waiting when we danced in the door, singing old songs together like two drunk teenagers carrying home the school trophy. All the Sire staffers were just as ecstatic. Even the cleaning lady knew we'd just been promoted. This deal could turn our oddball artists into international rock stars and, by extension, dazzle up the staffers' résumés forever after. Everyone was going to be a winner, especially the bands, and that's all I really cared about.

Looking back, I was no match for Mo Ostin, a brilliant and smooth operator who'd been negotiating multimillion-dollar deals for fifteen years alongside killers like Mickey Rudin and Steve Ross. And I wasn't just inexperienced at big business, I was dizzy with excitement about the scene Sire was sitting on. Don't forget that at that ripe moment, in 1977, punk felt like New York coming back to life after more than ten years of British and West Coast dominance. When I was a small boy, New York had been the heart of the global record industry, but one by one, other cities like Nashville, Memphis, Detroit, Chicago, Los Angeles, and London all rose up and became synonymous with particular record labels and genres of music. All that diversity had been healthy for the industry as a whole, but somewhere along the way, dear ol' New York had slipped into relative decline.

Admittedly, not everyone knew what to make of punk. Around 1977, a lot of people hated it, but a change was in the air, and right across the record business, the term was suddenly on everyone's lips. Britain had been gripped by Sex Pistols fever over the previous year, and God knows the Brits love nothing more than a dirty scandal to complain about. In New York, it was the Ramones, the Dead Boys, and Richard Hell who personified this crowd-spitting, gutter-puking, bed-pissing subculture. On one hand, it didn't do us any harm to encourage journalists to bullshit hifalutin theories about this so-called punk movement that to me was just a return to the fast, immediate, ugly-faced rock and roll I'd loved in the mid-fifties. If the punk ticket got kids to run out and buy our records, fine. I wasn't going to complain.

The problem was radio, especially in America where the word

punk sounded about as appetizing as *jerk* or *scumbag*. In England, it didn't have those connotations. We needed all the help we could get, so I stumbled on the idea of new wave, pilfered from the French cinematic movement Nouvelle Vague. I don't know if I first read it somewhere or heard it in a conversation, but it popped into the air and became my standard telephone spiel to win over every plugger, program director, and hippie jock. "No, Talking Heads aren't *punk*," I kept telling everyone, "they're *new wave!*" Ain't the art of selling all about perception? You have to have hot product to get away with it, of course, which we did. Plus, it was broadly true; Talking Heads didn't sound *anything* like the Ramones or the Dead Boys, and they certainly didn't deserve to be kept off American radio just because the Sex Pistols were winding up the Queen of England.

The *new wave* term caught on fast because so many other publicists, managers, and record labels buzzing around the same scene had to tease the same long-haired gatekeepers of Top 40 radio to get hip to the street. And it was effective. There hadn't so much hair chopping since the recruitment centers of the Vietnam War. The idea of a "new wave" was so successful in changing perceptions, I think it even had an effect on the music itself. Talking Heads, Blondie, Ian Dury, the Stranglers, the Clash—if you listen to all these acts, you can hear a giant sonic leap between 1976 and 1978. They'd all been trying to capture the rawness of their early gigs, but as the audience grew and airplay on FM radio became a possibility, all these so-called punks started making tighter, slicker, more commercially ambitious new-wave records.

I'm sure some purists out there regret this, but I don't. There's only so long any artist can keep living in vans, playing to sixty people. Try it yourself. It's every artist's dream to sail the airwaves on a seven-inch masterpiece. Lesser talents of the punk era who now claim they never wanted to get on the radio are only kidding themselves. In most cases, the cream rose to the top, and a lot of what didn't has been lunching out on punk mythology ever since. In reality, the best "punk" bands generally disliked the term and had only ever dreamed of making great rock and roll. They all fed off punk energy and humor when it was new and interesting, but as creative people do, they got bored quickly and kept pushing themselves into new territory. Some had the talent to do so; others didn't.

Sire was undergoing major changes, too. We were still an indie in mentality, working out of the same old brownstone, but the combination of the Warner joint venture and the commercial success of the whole CBGB scene gave me the means and the credibility to sign far more acts than before. Increasingly, we were becoming an A&R office plugged into a giant marketing and distribution machine that fired out twenty new releases every month. Warner constantly needed hip records, and I was only too happy to keep feeding the monster. I knew we were on a roll.

I swung my binoculars over to London, which was once again teeming with fresh meat. One of my main sources was a record store in Notting Hill called Rough Trade, a tiny Aladdin's cave of weird and wonderful indie activity that opened in the summer of 1976. I'd fly in from New York, dump my bag in my flat on Gloucester Place, then head straight over to rummage around and talk to people. That was more or less how I signed Sham 69 and an interesting character I actually met in the Rough Trade store. His real name was Daniel Miller, but he performed as the Normal. All he had to play me was a self-produced, self-pressed seven-inch with two tracks called "Warm Leatherette" and "TVOD." I released his single in the States not expecting many sales; his record was as avant-garde as it gets. I just had a gut feeling about *him* in the way I'd had a feeling about Mike Vernon a decade before. Sometimes you look into people and just know they've a bright future.

I hired a local A&R man, Paul McNally, and an assistant,

Geraldine Oakley, to keep me up to date on English news. If I liked a record, we'd check out the band live, which was the only way of knowing what they were really made of. That's how I heard "Teenage Kicks" by the Undertones. Paul and I were driving to see the Searchers when the song came on John Peel's BBC Radio 1 show. It was such an obvious classic, I almost wet my pants. I sent Paul to Belfast to see the Undertones playing live, and there, he met Terri Hooley, the owner of Good Vibrations, the indie label that first released the single, and we struck a deal to release "Teenage Kicks" and other Undertones records in the States. In those months, I also signed the Rezillos, a punk group from Scotland.

I'm making all this sound easy, which of course it wasn't. To find the best stuff, you had to put in the miles and move fast. When I was in London, Paul and I went out to gigs almost every night, and if we had to, we'd bundle into his car and drive off to towns and cities outside London. If we didn't find what we wanted, which we mostly didn't, we'd console ourselves with a shark's fin soup in the Gallery Rendezvous, a late-night Chinese restaurant on Beak Street. Or, if we got back to London at dawn, the tradition was fresh bagels on Brick Lane. The fact my body clock was running on New York time probably made all this midnight English hunting a bit easier.

One of my great disappointments of that otherwise fantastic year was not breaking the Paley Brothers, who I got Phil Spector to produce in LA. They were the kindest guys you've ever met, and Andy Paley was a great songwriter. Jimmy Iovine, who would later become a giant in the music industry, was an up and coming engineer at the time, and had his first credited production as an Executive Producer on their E.P. When I met with Andy and Jonathan to discuss producers, Andy suggested Jimmy, who was a protégé of Ellie Greenwich. Jimmy had already engineered the John Lennon album *Rock & Roll* produced by Phil Spector. Andy told me that

Jimmy was a great engineer and that he could work under pressure. I played Jimmy the four songs I wanted to cut with The Paley Brothers, and he loved them. The boys came down from Boston and stayed in the Holiday Inn on West Fifty-Seventh Street and drove to House Of Music in Orange, New Jersey every day to make the E.P. With overdubs and mixing it took three days. Jimmy brought in the late Ray Bittan (of Bruce Springsteen's E-Street Band) to play organ and piano. Jimmy booked horns for one song. The Paley Brothers brought in Jersey native Leigh Foxx (now with Blondie) on bass. Other than that Andy and Jonathan covered all of the instrumentation. The four song E.P. "Rendezvous," "Ecstasy," "Come Out And Play," and "Hide & Seek" is a classic on many levels and is often cited as a power-pop trend setter. In fact, Rhino named their first POWER POP collection after the song "Come Out & Play." Ahead of its time in many ways. It still stands up today. But for some reason, the spark didn't ignite. We had other disappointments, too. In Germany, I picked up "The Rivers of Babylon" by Boney M from Trudy Meisel at Hansa Records in Berlin, which broke into the Top 40 on the *Billboard* Hot 100—pretty good, but nowhere near the smash hit it was in Europe. I always needed to provide some straight-up pop hits to justify all the weirder stuff that Mo's crew in Burbank didn't always like. I also needed to ensure we had career artists, which meant spending more time and money on production than I could afford in the old days.

Along with Ken Kushnick, I took David Byrne to the calypso carnival in Trinidad during Mardi Gras of 1978, knowing David would love the color and warm sounds of the West Indies. Shortly afterward, Talking Heads set up in the Bahamas with Brian Eno and took their time to record *More Songs About Buildings and Food*, their second album, which we released that July. The unusual choice of location was partly their manager's idea. Gary Kurfirst was an old friend of Island Records founder Chris Blackwell, who agreed to rent them his Compass Point studio at buddy rates. It was a comfortable, state-of-the-art studio being used by a host of Caribbean stars like Burning Spear, Althea & Donna, and of course Bob Marley. From those warm, bigger-sounding sessions, a cover of the Al Green song "Take Me to the River" became Talking Heads' first hit on U.S. radio. David Byrne's songs were still as lyrically inventive as in the CBGB days, but as a band, their sonic focus took a big step toward funky rhythms and Eno-style art rock.

I think Warner bought into Sire, when punk first blew up, because it was the way to get hip and to do it pretty damn quickly. Mo wanted punk and new-wave acts all to himself. He personally ran around for months chasing Malcolm McLaren to sign the Sex Pistols to a big North American deal, which always struck me as a wild-goose chase. Once the Sex Pistols dumped their songwriter, Glen Matlock, only to replace him with Sid Vicious, who couldn't even play, I always suspected they wouldn't last. A band can't survive on clothing and publicity alone; you need songwriters to keep the engines firing.

There was one new-wave band, however, that Mo snatched right out of my hands. Michael Rosenblatt—whose father, Ed Rosenblatt, was head of marketing and sales, one of the most senior positions at Warner's, and great friends of the Ostin family—had discovered the B-52's. The honeymoon, if there ever was one, was officially over.

The story began thanks to one of my junior staffers, Michael Rosenblatt, who was only twenty-two at the time. I'd hired him as a favor to his father, Eddie Rosenblatt, who was Warner's sales chief and a key player to have on our side. In the early days of the joint venture, we'd been invited to a Rosenblatt barbecue, and Linda picked up the hint when Eddie called over his son and gave us chapter and verse on how much Michael loved underground music.

Looking back, Eddie had the good sense to get his son a break in a smaller, hotter label in a different city. I'm sure Eddie could have got Michael a job in Burbank, which probably wouldn't have turned out as well. Anyway, when we got back to New York, it was Linda who kept barking at me to offer Eddie's son a job, and I'm glad she did; we'd all benefit from the exchange.

When young Michael arrived in New York, he was so eager to learn, he ventured down to CBGB one Tuesday evening in December 1977. Sitting on his own, he watched a gang of men and women take to the stage. "Hello. We're from Atlanta, Georgia," announced the singer, and the B-52's launched straight into "Planet Claire." Michael skipped into work the next morning with news of this wildly original party music he'd heard in CBGB. The problem was, the number they gave him was the Greyhound Bus Station in Atlanta, where two of the musicians worked. The B-52's were so broke, they didn't have a telephone.

After a bit more investigation, I flew down to Georgia to see them play and thought they were an absolute hoot. Not only did I want to sign them, I wanted to make sure they had a manager, the plan being—like all our new-wave bands—to keep them touring and developing professionally. While setting up the deal, I introduced them to Gary Kurfirst, but what does he turn around and do? In the negotiations between the B-52's and my corporate masters, Gary caves to Mo, who wanted to sign them directly to WBR.

What apparently happened was that Gary was trying to broker some kind of a territorial split whereby Sire would get North America and Island would get the UK. Mo, however, looked straight at him and asked, "Why are you going to so much trouble, Gary? Sire and Island come through us anyway. You might as well sign your band directly to us." And because Gary was already managing Talking Heads and needed to keep everyone at Burbank sweet, it was easy for Mo to get his way. In fairness, Gary asked for our logo to appear on the record, because, apart from the guilt-acknowledging gesture, Sire was a stamp of new-wave quality that scenesters recognized. Mo, however, refused and took the B-52's all for himself—pretty cavalier considering they were Michael Rosenblatt's first A&R scoop and Mo was an old friend of the kid's father.

The B-52's saga was an eye-opener. Officially, Mo's contract's man, David Berman, was blamed for the "mix-up" on some technicality, but I never bought a word of it. I was starting to understand why the guys at Atlantic all thought Mo Ostin was Machiavellian. There may have been some East-West rivalry that our common emperor Steve Ross encouraged to get all his little arms competing, but it definitely had something to do with the way you couldn't even talk records with Mo. Well, you could, and you had to, but there just wasn't that common passion that binds even the fiercest competitors. Some of us grew up with music, and others just approached it as career. I mean, if you're not *playing* the records you produce, if you're not one of the fans, then why the fuck are you doing it? For the money, the power, the smug thrill of hanging out with rock stars?

Culturally, I was much closer to Ahmet Ertegun, a music addict with a childlike appetite for life. For twenty years, Ahmet had spent his own money building Atlantic from nothing into one of the greatest ever independent record labels. That meant a lot to me. Yeah, Ahmet was also the son of a senior Turkish diplomat and knew how to play boardroom politics with the same dagger-wielding intrigue as Mo. The difference was that Ahmet was always trying to corrupt those corporate stiffs in Warner Communications. He'd lure Steve Ross to gigs and play the larger-than-life showman. He'd borrow the private jet and throw crazy parties, usually with the help of his bubbly wife, Mica. With his brother, Nesuhi, Ahmet talked Steve

Ross into building a glamorous soccer club, the New York Cosmos, which brought Pelé and Franz Beckenbauer to America and launched soccer as a national sport. I admired Ahmet's attitude. He was out to have a blast and convert the suits, whereas Mo was always kissing corporate ass, more interested in learning all their Wall Street tricks to turn rock and roll into big business.

Would I have preferred to be in bed with Atlantic rather than Warner? Yes and no. The Erteguns had long-standing strong connections with music folk in the UK and Europe. Because of that, I felt I would be more valuable to WBR. In addition, at that time, WBR was also the hotter label of the whole Warner group, with plenty of talented people, most of whom truly believed in Sire.

Every few months, I'd have to fly out to Los Angeles to meet Mo and go over my business—usually money to sign bands or marketing funds to get them happening. We'd usually meet for lunch or dinner at Peppone, a great Italian in Brentwood, which was very close to his house. On a few occasions, we met up in the Beverly Hills Hotel, which was basically Hollywood's trading floor and a popular place for record industry meetings. I'll never forget the first time I met Mo there for breakfast. I'd already been to the Beverly Hills Hotel many times as a tourist, but everything felt so different once I was part of the local family.

One beautiful morning, I pulled up in my rented car. I strolled through the pink lobby and back outside onto a patio where a trellis wrapped in vines covered a restaurant area overlooking the pool and gardens. And sitting at the end table, there he was, the little man with the big glasses.

"Seymour!" said Mo, standing up. "Wonderful to see you! How was your trip?"

"Great," I said. This was Hollywood, no place for the truth about feeling depressed or constipated. At home, we New Yorkers would laugh at this smiling Californian fakery, but you'd walk in and instantly become one of them. You'd even start wondering if they were actually happier than we were.

"I'm so glad we can talk things over in person," he said. "Please, sit down. I'm all yours for breakfast."

Since dawn, I'd been holed up in my hotel, running on coffee, which was no condition to step into the ring against Mo Ostin. In such circumstances, small talk can get ugly if you don't order food straight away. There needs to be impending hope hanging over the table. All those knives, forks, and teeth need to be given peaceful, satisfying jobs.

"Excuse me," I said to a waitress. "Can I get a cheese omelet?" I said, handing the unread menu to the waitress.

"And I'll have the fruit salad," added Mo.

This was typical Mo Ostin. He'd drag you out to California for a happy-family breakfast, but he ordered like he'd eaten at home before coming. Thankfully, the food arrived after a tolerable amount of small talk about my flight, my hotel, the weather, my daughters, his wife, anything except music.

"How's your omelet?" he asked like he actually cared.

"Great . . . Listen, Mo, why is it so difficult to get money out of Warner? Anytime I try to sign anything, your guys tangle me up in red tape."

"Really, do they?"

"Yeah, they do."

Mo had this clever trick of silently shaking his head whenever he wanted to appear shocked and surprised but didn't want to express an opinion. I knew he was orchestrating all these procedures as a method of control. I also knew my nickname inside Burbank: "Seymour Stein, see less money!" For Mo and some of his directors and managers, I'd always be the cheap-signing record man from Brooklyn. Yes, I chose to operate in modest means and would have been happy to make a small profit on a new band just by word of mouth and have the time, belief, and patience to break them on the second, third, or even fourth album. That's what being an indie, to me, is all about. They must've known that was the label and philosophy they bought into with Sire. That was the way the record men I admired, like Syd Nathan, the Chess brothers, and Ahmet and Jerry at Atlantic, did it. When you're gambling with your own money, it's not the same, believe me.

As I was talking, I noticed that Mo seemed distracted by something behind me. I turned around and saw Clive Davis sitting at another table, eating by himself. I had great respect for Clive. No other lawyer I knew had successfully made the transition to music man the way Clive Davis did. Paul Marshall was the lawyer I respected most because he understood the inner workings of the music business and personalities, and he also kept a close eye on what was happening all over the world. It was apparent to me, even then, that Clive had great ears and had made the right decision moving into A&R. That said, and while I had great respect for Clive, the late seventies hadn't been easy for him. His Arista label almost went bust, but in my opinion, the German indie/major Ariola, a subsidiary of BMG, had made a wise decision to come to his rescue.

"Do you know he's losing the Germans a million a month?" Mo said gloatingly. Where I came from, people's money problems should never be laughed at, and I half listened to Mo's gossip until he popped the question a lot of people were asking at that time. "Do you really think he's gay?"

"As far as I know, he is," I said carefully.

"Well, I don't get it. On several occasions while at conferences on the road, we both wound up chasing some ladies. I think it may have been Clive's idea. Anyway, Seymour, I'm going to have to invite him to join us for a bit. You don't mind?"

"Okay, Mo. Fine with me."

As Mo sauntered over, Clive's face lit up. Mo patted Clive's back with one arm and with the other extended a welcome toward our table, a hearty gesture straight from *Little House on the Prairie*. I stood up and greeted Clive, although our relationship had not yet developed too far beyond formal gestures. Once reseated, the conversation went straight to the big retail season ahead. Mo asked what Clive had teed up for releases that fall.

"I've got some strong releases I'm counting on."

"Do you have anything new from Barry Manilow?" asked Mo.

"Unfortunately, I don't."

"What about a Barry Manilow greatest hits?" I innocently suggested, but the look on Clive's face turned the air blue.

"I couldn't possibly do that!" he quickly replied.

"Do you not have the contractual provision?" asked Mo.

"Oh, no, no." Clive who was, after all, a top lawyer, smirked. "It's a personal thing."

"How so?" inquired Mo.

"Barry is a wonderful human being, but he's *terribly* sensitive. I know a greatest hits would go platinum, at least, but I couldn't do that to him as a human being."

I caught Mo's eye. He was as lost as I was. "I don't get you," pressed Mo.

Clive Davis breathed in deeply, like he was getting ready to unload some awful burden. "Because *I* picked all his hits. I found the songs. For Barry, seeing the words *Barry Manilow's Greatest Hits* written across that sleeve might embarrass him. Because he and I both know it should really be called *Clive Davis's Greatest Hits*."

I must admit, I couldn't believe what I was hearing. A muscular spasm in my left leg kicked Mo under the table. Clive Davis's ego was legendary even in the record business where XXL is the regular size. Clive's greatest gift, as it was later proven, was picking songs, which he did an exceptional job on, not just for Barry but for many artists he worked with over his long career.

When Clive eventually disappeared back to his room for a phone call, Mo rolled up his trouser leg and showed a bruise forming on his shin. "Look what you just did to me!"

Mo laughed, and admittedly, I chuckled a bit. In that fabulous Beverly Hills moment, I knew how lucky I was to be seated at the big boys' table.

Right then, Mo made his move. He signaled to the waitress for the check and looked into me as only bosses can do. "Seymour, getting back to us, please just call me whenever you've a problem with any of my guys, okay? I'll do my best to fix it."

This was life in my new adoptive family. You'd call Mo with a problem, so he'd invite you here, and now you were here, he was telling you to call him next time you had a problem. Mo Ostin was so very smooth. The guy could have sweet-talked a pack of rabid wolves over a cliff. They'd have wagged their tails and jumped.

I guess like Napoleon, Mo had figured out that choosing the battleground is usually the secret to winning. If you had good reason to be pissed off about something, he'd always meet you somewhere exclusive, public, and on his own turf. I'd stayed at lots of beautiful hotels. My favorite palaces in Paris and Cannes were probably a class above the Beverly Hills, but a sentimental Brooklyn boy who'd grown up on classic movies was never going to throw a complete tantrum on Hollywood's front lawn. God forbid, Paul Newman might suddenly turn around.

How things had changed. I was thirty-six, right at that hilltop of life where you look down and see a belly bulging over your belt buckle. This, the other bulge in my pockets, and the news I'd get from my folks about their declining health were making me look at my own life differently. Whatever I still wanted to do on planet Earth, I'd better not waste any more time getting there. That's what success does—you get to where you always wanted to be and realize there was all this other stuff further down the priority list that probably should have been higher up. Even for a shellac-blooded shark like me, you just can't eat and sleep records twenty-four hours a day, certainly not in the afternoons, which I found was the soggy part of my working day. Without even realizing it at first, I was developing a new obsession, especially on my frequent trips to London.

I'd always been picking up antiques since I first started making money. At first it was mostly Chinese, ivory, and netsukes, also Qing Dynasty porcelain, all of which I'd learned about from Syd Nathan. I'd always loved Cantonese and Szechuan food and felt a personal connection to the Orient. Since I was a teenager, the intricate beauty of Chinese porcelain just sucked me further down that Silk Road of the imagination, but it wasn't until I discovered the London auction houses like Sotheby's, Christie's, and Phillips that my curiosity became a full-blown passion.

As so often, it all began through a series of accidents. There was this English executive I knew from the sixties who I'd kept doing business with; his name was Roland Rennie, a talented record executive who'd been gradually losing his way. When I first met him in the sixties, he'd been perfectly normal and had almost single-handedly steered Polydor out of its old-school past into the heart of the swinging sixties. His office scored so many major hits with the Who, the Bee Gees, Cream, Jimi Hendrix, and others, his German owners kept flying over to London to celebrate. They'd have these grotesque, thigh-slapping lunches and expect everyone to drink themselves sick, an annoying German habit even the English found tiresome. Over time, all the success got to Roland. He had to be moved around the company and first went to Phonogram, where he found success and also groomed the talents of Nigel Grainge (elder brother of current Universal supremo Lucien Grainge), who had started as a clerk and ended up one of the top A&R men in the business, with his own label, Ensign, a joint venture. He finally wound up running the publishing division at the time, Chappell Music.

Roland had lost his lucky star along the way, but he remained a bright-eyed character who'd never lost his ears. He seemed to trust mine, so, whenever I had something special and needed cash, like when the Ramones first came out, I'd call into his office, offer him a sub-publishing deal, and usually walk out with a check. I'd done it so often, I even had a little song to warm my throat on the way to his office. By changing one word in the Dixie Cups classic, "Going to the chapel and we're gonna get *money*," I'd always arrive into Chappell Music focused and in good spirits. The only catch was that Roland was never on time, so I often found myself hanging around his reception until he returned. Nearby was New Bond Street, so instead of sitting there making his secretary feel uncomfortable, I started killing time watching the auctions at Sotheby's.

I found Sotheby's fascinating. All these old eccentrics bumbled about studying beautiful antiques. It was the auctions, however, that I found absolutely thrilling. I didn't dare buy anything for ages, nor even open my mouth, but I started reading books and collecting catalogues from the specialist dealers, and although I checked out auctions in New York, I never felt the same zeal and determination as when I was in London.

London also had the Portobello Market where I enjoyed nothing better than to mooch around early on a Saturday morning, rummaging through the high-class junk before the crowds arrived. By late morning or early afternoon, I'd usually walk to Rough Trade to see what was happening there. Antiques seemed like a natural partner for records; you had to learn genres, meet dealers, spot details, figure out value, and above all, *find* the treasure. I knew I was good at turning songs into cash. Now I'd found a way of banking the cash back into art. If you were really smart, antiques even offered the best interest rates, plus, of course, waking up to all these exquisite objects sure as hell made life prettier than papering your walls with bank statements.

I'd long been an Anglophile, but by the late seventies, London had become my other self. My flat on Gloucester Place had become more than just a second residence; it had the feel of a real home and contained most of my prettiest antiques. I was signing so many English groups and spending so much time in London, my own family were starting to poke fun at me about my Brooklyn-British accent that I'd developed over the previous decade. As anyone who's spent any time in a foreign city will tell you, you have to adapt. The secret to traveling is to melt into your surroundings like a wildlife cameraman. Because, believe me, if you speak raw, unpasteurized Brooklynese in an old-world capital like London, you may as well be popping up out of manholes like Bugs Bunny, asking, "What's up, Doc?"

In New York, I'd always been absent; off on business trips, stuck in the office, at a gig, but by late 1978, I'd practically moved out of Central Park West. With all my running around, I know Linda thought I was trying to keep my distance from her, which in a way I was. Except it was more about myself. What a tangled web we weave when we practice to deceive. I'd been lying to myself all along. I was gay. Not bisexual, not confused, just gay. And I knew I couldn't continue with this Mr. and Mrs. Stein charade much longer. Anytime I stepped through that door on Central Park West, I got tense and nervous like the character in the Talking Heads song. It wasn't that I didn't love my family; I definitely loved the girls and still felt a strange loyalty and companionship toward Linda. What was eating me up inside was that I'd created this confusion that was hurting us all. All they wanted was for me to be a regular husband and daddy. I could see it in their eyes: "Why won't you just be *normal*?"

You can keep running, but sooner or later, the truth will catch up. The late seventies was when gay culture went from being *tolerated* to becoming quite fashionable. Thanks to disco, it reached a point when straight people were indulging in what people jokingly termed *trisexuality*—you'd *try* anything. Linda and I spent plenty of wild nights in Studio 54, which, to be honest, was more her bag than mine. It now turns out that most of the writhing, whooping, half-naked characters on the dance floor were being paid with drink vouchers to provide entertainment for all the fat, middle-aged VIP schmucks sitting around paying for the overpriced champagne. It was all harmless fun, but if you looked around the edges, there was plenty of genuine madness going on. There were always hunky ice hockey players who weren't gay, but they were so revered as icons of male beauty, they'd let drooling queens suck their cocks under the table in return for some coke.

There was one afternoon when the craziness of our marriage knocked on our front door. Linda was running off to catch a plane, for once leaving me alone in the Central Park apartment. Minutes after she rolled her suitcase out the front door, the buzzer rang. I thought Linda had forgotten something—but it wasn't Linda. Had it been anyone other than Dee Dee Ramone, you'd have thought it was just somebody in the neighborhood dropping by to say hello. But Dee Dee was the last person you'd associate with innocent coincidences. I just knew he'd been hiding on the street until Linda got into her cab. After all, she was his manager. He probably knew where she was flying, when, why, and on which airline.

He appeared at the door with a filthy, horny face I barely recognized. He moved into the hallway and pulled a cigarette slowly from his packet. Like a diva in a 1950s movie, he placed it slowly in his pouting lips and reached his neck forward, signaling for a light. Mortified, I pulled a lighter from the hall table and flicked. He sucked on the flame and gently blew his first puff of smoke in my face. He then walked past me into the bedroom where Linda and I shared our brief, tumultuous marriage. In the most improbable striptease I've ever witnessed, Dee Dee peeled off his hallmark Ramones uniform. First the little T-shirt and then the sneakers and shredded jeans. He then lay on the bed naked like some eunuch in a Renaissance painting. His eyes and body position said it all: *Take me whatever way you want. I'm your bitch.*

Dee Dee was a long story of drugs and delinquency. He was more insane than any of us, so far gone in fact that he'd already reached the point of no return where you don't even care what anyone thinks. I'd heard he did some prostitution on the side, but I'd never quite believed it. I'd met all his girlfriends. I thought I knew Dee Dee. I'd watched him onstage a hundred times, thrashing his bass like a good little Ramone. What bothered me wasn't that I happened to be his label boss; I just couldn't stomach how feminine he'd become. I like my men masculine. For a prostitute, Dee Dee obviously hadn't progressed very far up from public toilets. Had he just been himself, he'd maybe have gotten whatever he was looking for, which I can only guess was money.

"Just a second. I'll fix us a drink," I told him and made a dash for the kitchen, wondering what the fuck I was going to do. While making noise with ice cubes, I picked up the phone and dialed a special number that would make the phone ring back. I placed the receiver gently back on the cradle, which set off every phone in the apartment. I ran into the living room, where Dee Dee could hear me through the bedroom door. "What?" I shouted into the dead telephone line. "No. I don't see any fog . . . well, there's none here." It was one of my finest acting performances. "Oh, okay. See you in a bit," I said and hung up. Looking panicked, I told Dee Dee that Linda had turned back because fog had shut down the airport. He had to get dressed and go.

A white lie got me out of a tight corner. He probably sensed he'd been fobbed off, because he never tried that stunt again. Not that Dee Dee was the type of person who wasted time on regret or shame. As for me, my little secret was obviously no longer such a secret anymore, and even I was starting not to care that everybody knew I was gay. As I was about to discover, the thing about repressed sexuality is that it's not necessarily physical desire that'll lure you out of the closet but something far stronger.

There was this guy in New York, a friend of ours—I'll spare both him and you the details—but I started having a scene with him in a hotel. It wasn't only the most powerful sex I'd ever experienced, I felt a profound love for this man, and that love has never left me. I don't know how Linda found out, but when she did, she was like a cat cornering a mouse. It wasn't Linda's style to boo-hoo like a loser, "How dare you do that to my husband!" No, she lured him into another hotel and upped the ante. "If you don't have sex with me right now," she purred, "I'm gonna tell all New York you're gay." My poor lover did what he was told until *my* secret affair was trumped by *her* secret affair. Then, of course, Linda twisted the knife. "Do you know who I fucked, Seymour?"

"What?"

"You heard me. I'll give you just *one* guess. Now, who do you think it could be, Seymour? One guess."

I don't know if you've ever wound up in a situation like this, but even if Linda was insanely jealous, this seemed psychotic. It wasn't even a ménage à trois, which implies some kind of domesticated three-way agreement. I doubt the KGB even had a name for *this*. It was so insane, almost comical, we just about survived, which was probably Linda's strategy all along—to get even, to turn her victimization into a surprise attack that left *me* on the floor. It might have worked. The problem was, I'd fallen in love. The man, who shall remain anonymous, was the love of my life. And he'd been so sickened and damaged by the whole experience, he refused to talk to me for months. It was hard enough for him to reconcile his feelings for a man, never mind the humiliation of Linda's sex-revenge bullying.

I don't consider myself an expert on marriage, but I do know that a married couple can overcome all kinds of tests, even humili-ating affairs. Extramarital flings, as long as they're only about sex, will certainly get saucepans flying, but the one thing that will capsize a marriage irreversibly is when a husband or wife *falls in love* with an outside party. That's checkmate. Seeing how heartbro-ken I was about losing this man, Linda slid into her own inconsol-able mix of self-pity and bitterness.

She spiraled into such a state, she called up my seventy-three-year-old mother and started raving about me fooling around with a guy. Luckily, Linda was so incoherent and my mother so innocent and hard of hearing, nothing was understood. Linda had always blamed my mother for me turning out gay. Apparently, I'd been spoiled and pampered into a mommy's boy. We were back to Mabel's "mocky" theory; it was all Dora's fault for not making a real man out of me. For all her temperamental faults, I'd like to think that Linda was too smart to believe such bullshit; she just wanted to stab me in the heart, as heartbroken people generally do. Telling my dear old mother was of course the ultimate act of war, the nuclear button.

The closing act of a marriage is when the combat turns finan-cial. I knew our separate lives were costing me a lot of money, but I just ignored away the problem down the corridor to Sire's book-keeper, a little middle-aged Jewish lady named Lynette. I ran away from all this chaos for as long as I could, but I was eventually confronted with a pile of bank statements left on my desk. Linda wasn't just spending heavily; the more she hated me, the more she spent like a Saudi princess. And I mean irresponsible, pathological spending, like dollar bills were being plucked from some magic beanstalk we had growing up through the floorboards of Sire Records. Who the fuck did she think she was? I raged home like a bull, found her sitting on the toilet, and shoved the statements so hard in her face, she fell on the floor with her knickers around her ankles. She looked so terrified, I started breaking stuff all over the bathroom.

I'd finally lost it, I was so out of control, I almost wanted to hurt myself. The nastiness, the years of suppressed sexuality, the man I loved who wouldn't talk to me, the coke, the jet lag, the hatred of what I was doing to myself, the money it was now costing me, the money it was *going to* cost me, everything erupted into an ugly outpour of uncontrollable rage. We'd slapped each other before, but usually it was her throwing ashtrays or whacking me in the face. Linda was a tough fighter who not only scared *me*, but I know Danny Fields had heavy objects thrown at him, too. This time, however, my physical superiority showed in a way I'm still embarrassed about. If there's two things you'll regret in life, it's fights over money and slapping a woman, and on that fateful New York afternoon, I plead guilty on both counts.

This wasn't our first fight over money, of course. We'd had hundreds. "Ya cheap bastard!" was always her answer any time I complained about her spending. She was half joking but only half, because Linda possessed all the hang-ups of the textbook nouveau riche Jewish Bronx caricature. I'd always let it pass, because deep down I felt sorry for all her insecurities. At the time, Linda had no idea how wealth was made or how money had to be treated with extreme caution. She'd only been a society player for, what, the seven years she'd been married to me? And it wasn't just her. All the people who'd ever accused me of being a cheapskate were the same. There's no greater expert on how *you* should be enjoying your riches than a good-timer who hasn't a pot to piss in.

I knew the true value of money, because I'd been shown the ropes by real characters who'd lived through the Great Depression and World War II, the generation who beat Hitler and rebuilt the record business. They never wasted hard earned cash on Yves Saint Laurent or luxury shampoo; they invested in businesses and buildings. Nothing ruined people faster than easy cash and addictions. Last time I saw George Goldner, he came begging me for ten grand to help his kids through college. Like a fool, I gave it to him, and then heard he'd squandered it all at the track. Next thing I know, he was a funeral announcement in *The New York Times*. Addictions come in many masks, and since I'd known Linda, she'd gone from being a hardworking teacher to a hard-partying socialite who couldn't function without my credit cards.

She went crying to Danny Fields, telling him I'd gone psycho over a bottle of expensive shampoo. Maybe that's how she wanted it to look. Truth was, I'd snapped over years of dysfunction and tens of thousands of dollars. The girls never even ate at home. Linda was sending them out to restaurants every night. It may have been a bottle of shampoo that got thrown against the bathroom mirror, but that's not the point—Linda was driving me insane. Maybe I was insane to begin with. Maybe I really had ruined her life. Who knew and who even cared anymore? It had to stop, and it had to change. We had to get divorced. We'd hurled this threat at each other so many times, but now the house lights seemed to flash on like closing time. No more sticking around: exit, cloakroom, two cabs, please.

It wasn't even like we were staying together for Samantha and

Mandy's sake. Every morning, when our nanny, Teresa, took the girls to school, our bedroom door would be closed—whether I was there or not, and I usually wasn't. With the Ramones touring, even Linda wasn't there for weeks on end. It didn't make much of a difference if she stayed at home and watched TV; she'd smoke a joint, sip a vodka, and fall into bed late, where she'd remain zonked for hours. When the girls got home from school, she'd be gone, either working or living the high life. As for me, I was far worse. At least Linda managed the nannies. As Samantha and Mandy would tell me years later, the only sign of my existence was a perfect brown circle left on the kitchen table by my cup of coffee. They'd find it after school, like a halo only they could recognize as proof their elusive daddy was in New York.

In the bitter end, I got a call from the greatest ever music business attorney, Paul Marshall. For a lawyer, he was an old-school gentleman who'd seen so much mutually destructive courtroom combat since the late fifties, he knew everyone in the business and always tried to resolve feuds humanely. "Your wife was just here to see me," he announced. "She wanted to hire me as her divorce lawyer. Don't worry, Seymour, I'd never handle this, and anyway, I don't do divorces. However, I gave her the name of a really good divorce lawyer who's been around for years. He must be in his eighties now. He's tough, but he'll want to get this over with quickly. Now, Seymour, I care about you, and I know how this could really affect your business, and I know how much your business means to you. So, listen to me carefully. Here's what he's going to do: his wife is a marriage counselor, so he'll send you and Linda to her. I'm sure counseling will resolve nothing, but it will make him and his wife happy. If you can get yourself a good lawyer, he'll do nothing other than make as fair a deal as possible."

Everything happened exactly as Paul Marshall predicted. After some counseling sessions, Linda and I began to discuss calmly how she was going to survive on her own. I'd leave her the Kenilworth apartment and pay child support, but to make her own dough and separate our common business interests, she was going to have to set up a management company with Danny Fields. I knew my staffers couldn't handle Linda coming into Sire and barking at everyone. On one occasion, she got them all making birthday party invitations for one of the girls. The bigger problem was her telephone torture. If I didn't want to answer her incessant calls, she'd call every other desk and intimidate staffers until they begged me to face her. All these crossed wires had to be untangled and the roles clearly defined. So, Linda and Danny found an office on Fifty-Seventh Street and baptized their management agency Coconut. Most divorcees fight over children; we shared custody of the Ramones.

Dividing up the bits and pieces, we both felt a mixture of sadness and relief, because as soon as we were working on a plan, we got along okay. The day we signed our divorce agreement, Linda insisted on popping open a bottle of champagne. We raised our half-full glasses to the future and wished each other luck. It wasn't that we were happy. I can think of far happier moments we spent together. For Linda especially, it was not easy adapting to life with much less cash than what she'd gotten used to. Subconsciously, I think we both knew we'd be joined for life in a way that went beyond our daughters. I genuinely wanted Linda to do well, and deep down, I think she still admired me as an adventurer, irrespective of what a disaster I'd been as a husband and father. We knew we never should have got married in the first place, and yet neither of us regretted that we had. How many divorcing men and women can both look at each other and honestly say that?

Our seven years together had been a war zone. When we fought side by side, we always won, and when we didn't have a common enemy, we turned on each other. How many times did I sneak out to see the Ramones, Richard Hell, or the Dead Boys just to get some peace and quiet from Linda's high-volume personality? I swear to God, it was pure relief to just stand on my own in Max's or CBGB, going deaf in the distortion as people bounced around spitting on each other. Never mind. Life's no bed of roses. We both knew that. We'd soldier on as always.

6. THIS AIN'T NO PARTY

There's a song for every chapter in your life, and for Linda, our break up was Gloria Gaynor's "I Will Survive," which she played over and over like it had been personally written from her to me. Thing was, that whole party scene would not survive.

According to music business mythology, Disco Demolition Night supposedly signed disco's death certificate. It was an event in Chicago in the summer of 1979 organized by a pair of rock radio jocks who hated disco so much, they invited baseball fans to burn disco records before a White Sox game against the Detroit Tigers. Thousands converged on the stadium and sparked a bonfire of the vanities that degenerated into a riot.

As much as I love a good story, this was a minor news item that has since been parodied and exaggerated out of all proportion. Since when did the record business ever care about Christian rockers in the Midwest? I mean seriously, apart from selling them our AOR dreck? Remember in the midsixties when John Lennon said the

Beatles were bigger than Jesus Christ? Far greater numbers started burning Beatles records in bizarre scenes all over the country. It never stopped the Beatles selling records by the shipload. If anything, it strengthened their image.

Disco died and was reincarnated exactly where it was born: in the clubs of New York City. Studio 54 was where the record moguls, the disco stars, and *Billboard*'s chart fixer Bill Wardlow hung out. So, the party was over, literally, when the cops raided Studio 54 in December 1978 and nailed its owners on tax evasion. You had to feel very sorry for Steve Rubell and Ian Schrager actually winding up in jail. I can only presume they'd refused entry to a mayor's wife or a police chief's mistress.

It probably wouldn't have mattered anyway, because by then, the Jerry Halls were sick of standing out in the cold trying to fight their way in. The rock star brigade had already migrated to Trax, a rockier joint on Seventy-Second Street and Columbus Avenue. Meanwhile, all the creative energy was heating up downtown, where the younger art crowd lived. CBGB was still going strong, and I remained loyal to the end, but of the new places, the place I loved most was the Mudd Club, opened in 1978 on White Street in Tribeca. It was a bar with a stage for bands, a deejay room upstairs for parties, and a gallery area for exhibitions. For a while, the Mudd Club was *the* place where you'd bump into the likes of Andy Warhol, Allen Ginsberg, Klaus Nomi, Lou Reed, David Bowie, and various other superheroes of the artistic world.

On 36 West Sixty-Second Street, there was also Hurrah, which had opened in 1976 and was the first to use giant video screens, way ahead of MTV. The biggest new place, however, was Danceteria on Thirty-Eighth Street, which had three floors—one for live gigs, a big dance floor, and a top floor for exhibitions and performance art. Opened in 1979, Danceteria attracted more of a younger, fashion crowd, but its main deejay, Mark Kamins, fast became New York's hottest mixer-upper of improbable sounds. I was approaching forty and traveling a lot, so I wasn't exactly hanging out, but I'd head down to all these places to check out bands and look around. Influences were coming in from all angles, but it was clear punk and disco were mixing up and evolving into something new. What that was, nobody had yet invented a name for.

Of all the people in my circle, those most plugged into the downtown scene were Talking Heads, who were so hot, they didn't have to follow any fashions—the hip crowd was busy chasing after *them*. Chris Frantz and Tina Weymouth had moved out to Long Island City, just a fifteen-minute drive into town, so when they weren't on tour, they'd party all night moving around between these clubs, looking at bands, getting invited into the deejay booths, and misbehaving as musicians their age might do. As the sun came up over the Williamsburg Bridge, Chris would drive them home in some frazzled states, thankfully never crashing their new Honda Prelude into any early-morning milk trucks.

Their apartment was a three-thousand-square-foot space in a brownstone factory on the corner of Vernon Avenue and Forty-Fourth Drive. It had been converted into several artist lofts but still had the old freight elevator, which opened straight onto the street, a small luxury if you're constantly lugging drum kits and amplifiers. It was the perfect HQ for rehearsals and huge parties, of which there were many. Their circle of friends included the B-52's, Brian Eno, Debbie Harry, Seymour Avigdor, new-wave composer Arthur Russell, writer Albert Goldman, actress Karen Allen, photographer Lynn Goldsmith, even David Lee Roth. Danceteria deejay Mark Kamins often entertained those parties, just pulling stuff out of Chris and Tina's record collection.

They didn't even have to worry about making noise—only its quality. Upstairs was inhabited by trumpeter Don Cherry, jazz royalty and probably the number-one pioneer of world fusions in those days. His band at the time included tabla master Trilok Gurtu and various jazz rockers from Lou Reed's band. When Don Cherry heard Chris and Tina rehearsing in the afternoons, he'd sometimes pop downstairs with his *donso ngoni*, a stringed instrument from Mali, on which he'd pluck rhythmic melodies inspired from West Africa. Even his kids, Neneh and Eagle-Eye, who also lived upstairs, were budding young musicians. Across from the Cherry home was the Modern Lovers' bass player, Ernie Brooks. Next door was Tina's older brother Yann and his girlfriend, Julia MacFarlane, both pioneer architects who worked from home, designing I. M. Pei projects for the Louvre and elsewhere.

It made sense that Talking Heads would record their third album, *Fear of Music*, in Chris and Tina's loft. The producer was again Brian Eno, by now living permanently in New York following his Berlin period with David Bowie, who had also just moved to New York. Their plan was to park a mobile studio truck on the street below, where Eno's machines were wired up to the musicians on the third floor. And because they were listening to so much African music, a bunch of fast groovers grew out of those sessions, some of which even picked up sirens and traffic noise from the street below. Tracks like "I Zimbra," "Life During Wartime," and "Cities" got heavy action on the dance floors of Danceteria, Hurrah, and the Mudd Club. In fact, while recording the album, Talking Heads tested out some of these new songs on the stage of the Mudd Club.

We released *Fear of Music* in the summer of 1979, and although Talking Heads were still too radical to get major-league rotation on Top 40 radio, the album got glowing reviews in New York and London. That's really when the critics started raving unanimously about David Byrne as an important voice of the times. Musically also, Talking Heads were probably the hippest sound around, not that they or any of us inside Sire quite realized the effect they were having on producers, club deejays, and other bands. I think even they were too busy to notice it themselves. Some things take a few years to sink in.

Inside Sire, I'm happy to say we were too busy ourselves basking in the sunshine of our latest smash hit, "Pop Muzik" by M, a fabulous pop art record I'd snatched in London before any Americans heard it. It first blew up in London and then all over continental Europe, but success doesn't get any higher than number one on the *Billboard* Hot 100, and in November 1979, that's right where we stood, top of the world, looking down on Michael Jackson's "Don't Stop 'Til You Get Enough." As old-school disco began to lose its sparkle, new wave was still going strong.

I had another silver bullet already loaded in the barrel. In purely A&R terms, the Pretenders were a fine example of how the best discoveries sometimes fall into your lap just by getting out, failing at first, but accidentally making new contacts that lead to something better. Back in 1977, I was at a Generation X show where I saw a familiar face hovering around looking very interested. His name was Dave Hill, the A&R man for ABC's brief attempt at a London branch called Anchor Records. It was such a disaster label that after about a year, Anchor was referred to in the English music business as Wanker, but because ABC was my distributor at the time, I joined forces with Dave to improve our chances of bagging Generation X. The plan was that I'd take their North American rights and Anchor would get the UK. In our efforts to charm the band, we even met Billy Idol's parents, Mr. and Mrs. Broad. All, alas to no avail. Chrysalis won the contest, which in hindsight, turned out to be the right choice. Terry Ellis and Chris Wright did a good job with Generation X and later made Billy Idol an international pop star.

When Wanker folded shortly afterward, Dave Hill did what most redundant A&R men do: he started managing a band he'd been eyeing up but couldn't sign. So, he telephoned me in late 1978 and explained, "I'm managing this really great band. I know your taste, and you're going to like them. The lead singer is actually an American girl; you might know her in fact—Chrissie Hynde? She writes for *NME* [*New Musical Express*]."

"Don't tell me she's a writer and wants to be a singer." I laughed. I had nothing against writers, but whatever it was about the late seventies, an alarming number of music journalists suddenly wanted to be punk stars. It was both a constant nightmare and a running joke for Linda, who had to befriend all these journalists to get the Ramones into the press. Unfortunately, she kept having to fend off their bullshit demos and schemes to get famous.

"No, this girl is different," said Dave, who was no fool. "She always wanted to be a singer, but to continue living in England, she had to get an office job. Forget I even mentioned *NME*. You'll like her. I know you will."

"Okay, okay, I'll come and see her."

In early February 1979, I first saw her group perform to fewer than a hundred people at the Moonlight Club in London's West Hampstead neighborhood. The location alone struck me because it was the exact same place underneath the Railway Hotel, just down the road from Decca's studios, where Mike Vernon took me in the midsixties. Back then, it was a mainly jazz and blues haunt called the Klooks Kleek, where many famous concerts were recorded by running a line up the street into Decca. I always followed my gut instincts, and just by walking into this refurbished venue, I sensed imminent magic. Sure enough, when the Pretenders stepped up, I was completely knocked off my feet.

There was an edgy confidence about them and lots of interesting songs that hit you first listen. To sign them, I had to do a label deal with Dave Hill, who had the good sense to set up his own little indie, Real Records, to which he'd signed the Pretenders before shopping them to me. It wasn't cheap, but even Warner knew we were onto a surefire hit and coughed up the money without any moaning.

Being an American exile in London, Chrissie Hynde was naturally very excited about her little career suddenly gearing up for a major-league homecoming. While the ink was still wet, she called into my apartment on Gloucester Place and suggested we go out for a walk.

"Do you know the rooftop on that building?" she asked, pointing at the building beside mine.

"No. Why?"

"You don't know it? Wow, it's one of my favorite spots in London." She beamed, like it was all an amazing coincidence. "I go up all the time. I walk in, and nobody says anything. C'mon, follow me. You've got to see this." She led me through a door and into an elevator. Getting out at the top floor, I followed her up another flight of stairs, which opened onto this spectacular rooftop garden overlooking London. "I come here to think and work on my lyrics," she said. "I really love this place."

I instantly liked Chrissie Hynde. She was from Akron, Ohio, and had witnessed London's punk scene from the inside, first working for fashion designer Vivienne Westwood, who was of course Malcolm McLaren's girlfriend and partner in the clothes store where so much of the Sex Pistols story began. After a few false starts in other bands and then a job in the *NME* that she never fit into, Chrissie found the perfect guitarist and collaborator in James Honeyman-Scott, who had a bright, jangling style of his own. They were a powerful duo backed by a tight drummer, Martin Chambers, and a hard-hitting bassist, Pete Farndon.

Technically capable singers are two for a buck, but what Chrissie Hynde naturally possessed was a unique-sounding voice and a gift for songwriting. She was a tough young lady who'd been living on her wits for a long time, but she also had a very sensitive, thoughtful side, and I think that mix of hard and soft gave her songs depth and personality. At the time, she was romantically involved with the Kinks' front man, Ray Davies, who wrote "Stop Your Sobbing," which the Pretenders covered. Everyone at Sire and Warner, however, agreed that "Brass in Pocket" was the obvious single, so we splashed out on a video, which was uncommon in those days, especially for an unknown act. In early 1980, "Brass in Pocket" broke into *Billboard*'s top twenty, ensuring the self-titled debut album was a hit.

All this was Sire's first sustained run of mainstream chart success that seemed to confirm our arrival into the major league. We'd been able to sell hip albums before, but always having something in the singles charts was new. The opening of Sire's London office on Floral Street in mid-1979 partly explains this bumper harvest. I'd bought the building myself, knowing that Sire urgently needed a physical presence in London, which was clearly going through an exceptionally creative period. As well as my main man Paul McNally, I hired two loyal staffers, Maxine Conroy and Geraldine Oakley, who collectively formed the backbone of my small English operation, which I have to say really did punch far above its weight. Maxine, although English, had worked for me in New York but met Paul Conroy when she picked up the Madness tapes and artwork from our joint venture deal with Stiff Records. After their marriage, she moved back to London.

New sounds were coming in from all corners of Britain, so much so, a new genre term even popped up in 1979. Although *ska* was an old Jamaican word, a new-wave British variety suddenly burst onto the scene, thanks in large part to an indie label called 2 Tone Records. It was founded by Jerry Dammers, the piano-playing creative force behind the Coventry group the Specials. They self-released the Specials through 2 Tone and quickly scooped up Madness, the

Selecter, and the Beat, all brilliant bands who could write songs and play knockout live shows. My favorites were Madness and the Beat, who I went after while London's labels all trampled over each other in the stampede to sign the Specials.

Getting Madness was nonetheless a bit of a tussle. The hottest of London's new-wave independents was probably Stiff Records whose boss, Dave Robinson, saw Madness at his own wedding and was as determined to sign them. They'd actually been booked by Paul McNally, so I almost got Madness for the world, but to avoid a major fight, I worked out a compromise with Dave Robinson, whereby I'd get North America and he'd get the UK and most of the rest of the world. The band agreed, and we all lived happily ever after.

The dark horse, however, proved to be the Beat, who nobody gave much attention to. They actually got signed from 2 Tone to Arista's London office by a talented A&R man named Tarquin Gotch. Fortunately for me, he didn't make a strong enough case to Arista's head office in New York, who foolishly passed. I pounced on their North American rights and enjoyed both commercial success and many happy memories with the Beat, who we had to rebaptize the English Beat to avoid confusion with another group. We got them touring with Talking Heads and the Pretenders, almost double bills that never failed to blow away audiences everywhere they played. I really did enjoy that whole new-wave ska scene. Just a few bands made some of the hippest party music ever recorded.

There was another pioneer act I signed that year that I count among the brightest lights on my A&R résumé. I first saw Echo and the Bunnymen in August 1979, at the YMCA on Tottenham Court Road, just three guys with guitars performing a few songs as warm-up for Joy Division. Their singer and songwriter, Ian McCulloch, was a twenty-year-old baby face, but there was already something of an old soul about his voice and lyrics. From the first song, I was hypnotized by the kid's strange power. With their drum machine, heavy echoes, and dark guitars, their sound made you think of Suicide mixed with something of the Velvet Underground, but they also evoked a northern English mysticism of their own that really sucked you in.

They were from Liverpool and were nothing like the Beatles, of course, but the spookiness of songs like "Pictures on My Wall" captured the brooding I'd felt so strongly on my visits. Liverpool in the late 1970s was not the majestic metropolis it had once been. In its day, Liverpool, which was the home of Cunard and the White Star Lines, rivaled London. Although no longer true by the time I came there in the seventies many of its beautiful old buildings, and the great bands and clubs that had become famous in the 1960s, were still around. I was fascinated by this enchanting city, which is a town of great character and humor. As a Brooklynite, I understood their mix of old religion and blue-collar attitude. Lou Reed and Alan Vega were both Brooklyn Jews like myself, so whatever holy spirits Echo and the Bunnymen were trying to evoke, they were close relatives to the ones I'd grown up with.

Straight after the show, I met the band and their two managers, Bill Drummond and David Balfe. Not only did I want to sign Echo and the Bunnymen, I was actually the only hunter on their tail. I knew that was probably only a matter of days, because they were already getting high-profile gigs and were about to play on John Peel's radio show on BBC Radio 1. At the same venue that night, I saw the great Teardrop Explodes, who I would have loved to sign as well, but with Mo breathing down my neck, I knew I'd be lucky to get Echo and the Bunnymen. After the gig, I stopped by the new office on Floral Street and telephoned Burbank. Unfortunately, I got bounced around until my good intentions came down with a thud on David Berman's desk.

"Sorry, Seymour," he announced. "You've spent all your budget for the year."

"But listen, we gotta get this band. They're gonna be big!"

"Well, can you not keep them on hold until the next financial period?"

"No, somebody else will get them by then. We've gotta move right now."

There was no point crying down a long-distance call to Mo's chief bean counter, who I knew was just following orders. What I wouldn't know until years later was that Mo had addressed his top staff about me in a meeting. "Have you ever seen such a bloated roster?" he gasped. "He can't stop signing. It's a sickness!" I don't doubt that my lucky roll must have seemed a bit crazy at first, but I totally believed that most if not all these bands would pay off in the long run. The problem always came back to Mo and his inner circle thinking California was the center of the solar system. Maybe it was in the early seventies, but they were thousands of miles from where tomorrow's sounds were happening. Undoubtedly, they did make some important international signings, mostly licensed from UK indies. But they had the benefit of being well-heeled to wait and pay big bucks, which Sire didn't have and which was not a way I wanted to operate.

I had to figure out a plan B right there in London, so I stayed up all night thinking. Top of my hit list was the head of Warner's UK publishing division, Rob Dickins. He was eight years younger than I was, had sharp ears, and always struck me as someone with a bright future. When it comes to choosing partners for music ventures, you never can tell, but Rob's father had been one of the founders of *NME*, Britain's leading music magazine.

I called into Rob's office the next day and played him a demo of Echo and the Bunnymen. He immediately recognized the good songwriting and original sound, so I pitched my idea. "Mo won't let me sign anything for the next two or three months, by which stage this band will be somewhere else. You've got great ears. You should have your own label. Let's start one together. We sign this band immediately, then we set up deals with Warner in London for the UK, with WEA for international, and Sire for North America?"

"Okay," said Rob. "But I'm not leaving my job. I'll have to do this on the side." Rob not only put up all the money to sign Echo and the Bunnymen, but so strong was his belief in the band that he worked his ass off to break them.

"Of course, Rob. We'll keep the whole thing dead simple and inside Warner. Believe me, they'll be glad we did this in the end, you'll see. I basically need you to be the band's contact here in London, which won't take up too much of your time. But I just wanna say, I think you'll make a great record man."

Insomnia and jet lag were the banes of my life, and this was one of many situations when I was nodding off midsentence like a hippie on downers. I had to get to bed, so I got up to leave. "Hang on, Seymour. We're not finished yet. What are we going call this label?"

"I don't care. You come up with any name you want."

"No, Seymour, we're not gonna start a label unless we *both* come up with the name."

He was dead right, so I sat there for hours, dizzy but still running on nervous energy. On his wall, there was a framed poster for the Stanley Kubrick movie *A Clockwork Orange*. Looking at the images, I remembered the name of the stylish bar where the gang members pour milk from the tit of the white statue.

"What about Korova?" I suggested.

"That'll do!" Rob smiled, obviously a big fan of the movie.

That little maneuver sneaked Echo and the Bunnymen into Warner through the back door. It also drew Rob Dickins out of publishing into cutting-edge record production, and what a bright future that would turn out to be. I advised the band to ditch the drum machine for a human, which they were already thinking about doing anyway. We'd have to wait a few months to receive their first album, *Crocodiles*, which I knew would make a bigger splash in England than in the States. Their sound was too dark for American Top 40 radio, but songs like "Rescue," "Pictures on My Wall," and "Do It Clean" were played by college radio stations, downtown clubs, and in specialist record stores.

In this magical period of signing pioneer bands almost every month, what I never saw coming was the small print of the Warner deal coming home to roost. According to the agreement I'd signed in late 1977, Warner Bros. Records could automatically buy the other half of Sire for $1 million, plus a token percentage of company value based on business. This meant that in 1980, during a major recession when record sales right across the board were down about 20 percent, I had to accept whatever Burbank's bean counters calculated as Sire's other half, and there was nothing I could do about it except negotiate an executive salary as Sire's chairman.

I hadn't really taken in the reality of not owning my company anymore, but if anything symbolized the seismic changes taking place both in my life and the record industry in general, it was that Sire had to move out of the old brownstone on West Seventy-Fourth Street and be put into WBR's East Coast office at 3 East Fifty-Fourth Street. The indie days were fading fast. Despite Mo's promises to keep Sire an indie, it was slowly becoming a Warner imprint. I still had a team of my own, though smaller, but nevertheless was determined to keep making the most of what we had, even though it was obvious Mo was doing everything to control me.

While I was dealing with all of this, Talking Heads were off around Europe on their Fear of Touring, this time with guest musicians like Adrian Belew and Busta Jones. Apart from the electrifying shows I caught here and there, I had no reason to think anything was turning sour in their dressing room. What I didn't know was that in late December 1979, the night they wound up the whole tour in West Germany, some journalist lady had come from behind the Iron Curtain to interview the band. For whatever reason, David Byrne was demanding to do his interviews separately and talked to the journalist alone behind closed doors. When Tina, Chris, and Jerry were called in afterward, the journalist innocently asked them, "What are you going to do now that David Byrne's leaving the group?"

Chris, Tina, and Jerry were totally stunned. They were also well accustomed to David's strange behavior. Because they'd been on the road for six months and just wanted to get home for Christmas, they bit their lips, tidied up their gear, and took the plane to New York. "Let's just catch up with some sleep before dealing with this," they told each other. After all, maybe it was bullshit? Maybe it was the journalist's bad English? The problem by then was that nobody dared confront David Byrne about much. The other Heads preferred to tread on eggshells, which is what I, the manager, the crew, Brian Eno, and just about everyone else did, too. Believe me, there's nothing easier or more normal than to appease a troubled genius. Not least because we were all in awe of him.

A few weeks later, Chris Frantz got a call from Brian Eno, who was producing something privately with David Byrne. Chris was not really told what the project was, but being a team player, he laid down drums on an instrumental track that would eventually be called "Regiment." Still scratching his head, Chris went home to his wife having to explain that Busta Jones was on bass. He then called Jerry Harrison and broke the news that Robert Fripp was the guitarist. All this must have looked and sounded a little ominous to the other members of Talking Heads. In the end, Brian Eno and David Byrne's side project would become *My Life in the Bush of*

Ghosts, an experimental album exploring their African influences from a more technological angle. Its release, however, would be held up for almost a year due to contentious samples.

They moved work to a studio in San Francisco called Different Fur, but when they came home to New York in early spring, Chris and Tina decided to confront Brian Eno, who seemed to be pushing David Byrne into a solo direction.

"Will you produce Talking Heads' next album?" they asked.

"No," replied Eno uncomfortably without explaining why.

"Well, will you come over to our loft and jam with us?" they asked.

"Sure, but what can I play?"

"Play one of our keyboards. Create sounds. Have fun. Let's try out something new."

"Okay," agreed Eno, who already knew how to get there.

When Brian Eno arrived, Chris, Tina, and Jerry had already spent days taping jams on a cassette recorder. They played their demo, which Eno liked, and then they all started jamming with Eno on synths. Once things started to cook, they called David Byrne and invited him to join in, and of course David was too curious to stay away. What followed was like one of those old cartoons where musical notes are pouring out of a window. A collective decision was made by all four Talking Heads and Brian Eno to move work down to Compass Point in the Bahamas and work as a five-piece team. Those sessions would become *Remain in Light,* probably their most acclaimed album among hard-core fans, but by no means their bestselling.

All the African experimentalism they'd started on their previous record was taken a step further, as with their masterpiece hit "Once in a Lifetime." That's also when David Byrne started making arty videos with his then girlfriend, the talented dance choreographer Toni Basil. Out in Los Angeles, they shot a video for "Once in a Lifetime" featuring only David Byrne spinning around on a wheel, trying not to puke. When the other Talking Heads were presented the video as a fait accompli, they were understandably a bit taken aback, but Chris, Tina, and Jerry had to admit it looked pretty cool. For another track, "Crosseyed and Painless," Toni Basil found a dance troupe called the Lockers, who performed what was then called robotics or creeping, the precursor to break dancing. There's even moonwalking in that video, years before Michael Jackson made it famous.

To re-create their bigger sound onstage, Talking Heads went back out on the road with something like ten musicians and as many crew. They put on a brilliant show, but at the end of that tour, they hit another brick wall. The band's accountant crunched the numbers and, ouch, they were almost broke. People today probably have difficulty believing this, but it cost five bucks to see them play in venues that held one or two thousand people. Their first four records had sold nearly a hundred thousand copies each, good numbers, but they kept breaking the first commandment of show business: *thou shalt not overspend.*

I don't know if it was money, heavy touring, or David's solitary nature, but all the unspoken shit that had been building up inside that dressing room started to hit the fan on my desk. In came the manager, Gary Kurfirst, who announced that now David was writing songs for a Broadway musical called *The Catherine Wheel.* He wanted money to produce the soundtrack as a solo record for Sire. What? We were already having such difficulty clearing the samples for *My Life in the Bush of Ghosts* we hadn't even released *that* side project yet. I nonetheless agreed to an advance without ever asking David myself if this spelled the end of Talking Heads. I chose to shut up and give him what he wanted, knowing that when David

Byrne set his eyes on some new artistic mountain, you'd only get injured holding him back. He was someone I'd always support even if he wanted to make a concept album about toothpicks.

Gary Kurfirst found himself in the tightest spot of all, because he was negotiating David's solo deal but had to share the information openly with the other members of the band, who of course were feeling left out. Next thing I knew, he was back on the phone saying Chris and Tina wanted money to make their own side project. Then, of course, Jerry Harrison wanted his solo album, too. All this was turning into a mess, and it's not like I didn't have plenty of other things happening. I'd always lived by the philosophy that songs were the magic ingredient in music, so I reasoned that David Byrne, being the main songwriter, deserved special treatment. I did offer Chris and Tina a deal, although—and here was my diplomatic goof-up—a smaller advance than what I was giving David.

Gary came back to tell me that Chris and Tina were taking an offer from Chris Blackwell of Island Records—modest enough, but bigger than mine. I could have upped my original offer, but I let it go. Gary was an old friend of Chris Blackwell's, and when it came to dub, Island was a logical fit for whatever rhythmic experiment Chris and Tina had in mind. So, I just concluded, "Yeah, whatever," thinking all this was a classic case of a band getting lost up their own asses. Who'd have guessed they'd start pulling out gold discs?

Calling themselves Tom Tom Club, Chris and Tina began jamming with one of Chris Blackwell's protégés, Steven Stanley, a Jamaican keyboardist and producer. Their first experiment was "Wordy Rappinghood," not really a *song* in the old-fashioned sense, but it was a funky whistler with a fabulous cartoony sound. Released by Island in February 1981, it made a splash in Europe, Latin America, and on the dance floors of New York. Tina's rhymes weren't exactly rap as we know the term today, but that twelve-inch caught the immediate attention of all the black pioneers who were inventing what we now call hip-hop.

Meanwhile, we were having serious difficulties with David Byrne and Brian Eno's collaboration *My Life in the Bush of Ghosts*. They'd sampled some truly obscure sounds, which had us chasing around after faith healers and the Council of Muslims in Britain. For religious reasons, some samples were denied, meaning a few tracks had to be redone or left off. The final cut of *My Life in the Bush of Ghosts* was nonetheless a fascinating creeper, a cult record that influenced so many experimental artists in its wake. We released it at exactly the same time as Island released Tom Tom Club. Although the release dates were accidental, it nonetheless set up a terrifying duel between the two sides of the *not-really-talking* Heads.

To be honest, I didn't know what to make of all this instrumental experimentation, but looking back, between *Remain in Light*, Tom Tom Club, and *My Life in the Bush of Ghosts*, new genres were being discovered right under my nose. These were the sounds of the eighties and beyond. The music scene hadn't stopped evolving since the Ramones hit London in 1976, but I think it's fair to also single out 1981 as another major milestone that points all the way into the digital era. This was the very beginning of dance music, hip-hop, electronica—all the generic terms we'd be using much later.

The year 1981 was also the beginning of MTV, the Sony Walkman, the Roland TR-808 drum machine, the Fairlight CMI sampler. John Lennon had just been shot, Ronald Reagan had just been elected, and everyone was hooking up to cable TV and buying VHS recorders. New technology was taking over in a big way. My corporate masters, Warner Communications, had bought into Atari, and even my own daughters couldn't get enough of all that arcade stuff like PAC-MAN, Donkey Kong, Space Invaders, Scramble, Galaga. Every kid was hooked. Between 1981 and 1982, the number of arcade machines in the United States tripled from half a million to 1.5 million. I guess all these bleepy electronic sounds were forging the ears of a new generation.

I was living on my own in a big new place on Central Park West, just down the street from the old Kenilworth apartment where Linda and the girls still lived. It was a three-bedroom beauty that I'd paid three hundred grand for. Unfortunately, I had to build a staircase to an upstairs room, and because the place was so big, it took a few years to furnish. Coincidentally, the Bee Gees manager Robert Stigwood lived on the top floor of the neighboring tower, not that I ever saw him. I was doing quite a lot of coke at the time, so when I wasn't traveling or working late, I remember sitting there in a sparsely furnished room for hours just flicking through the channels. Images were pouring in from all over the globe—revolution in Nicaragua, the Space Shuttle, the Ayatollah Khomeini, Leonid Brezhnev's funeral, Richard Pryor blowing himself up freebasing cocaine, "Bonkers candy bonks you out!"

Meanwhile, hip FM stations like WBLS, WKTU, and most importantly WLIR were playing the threads out of our records. Also on those stations, a new generation of deejays like Shep Pettibone, Marley Marl, Red Alert, Chep Nuñez, and the Latin Rascals performed what was called "cutting," a technique of rhythmically alternating between two copies of the same record to create all these chops, scratches, and dub-style echoes. There was also the "mega mix" using the same tricks but with different records. These live radio tricks and the growing demand for danceable records in clubs was what pushed labels such as Sire into releasing twelve-inch remixes of our coolest stuff.

Meanwhile, art house theaters were screening *Downtown 81*, a movie that documented our local music scene, including a hot new Latino band, Kid Creole and the Coconuts, whose percussionist, Coati Mundi, was putting out his own quirky records. Both acts were on an interesting indie called ZE Records, whose progress I was watching carefully. In the modern art museums, the big thing was video installations from around the world and the tribal art of Jean-Michel Basquiat, a New Yorker originally from Haiti who you'd see hanging out at the Mudd Club. Laurie Anderson released "O Superman," a cult hit among the performance art crowd, and although the landmark movie *Koyaanisqatsi* didn't come out until the following year, it was being filmed around New York to the music of Philip Glass. In Los Angeles, Ridley Scott was busy making *Blade Runner.*

It was an incredible time for creativity, most of it futuristic and global in flavor, and for me personally, the year's discoveries were only just beginning. In the early hours of April 28, 1981, I was wide awake in bed, reading a copy of *NME*, when one review glowed in the dark. Its headline read "Basildon à la Mode" and profiled a new English group named after French fashion magazine *Depeche Mode.* This was the kind of reading that'd usually slip you into the Land of Nod, but what kept me up all night was the name of their producer, Daniel Miller, the guy I'd first met in Rough Trade three years before. Since then, I'd released his second record, under the name Silicon Teens, a pretend group that was all his work. It hadn't sold much either, but I thought the guy had brilliant ideas.

"Mute maestro Daniel Miller has a notoriously sweet tooth," read the review, "one that's balanced by a taste for bitter extremes. . . . Due to their extremely shy natures the four have chosen to be chaperoned by producer Miller, whom they refer to as Uncle Daniel. . . . Depeche Mode come from Basildon. (Sentence Of The Week—Ed.) They are bass synth player Andrew Fletcher, an insurance man; David Gahan, lead vocalist, electronic percussionist and trainee window dresser; the silent Martin Gore, synthesist and banker; and Vincent Clarke, writer, synthesist and otherwise unemployed."

It was about 2:00 A.M., but alarm bells were ringing. I knew enough about Daniel Miller to know that if he was taking that giant leap from artist to producer, this new group had to be exceptional. The other detail that gave me the heebie-jeebies was the date of the article. I'd just picked up whatever was next to my bed, but when I examined the cover, this copy of *NME* was three weeks old—an eternity in A&R time. So, at 10:00 A.M. English time, I called my man in London, Paul McNally, to find out if Depeche Mode's American rights had been signed. He called me back saying that no, America was still up for grabs and that Depeche Mode were playing that night in some nightclub in Essex, about an hour east of London. I called up British Airways and booked a seat on the next Concorde—eight grand, an obscene amount of cash in those days, but I smelled something cooking.

With the five-hour time difference, it was already almost evening in England when my flight landed. Paul was waiting in arrivals and drove us straight to Basildon, a dead suburb where we had to ask directions to the concrete box of a discotheque called Sweeney's. In the crowd of about two hundred kids, I saw Daniel Miller standing behind the mixing desk; he was the gig's soundman. There wasn't even a dressing room, and the boys were getting changed in a stairwell, where I dropped by to say hello. This was their local nightclub, they hadn't even put out a single yet, and here I was, in their teenage eyes a powerful record executive who'd just flown in from New York by Concorde. God knows what they were thinking.

They got up and launched into what I can only describe as an electronic cabaret show. At that time, there were a few synth acts out, notably Gary Numan, who'd hit the big time with his 1980 smash "Cars." There was Visage, OMD, and others, but any time I'd seen any of these so-called new romantics in concert, I couldn't keep my eyes open. Synthesizers created impressive soundscapes on record, but keeping a crowd bopping for over an hour is a very different business. To my delight, Depeche Mode weren't standing around looking enigmatic in heavy makeup; they had bubbling rhythms, singable tunes, and a dancing singer who put in the effort to entertain his crowd. I looked around and thought, *If all these Essex kids are dancing like this all night, then surely Depeche Mode could be big all over England.*

Of course, there's only so much you can take in when you see a band for the first time, especially when you've just stepped off a plane and haven't slept in two days. I'd love to be able to say that I had visions of Depeche Mode selling out football stadiums across the world. I didn't. I mean, you really couldn't. They were four teenagers poking synths in a dump in the English suburbs. Getting on *Top of the Pops* was probably the sum total of their own wildest fantasies. Truth is, when I booked that plane ticket, I was banking on Daniel Miller. Deep down, I just knew he and his Mute label were headed for major success. Sometimes it's bands, sometimes it's the people behind them, and if you're very lucky, it's both.

Sire signed another of his groups, Fad Gadget, and later that summer, I stumbled on another gem from the same electro scene. As a freelance producer, Daniel Miller had just produced the first single of an underground group called Soft Cell. It wasn't Daniel who played me their subsequent stuff, because Soft Cell were signed to a UK indie called Some Bizarre, which in turn had an exclusive deal with Polydor. From Polydor's London office, we received a promo copy of "Tainted Love," which I knew was a potential smash. Polydor's UK boss Roger Ames and I went way back, so, with my A&R kid, Michael Rosenblatt, I flew straight back to London. "Say nothing," I told Michael, who was only twenty-four and eager to learn. "Don't let him know I want the album."

When we sat down with Roger Ames in a London restaurant, I had a gut feeling Polydor's office in New York had already passed on Soft Cell. If there was one thing you could count on, it was Polydor's New York staffers turning their noses up at wacky English pop. So, I kept ordering wine to get Roger as pliant as possible.

"I think 'Tainted Love' could work in the States," I told him. "But it's risky. Would you take ten thousand for the single?"

"Well, we don't really want to license the single, Seymour. Would you not take the whole album for fifteen?"

"Oh, all right, Roger. It's gonna be tough, but we'll do our best with the album."

I kept a straight face knowing this verbal agreement needed to be signed *immediately*. Soft Cell were being managed by a larger-than-life Cockney character by the name of Steve-O, who I knew was not lacking in connections and brass neck. It was a mystery that Soft Cell hadn't yet been shopped to every American major, so, before we got up and stumbled out of the restaurant, I scrawled the basic deal terms on a napkin and made Roger Ames sign. This rather curious-looking tissue paper was duly delivered to Polydor's contracts man, John Kennedy, who apparently cracked up laughing.

I'd landed a bargain, but to be fair, £15,000 wasn't nothing in 1981 for an unproven group, especially considering what it was. Soft Cell's singer, Marc Almond, was absolutely the gayest English-man I'd ever seen, which is saying something. It didn't make a difference if he was on- or offstage, he minced about in leather costumes, wearing this dirty grin like he'd just stepped out of the toilet of an S&M bar. I loved him. He was one of those "I yam what I yam" characters but with a unique voice that made everything he sang his own, including, "Tainted Love," which was originally a 1964 hit for Gloria Jones. The title of Soft Cell's album *Non-Stop Erotic Cabaret* was no exaggeration either. It was brilliantly filthy party music but with really romping, singable tunes.

We suddenly had three electro groups in the pipeline—Depeche Mode, Fad Gadget, and Soft Cell—which, as you can imagine, weren't the easiest signatures to explain out in Burbank. In 1981, the American market was still chewing on adult-oriented rock, and these new acts probably wouldn't have flown had they not been such reasonable signings. Luckily, it all came together exactly at the right time, about six months before the likes of Human League and Eurythmics blew up and suddenly the whole UK electro scene became big business in America. By the time the various albums were finished and release slots allocated, we'd be surfing what many Americans incorrectly term *new wave*—that second, early-eighties wave of synthesizers and funny hair that purists prefer to call *synth pop* or *electro*.

Meanwhile, in the Bahamas, the Talking Heads plot was thickening. By midsummer 1981, Island released a second and even bigger Tom Tom Club twelve-inch, "Genius of Love," which hit even harder than "Wordy Rappinghood." All summer, New York couldn't get enough of this sunny tune, and I mean *everyone* from the downtown clubs all the way up to the Bronx, where a then unknown group called Grandmaster Flash and the Furious Five looped the main hook and rapped over it, earning Chris and Tina an official place in early hip-hop history.

Of course, I hadn't signed Tom Tom Club, so when one hundred thousand copies of "Genius of Love" were imported into America from Island's main office in London, I was officially King Dumbo, standing there with his dick in his hand. I'm sure Chris Blackwell was having a good laugh at my expense. Fortunately, Tom Tom Club still had a whole album ready to go, and so Gary Kurfirst came back to me tut-tutting, "If you want a piece of the action, Seymour, you're going to have to cough up a lot more now!" I bowed my head, wagged my tail, and dug into my pocket.

With Gary Kurfirst acting as broker, Chris Blackwell and I

agreed to a territorial split on the album and the twelve inches, which, I'm happy to say, worked out for the best. The album was a huge hit, earning Chris Frantz and Tina Weymouth a well-deserved gold disc. With proper Warner promotion and distribution, "Genius of Love" even got a second lease of life, breaking into the American Top 40 the following spring.

Best of all, I think it's fair to say that Chris and Tina's unexpected success helped glue Humpty Dumpty back together again. Brian Eno and David Byrne's *My Life in the Bush of Ghosts* had been hailed by critics and musicians as groundbreaking, which it most definitely was, but sales were a fraction of Tom Tom Club's. That didn't bother *me*, but it sure as hell altered the team dynamics between the members of Talking Heads. Especially after November 1981, when David Byrne's *Catherine Wheel* project was released to relative indifference. It sold something like ten thousand copies, a big disappointment, although it did contain some beautiful moments, like "What a Day That Was," a song with a stunning chorus that would be revamped into one of the highlights of future Talking Heads shows. The weakness of *The Catherine Wheel* wasn't the writing; it was the flat sound.

The jury will be out for years to come on all this. I'd bet that David Byrne did not at first enjoy Tom Tom Club's commercial success, but he got over it and found a renewed faith in his old bandmates. What is undeniable is that for the next few years, he would put his solo ambitions on standby and throw all his chips into Talking Heads. Their manager, Gary Kurfurst, came out stronger, too. He'd calmly handled a messy situation and earned everyone's respect, mine included. Never again would anyone make the mistake of assuming Chris Frantz and Tina Weymouth were just a rhythm section. Jerry Harrison's versatility was another integral part of whatever magic sauce made Talking Heads taste so good. Songs definitely are the core ingredient, but in the crazy science of bands, a lot of what we can't define comes down to the chemistry of the people involved.

In November 1981, right beside David Byrne's *Catherine Wheel*, we put out Depeche Mode's debut album *Speak & Spell*, which created a nice little stir. Those four boys from Basildon had written some great pop songs, but with Daniel Miller working the boards, they also had a sound and chemistry that oozed through the vinyl. There were some hot numbers like "New Life," but the single had to be "Just Can't Get Enough," which we put out as a seven-inch with an alternate six-minute twelve-inch mix for the clubbers. Combined sales got Depeche Mode straight onto *Billboard*'s club chart—still a niche thing, but they were flashing on radars and getting the hip kids dancing.

Soft Cell, however, blew up massively. We put out *Non-Stop Erotic Cabaret* in that big November 1981 batch expecting action, but "Tainted Love" got hammered on Top 40 radio. It peaked at number eight on the Hot 100 and stayed on the chart for something ridiculous like forty-three weeks, totally unexpected for such a dirty English joke. Yes, sir, Yanks in places like Colorado and Texas were buying this ass-spanking piece of vinyl. There really is no business like show business.

I adored another song off that record, "Say Hello, Wave Goodbye," which was admittedly more of a slow burner, but its stunning chorus sent shivers down my spine. I tried everything to make it a hit, including knocking on the door of my old friend Bill Wardlow at *Billboard*, who'd been so helpful keeping "Tainted Love" in the charts for so long. He was gay and loved them as much as I did, but sadly, Soft Cell's elusive follow-up wasn't to be. I loved the song so much that a couple of years later, after the success of "Take on Me" by Aha, I suggested to my friend Andrew Wickham, who discovered the band and brought them to Warner Brothers, that the band might consider doing "Say Hello, Wave Goodbye." As far as I know they never recorded it.

There was another band I helped in that year who weren't even mine. Island had signed an Irish post-punk group called U2 who were making some noise in Britain and wanted to tour the States. Island had such a small U.S. operation, Warner was handling most of their local marketing, but U2 were so far down the pecking order that I did what I could to help out. It was their manager, Paul McGuinness, who I first met in 1981. He was in New York, staying with a friend of his, Michael Deeny, an Irish manager and accountant who'd I'd previously crossed paths with when he was handling an Irish band called Horslips that I'd wanted to sign in the seventies. I just happened to be having dinner in some restaurant when a bottle of champagne arrived from another table. It was from Michael Deeny and Paul McGuinness, who invited me back to their place to continue the festivities.

I don't think Paul McGuinness had a dime in those, but I'd heard U2's debut album, *Boy*, and thought they definitely had something. So, as a simple favor, I talked Warner into giving U2 tour support, not a huge amount of money but enough to get them driving around, playing whatever slots they could find. I can't claim any part in U2's success. They worked hard for what they eventually got. I'm happy nonetheless that my phone calls provided a few drops of oil in the wheels of destiny. Syd Nathan made calls for me when I was their age and desperate. Now it was my turn to pay back life. That's how it's always worked and always will.

I know I made mistakes along the way, but with so many fireworks going off in all directions, Sire had become the hippest label in New York. As new clubs kept opening and MTV grew in popularity, a whole new generation of punky-haired teenagers proved to be our most loyal and excited customers. Damn it, kids were growing up with that Sire logo spinning through their teenage years, and of all the little things I treasured most, that thought made me the happiest. If you've been a rebel or an outcast yourself, you'll understand the privilege of being able to pour sonic medicine back into the school yards and unhappy bedrooms that made you who you are. We're not actually doing it for the money. Money is *how* we keep doing it, but not *why*.

I hate to toot my own horn, but just look at the amount of hits, creepers, and dance floor stompers on Sire's catalog in those years. And I haven't even mentioned all the underground classics I signed that didn't always make the American charts but which have stood the test of time. Stuff like "One Step Beyond" by Madness, "Mirror in the Bathroom" by the English Beat, "I Melt with You" by Modern English, "Ça Plane Pour Moi" by Plastic Bertrand, "Moskow Diskow" by Telex, "Safety Dance" by Men Without Hats, "Don't Go" and "Situation" by Yaz, an offshoot of Depeche Mode. And what about Kid Creole and the Coconuts, that new-wave salsa group that began stirring in 1981? I licensed Kid Creole and the Coconuts at their hottest moment in 1982, but we unfortunately never managed to break them onto American radio, a personal regret, but, my God, songs like "Annie, I'm Not Your Daddy" and "Stool Pigeon" were surely among the very hottest records of that whole downtown scene.

Much has been written about CBGB in the late seventies, but the early eighties in downtown New York also deserves history's full attention. Even some of David Bowie's best songs, like "Ashes to Ashes," "Fashion," and "Let's Dance," fed straight off that funky downtown sound. I was hitting forty and couldn't dance, so I can't say I experienced the party like the club kids. I was just one of the talent hunters leaning up against a wall in Danceteria, admiring how Mark Kamins mixed up all these records so effortlessly. There was nothing new about playing punk, reggae, and krautrock back to back—the Brits had been doing it for years. In Danceteria, however, you'd get all the UK sounds remixed into something new, plus Brazilian, African, Indian, early hip-hop, Detroit techno, sounds you couldn't even place on any map.

I know Lady Luck was smiling my way, but I took to that globalist period like a duck to water. What gave me an edge was all those years traveling, listening to foreign pop music, and making contacts all over the world. I could pick up all the little references and, just as importantly, locate the sources. The beauty of the Warner joint venture in those first years was that I could sign almost whatever I liked. No matter how obscure or indie the music was, the records would still get major company distribution. Of course, not even Warner could turn every slice of vinyl into a hit—nobody can—but at very worst, almost every record reached the desks of radio stations, local newspapers, and TV channels. Everything got its shot.

The early eighties were magical years, blindly pushing the late seventies into a whole new world order and not even realizing the lasting effect all these sounds and global ideas were having on the next batch of kids coming up. It was like the whole music world had been spinning leisurely at 33 RPM throughout the couch-bound seventies. The combined forces of punk, disco, and new wave had pushed everything up to 45 RPM. Without me and others in my line of work, it was waiting to happen anyway. I'm nonetheless proud that Sire was part of that urgently needed explosion of big-city energy that got kids out and shook things up.

7. BORDERLINE

Musically, I had every reason to be happy. As an entrepreneur, however, I hadn't expected to feel such profound regret when I lost all ownership of the label. As I soon discovered, seller's remorse was a common affliction among dispossessed indies. And believe me, it's a slow killer.

Jerry Wexler in particular was sick with regret for years after he talked Ahmet and Nesuhi Ertegun into selling their label. Against Ahmet's better judgment, they voted to sell Atlantic and got $17 million, which seemed like a king's ransom in 1967. First, they had to split their winnings into four parts because Herb Abrahamson's ex-wife Miriam Bienstock was also a stockholder. Then, the year after selling, they enjoyed a bumper harvest of smash hits, clocking up a record $40 million in turnover. From there, Atlantic kept growing so big that their sale price became a complete embarrassment.

Tell me about it. It was the same general story for every indie that sold out. You got scared and panicked, never imagining just how much money you would make your new owner. And as the album market kept growing, the regret tended to get worse with time, especially once the compact disc arrived and retail prices doubled. That's the whole point of the two-tranche deal I'd walked into. For a few years, you enjoyed the best of both worlds—half-indie, half-major—which had you planting seeds furiously with their money, wrongly thinking the harvest would be half yours, too. By the time those seeds sprouted and began budding, the whole orchard was theirs.

To be precise, I didn't regret *everything*. I always knew that Warner was good for Sire's artists, who never would have gotten the same breaks had I stayed independent with the likes of ABC as distributors. Talking Heads in particular were big winners, and for that reason alone, my grumbles should be mixed with due gratitude and relief that I didn't fuck up *their* destiny. What was killing me was that I'd been so naive about other aspects of the deal.

In music business mythology, Warner Bros. Records is often referred to as Camelot. Mo's sycophants still believe it, but if there's one key witness on this earth who can validate or shatter the Camelot legend, it's surely me, right? Mo Ostin's table was about as round as a pulpit. It was a table for one, protected on three sides and sloping heavily toward his pocket area. Oh, sure, you could gather around and clap your hands like plenty of misty-eyed WBR employees did, but that's only saying something about their own faith in the mythology.

To put it bluntly, there was nothing "joint" about what I'd ventured into. It was about as joint a venture as a whale swallowing a fish. Warner Bros. were the owners, the bosses, the bankers, the publicists, and the distributors. To Mo, Sire was just a pile of masters, artist contracts, and an A&R office of about ten expendable staffers. For $2 million, Mo basically bought *me* and all the contents of my filing cabinet, before and forever after. He'd dazzled me with flashy terms and big round numbers, and then he let me sign away for a few relatively undisturbed years. Then, when my playtime was up, his bean counters reeled much of it in.

Why hadn't I talked to David Geffen? Hopefully, he might have kicked some sense into me. In 1972, Steve Ross had done exactly the same thing to Geffen's Asylum label. Even the most brilliant negotiator, David Geffen, had been charmed by $7 million and took a while to come to his senses. When he did, he was just an employee watching all his acts generate about $100 million. He'd even signed the Eagles, the biggest-selling band of the seventies. Geffen was the smartest record boss of us all, which tells you how cunning Steve Ross must have been. Ross had basically worked out the postwar record business mathematically; he understood its values and its time scales. Artists came and went, so you bet on the Erteguns, the David Geffens, and Mo.

Mo used Steve Ross's playbook on me. When Warner saw something happening, it bought in fast while the labels were still cheap and then fed them millions in operating capital for two or three years, which is about what it takes for new bands to break. From there, the buyer reaped the long-term returns. So successful was this method, Warner became the world's biggest major in less than a decade—not bad considering it began as a handful of indies competing against major labels, some of which, like Victor (RCA Victor), Columbia, and the Gramophone Company (EMI), dated back to the turn of the century, while still others, like Philips (Phonogram), Deutsche-Gramophone (Polydor), Decca, and Capitol, emerged between the teens and the 1940s. Most amazingly of all, its music division was the most profitable side of the entire Warner Communications conglomerate. Hot record labels were automatic cash machines compared to movie studios, soccer clubs, arcade games, TV channels, and magazines, all of which cost a fortune to operate in comparison.

To cut a long story short, Warner structured my deal so they held all the cards. A built-in buyout option enabled WBR to take my half of Sire when it suited them. I had become a glorified employee who had to get every demo, band, and budget sniffed, poked, washed, ironed, and folded by Mo and the Warner machine. Never again could I shake a manager's hand with total confidence and say, "For sure, you've got a deal!" For a corporate salary, my job was now to convince artists and their managers to hold off for some more time so that I could squeeze money out of a building in California. As I was learning, asking nicely just doesn't work inside a large corporation; only the squeaky wheel gets the oil. You actually had to rave down the phone and keep calling back like a pest until they cracked and gave you what you needed. Managers around Burbank used to say I was annoying, that I hounded them to get my artists money or special attention. I'd tell you who some of these critics were except that you'd never have heard of them, which sort of proves my point. Being liked was not my goal in life. My business was turning great music into hit records.

Sire's worsening corporate predicament, to be fair, also had something to do with a recession affecting the whole industry in the early eighties. Like every other major, Warner had to reduce spending across the board, so even though I knew I was on a roll, my budgets got cut back like everyone else's. That said, it *was* personal; Mo felt I'd gone on an irresponsible shopping spree, the Pretenders had made a big splash but had drug problems, Talking Heads were still on the field but were looking a bit shaky internally at that point, the Ramones, in Mo's mind, had probably reached their limit, and we'd had lucky strikes and one one-hit wonder along the way. None of Sire's bands had taken off big-time, not by WBR's major major-league standards, and Mo didn't have the ears to hear what was just around the corner.

Mo being Mo, he didn't want to completely demoralize and humiliate me; that would just threaten the whole investment and potentially lose him points in Steve Ross's good book. He needed to smile me through tolerable levels of pain; I was to be kept alive, just healthy enough to keep Sire growing, and who knows, maybe find the occasional zero-risk moneymaker.

I don't know if it was all this regret that made me sick. It certainly couldn't have helped what I was doing to myself, anyway. Working around the clock like the transatlantic bachelor that I'd become, I was blowtorching the candle at both ends, and in mid-1982, I started getting pains in my chest. I thought I was getting a heart attack, so I didn't waste any time seeing a doc. An EKG showed that the hole between the left and right ventricles was infected. My rare condition had a name: subacute endocarditis. The good news, however, was that it was fixable with open-heart surgery. I was checked straight into Lenox Hill Hospital for four weeks of penicillin to clear up the infection before they decided what to do about the deformation. And right there, feeling sorry for myself in that ass-numbing bed, was where the record man's equivalent of Florence Nightingale walked in. Yes, you guessed it, she wasn't really a nurse, though sometimes I do wonder if singers are types of faith healers.

The series of events that brought Madonna to my hospital bed began months earlier when Mark Kamins started dropping hints. Danceteria was still the number-one downtown club, and Mark was arguably New York's hottest deejay. Unfortunately, he wasn't making enough money and knew he had to broaden his professional horizons while he was in such demand. We'd asked him to remix a David Byrne solo track called "Big Business," but Mark was dreaming of becoming a real-deal producer and asked me for help. I told him flat out that no big artist would *ever* risk working with an unproven producer, even if he was New York's hippest deejay. Remixes? Fine. But doing albums from scratch? No way. Like everyone else, he'd have to earn his stripes by finding nobodies and making them sound like stars. The best producers, I explained, are also A&R men who *find* and develop.

I knew it wouldn't be easy for Mark Kamins to make that jump to production, because he couldn't play an instrument, and the best producers are generally musicians to begin with. He had something else, however. He already had a sound. Just the name *Mark Kamins* evoked a sonic picture in people's ears, which is surely the sign of an exceptional deejay. He was also a natural-born digger who knew how to find really interesting stuff. So, doing as I'd done throughout my career when I encountered a red-hot talent magnet, I gave Mark $18,000 and set him a challenge: "Go find a few acts and make six demos for three grand each." Crazy as it sounds, I chose the figure of eighteen for reasons of Jewish numerology. It's the magic number of *chai*, the Hebrew symbol for life.

Maybe I was being naive, but I just presumed eighteen grand was as good as a gentleman's handshake. Imagine how I felt when I read about Mark Kamins working for Chris Blackwell at Island. *The fucker!* I thought. *Where did my money go?* It transpired that while I was off traveling and doing my usual thing, Mark had actually played his Madonna demo to various companies. Thankfully, I didn't know until years later that he'd actually played it to Chris Blackwell first and then somebody at Geffen Records, both of whom turned him down.

Never mind—youth and ambition were never known for their table manners. Mark was so desperate for a break, he was schmoozing all the labels he liked. I can't blame him; he was spreading himself wide like I did at his age. He also played his demo to one of my staffers, Michael Rosenblatt, with whom he had become friends. Nobody really heard the fireworks going off in Mark's head. They all thought he had love hearts in his eyes, and it's true that he *was* romantically involved with Madonna when he was hawking her demo around town. Call me an old shellac-blooded cynic, but I don't believe Mark Kamins was capable of putting romance before music. I'm sure a lot of stunning party girls floated around his deejay booth. His compass was his ear, not his dick. He *knew* Madonna was no ordinary young lady, and look how right he was proven.

What actually happened was that one night in Danceteria, he had been approached by this dancing beauty who introduced herself. Madonna charmed the pants off him, literally, and played him a self-made demo of a song she wrote called "Everybody," which she'd made with a guy called Steve Bray. Mark then reworked and revamped the whole tune from scratch in a better studio with better musicians. He even had the sense to test his mix on the dance floor before shopping it around. The crowd seemed to respond enthusiastically, so he made copies and went hustling.

I couldn't believe that I hadn't been played this demo yet, so I arranged for my secretary to send the cassette into Lenox Hill Hospital, where I duly slotted it into my Sony Walkman. As penicillin dripped into my heart, I lay there and listened to Mark's first find. I'm sure I was going nuts in that little room, but I immediately felt an excitement. I liked the hook, I liked Madonna's voice, I liked the feel, and I liked the name *Madonna*. I *liked* it all and played it again. I never overanalyze or suck the life out of whatever I instinctively enjoy. I reached over and called up Mark. "Can I meet you and Madonna?"

He called back saying they'd drop by the hospital that evening. "What?"

"I know. I told her you were sick, but she really wants this."

Maybe it was the thought of Chris Blackwell that got me twitchy, but I just said, "Okay, see you this evening," and hit all the panic buttons. "Get me a pair of pajamas," I told my secretary. "Oh, and send me in a hairdresser as quickly as you can." I then pushed the buzzer for nurse assistance. "Someone important is coming in. I need to wash. Can you unplug this drip while I have a shower?" I'd been rushed to the hospital a few days previously and hadn't really emerged from the bomb crater I'd suddenly found myself lying in. My armpits were probably growing fungus, and all I was wearing was one of those embarrassing hospital gowns like some lobotomized weirdo in *One Flew Over the Cuckoo's Nest.*

First, Ken Kushnick called in and gave me the lowdown. Then Michael Rosenblatt arrived and gave me his take. By the time Madonna walked in with Mark Kamins that evening, I had been fully briefed and tidied up by a team of ladies. My hair was good, I no longer smelled like a French farm laborer, windows had been opened, piles of magazines and tapes had been neatly stacked. All that was missing was the pipe, the monocle, the book, and the beagle asleep at my feet. Of course, Madonna took one look at the tube stuck into my skin and squirmed. Not that she really cared about my predicament. She'd come to get a record deal before some old record guy croaked, along with his check-signing hand.

She was all dolled up in cheap punky gear, the kind of club kid who looked absurdly out of place in a cardiac ward. She wasn't even interested in hearing me explain how much I liked her demo. "The thing to do now," she said, "is sign me to a record deal." She then opened her arms and laughed. "Take me, I'm yours!" She was goofing around doing a Lolita routine because I *was* twice her age. Or maybe I really was smiling back at her like a dirty old man, because she didn't take long to cut through all the small talk and go straight for the kill. Peering into the back of my head with those Madonna eyes, she said, "And now, you give me the money."

"What?" I snapped back, which was unusual for me. As a rule, I'm always careful around artists, but Madonna had bigger balls than the four men in the room put together.

"Look, just tell me what I have to do to get a fucking record deal in this town!" she hit back, sounding deflated.

"Don't worry, you've got a deal," I assured her.

And with that exchange, we finally met each other on level ground. Madonna had a power over men, a power over *everyone* that I think she was too young to control or even realize. For obvious reasons, her magic didn't work the same way on me, which I think was a good thing for us both. I doubt she knew I was gay, and all I knew about her was the tape I'd heard. I had no idea she was stone broke and secretly hoping to leave the hospital with a check.

Lots of people have written about Madonna's natural star power, and it's absolutely true that even when she was still a complete unknown, she filled up every room and oozed a dazzling aura that even a hardened vet like me wasn't immune to. I gave her my promise and told her to go find a lawyer, but I still had to get the money and all the passport stamps from Burbank, which, under the circumstances, was not a foregone conclusion. The deal we agreed to was modest: Madonna would get an advance of $15,000 per single, for a total of three singles, with an option for an album. On top of that, there was an additional publishing deal by which she'd get a $2,500 advance for every song she wrote. It was more of a test run than a full deal, but that's all she needed, and under the circumstances, that's about all I could offer.

Knowing what we know today, that tiny agreement looks rather comical. However, all she had right then was one clubby song that you couldn't get on Top 40 radio. She wasn't a musician, she didn't have a band, all she really had was the name and sound of Mark Kamins behind her. He'd produced "Everybody" as a six-minute twelve-inch for clubs like Danceteria, so, in real terms, I was taking a small bet on Mark's first studio production for the sheer interest of seeing where it would go. To be honest, I was doing him the good turn; there was no reason to believe I was looking at a female Elvis. The fact Madonna wasn't even on the cover of her very first single tells you how much it all began as a downtown dance experiment. I would eventually see Madonna as a regular pop artist—we all would—but at that first meeting point, my job was to get both Mark Kamins and her in the net before anyone else. We'd get to the next bridge when we came to it.

The biggest joke of all was that I couldn't even get the fifteen grand out of Warner. I spoke to Mo while lying in Lenox Hill Hospital unsure if I would survive. He said absolutely not. He told me I was signing too many acts and didn't want me to sign any more for a while. I told him Madonna was special, like no one I had ever seen or heard before, with immediate appeal to international and domestic audiences. Still, he refused.

As we now know, Madonna ended up selling over three hundred million records for Warner. Over two decades, she clocked up twelve number-one hit singles and forty-eight top tens. She scored eight number-one albums, and all that's just in the States alone. Madonna is as big as it gets, up there with Bing Crosby, Frank Sinatra, Elvis, the Beatles, and Michael Jackson. So let me just repeat that detail for posterity: had Mo gotten his way, Madonna would *not* have been signed to Warner Bros. He was never very talkative about his initial resistance, so I can only presume he thought the deal was pointless twelve-inch bullshit that wasn't even worth the small change. Thankfully for all of us, the deal was saved by the blind faith of Ahmet Ertegun's brother, Nesuhi.

Nesuhi Ertegun had been one of Atlantic's old crew with Ahmet and Jerry Wexler. But in 1970, when the Warner group came together under Steve Ross, he'd been given command of Warner's international division, which handled all the labels overseas. Nesuhi was a slightly eccentric jazz connoisseur from a bygone age, and although his division had become a giant component in the Warner group, he did his best to avoid all the corporate politics. He couldn't bear Mo's maneuvers any more than most, so I figured he'd believe me and would be sympathetic to Madonna's cause. All I had to do was track him down to the South of France, where he was on vacation, and tell him the truth.

"Nesuhi, I'm so sorry to disturb you on vacation, but I've got a young artist. She's great, but Mo's trying to sink it. I hate having to ask for this, but please, I need your help. It's just a fifteen-grand deal."

I guess Nesuhi could hear the passion and despair in my voice. He didn't even ask to hear the demo; he was more interested in hearing about my health. He told me to rest up and, yes, he'd gladly pick up the tab. "Don't be nervous," he tut-tutted. "My brother tells me you're in the hospital. It's not good for your heart. I want you to forget about this, and let me handle it." You had to love the Ertegun brothers. They had true class and were both great music men.

So, I'd break out in a rash whenever I heard this nasty myth about how Madonna somehow screwed her way to the top. I could see she was the real deal. I certainly didn't know then just how big she would be, but I did believe with all my heart she would be really big. I defy anyone to screw their way to number one and stay there for well over three decades. It can't be done. But please, be my guest—have fun trying! If you only knew how twisted and perverse the office politics could get inside the Warner group, you'd understand what it meant that I had conspired with Ahmet's brother to wriggle through a deal that Mo had totally rejected.

At the time, there was a bitter cold war raging between Mo and Nesuhi as a result of so much product from all the WEA labels fighting for attention from our overseas labels. Mo wasn't at all happy with the quality of export service he was getting and kept threatening to team up with European companies like Island,

Chrysalis, Virgin, and Ariola to release WBR artists internationally. To me, Nesuhi was the most distinguished boss among us all. I didn't know the ins and outs of their ongoing wrangles, but Mo seemed awfully tough on him. All these European markets had their own tastes and regional peculiarities, there was nothing unusual about any of our records being turned down for being too American or too whatever else. It takes something truly special to sell all over the world.

Anyway, you can imagine how it looked to WBR staffers that Madonna's first contract was actually with Sire and Warner Music International, and that it had Nesuhi's signature along with my own. Initially, this arrangement suited me fine, because apart from Mo not wanting her, I felt the clubby sound that Madonna and Mark Kamins had created was tailor-made for Europe. So, far from Madonna getting any free passes, her billion-dollar career at Warner began as a gate-crashing outsider. With her little three-singles deal, she had to prove to every one of Mo's obedient managers all the way down the chain of command just how irresistibly good she was.

As for the men in her life, she did have something going with Mark Kamins when "Everybody" was made. However, both Mark and her next boyfriend, Jellybean Benitez, were just club deejays. She may have had other flings around that time, but trust me, no big shot picked her up and sprinkled her with stardust. Not Mark, not me, not Svengali, not the Wizard of Oz. She was just a very passionate young lady, *living* it, and who knows, maybe she thrived on falling in love. But hey, she was just twenty-four. It's funny how we don't cry foul when a twenty-four-year-old male rocker turns a trail of pretty women into a storyboard of high-voltage songs. Okay, now a girl was chasing her mojo through all these handsome, talented guys. Do you have any idea how much I would have loved to do that at her age?

David and Dora Steinbigle, and Linda and Seymour Stein at a celebration of David and Dora's fortieth wedding anniversary. (*Seymour Stein*)

Seymour at age thirteen, en route from New York to Detroit, with his aunt Edith Weiberg and cousins. (*Seymour Stein*)

Brett Ratner and Mandy Stein. (*Seymour Stein*)

Seymour with Antony Langdon. (*Seymour Stein*)

Married life. (*Seymour Stein*)

Linda, Mandy, Samantha,
and Seymour Stein at
Samantha's wedding.
(*Seymour Stein*)

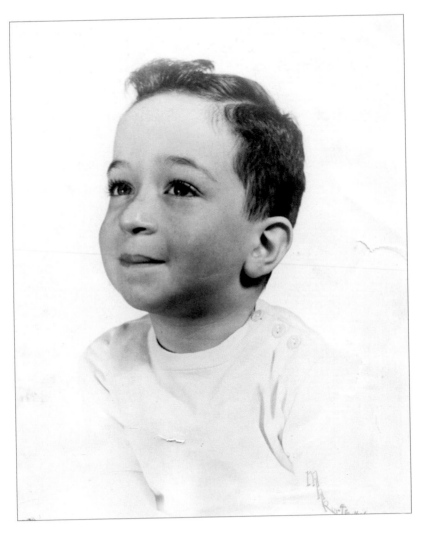

Baby picture. (*Seymour Stein*)

Seymour with Lenny Kaye. (*Bob Gruen*)

Seymour with Larry Uttal. (*Bob Gruen*)

Seymour with Joe Galkin and mentor Paul Ackerman. (*Bob Gruen*)

Seymour with Syd Nathan. (*Seymour Stein*)

Seymour with Bette Midler and Henry Edwards. (*Bob Gruen*)

Seymour with Danny Fields, Bowie, and the Ramones. (*Bob Gruen*)

Seymour with Tommy Ramone and Lenny Kaye. (*Bob Gruen*)

above: Ice-T introducing Seymour at the 14th Annual Rock and Roll Hall of Fame Induction Ceremony. (*Bob Gruen*)

right: Seymour with David Byrne and Madonna during the 14th Annual Rock and Roll Hall of Fame Induction Ceremony. (*Getty Images*)

below: Seymour with Bette Midler and Danny DeVito during the 14th Annual Rock and Roll Hall of Fame Induction Ceremony. (*Getty Images*)

MADONNA

SIRE

Photo credit: Lorraine Day

RICHIE
DEE DEE

JOEY
JOHNNY

RAMONES

Photo Credit: George DuBose

SIRE

RAMONES

RAMONES

MALCOLM FOSTER
ROB MACINTOSH

MARTIN CHAMBERS
CHRISSIE HYNDE

January 1984

PRETENDERS

SIRE

MARTIN CHAMBERS   ROB MACINTOSH   CHRISSIE HYNDE   MALCOLM FOSTER

January 1984

PRETENDERS

SIRE

PAUL WESTERBERG

SIRE   reprise

The Replacements

SIRE   reprise

LOU REED

SIRE

k.d.lang

SIRE

Barenaked Ladies

Billy Duffy   Craig Adams   Scott Garrett   Ian Astbury

THE CULT

The only guy she relied on in the early years and who never gets a mention was Martin Burgoyne, her roommate. Martin was gay and used to be a bartender in Studio 54. He knew everyone in New York and showed her around all the clubs, introduced her to Andy Warhol, whisked her through the side doors into all the right places. They were a real pair, pointing at men in the crowd, plotting, misbehaving, having fun. Martin was artistic; he danced in her first live performances and did some of her early sleeve designs. She worked out all her early songs, outfits, and moves with Martin giving her his honest feedback, but even he was just a friend, confidant, and cheerleader; he had no power over her strong personality.

Madonna outgrew Martin's talents pretty fast, as she did everyone else's. At one point, she had to discreetly ask Michael Rosenblatt to refuse Martin's sleeve design for her debut album because it just wasn't iconic enough. They would always be inseparable friends, and Martin continued following her everywhere, whether it was on her club tours or to her many record company meetings—as did some of her other friends. At Sire, we used to joke that before Madonna even had a manager, she had a court of valets and minstrels following her everywhere; that's what a natural princess she already was. Sadly, Martin was among the first to die of complications from AIDS and never got to see the full extent of Madonna's success. I'm sure that hurts her to this day. Martin died in Madonna's arms.

The thing to remember about Madonna's early days is that she was stone broke in New York City without any safety nets. Just look at her early photos; it's all dime-store junk, wristbands, hairspray, heavy makeup. She was certainly a looker, but I was not interested in her appearance, no more than I signed the Ramones because I liked their ripped jeans and All Star sneakers. The only reason so many young punks ran out and dressed up like the Ramones was because of the music, and it was the exact same for

Madonna. Her first believers were music geeks like Steve Bray, Mark Kamins, me, Michael Rosenblatt, Jellybean Benitez, and a few others. What we all heard was something in her voice.

It was more her personality that drew in disciples and over time gathered an army. Seriously, try hustling a six-minute video in 1982 with virtually no money. She got use of the Paradise Garage, rounded up some dancers, and found a camera crew who'd work for almost nothing, and by motivating and directing a large group of people, she got what she wanted. Mark Kamins produced a clubby nine-minute remix of "Everybody" for the B side and remained invested in the project, but by then, Madonna had taken full charge of the show and was looking for new material with her new beau, Jellybean Benitez. Pop songs like "Holiday" and "Lucky Star" came next, which she also managed to put together with hardly any money.

Of the Warner staffers, Madonna's earliest supporter was Bobby Shaw, who worked out of the New York office and did a great job of breaking her in the clubs. Out in Burbank, the New York–based publicist Liz Rosenberg was probably the earliest believer, but others quickly followed, such as Craig Kostich, who ran the dance promotion department, and Carl Scott in artist development. Madonna was basically a force of nature who *knew* she had a giant destiny. There was no stopping her. Each studio collaboration bore at least one great tune, every photo shoot produced at least one knockout image, every company meeting converted new believers. Everyone probably did want to fuck her, but isn't that the whole point of show business? It's not supposed to run on money. Whether we're fans, back-line handlers, session musicians, or photographers, we're all secretly dreaming of fucking the singer, right? Just like it was with Frank Sinatra or Lena Horne.

With her three-singles deal, Madonna just kept raising the stakes until a growing number of voices up and down the hierarchy started agreeing that, hell yeah, this hot chick should maybe be given a bigger break. We had the option for an album, and we didn't even have to spend that much money on its recording. All we had to do was keep going and put the singles together into a pop album with her face on the cover. Admittedly, the material she'd made thus far was a bit uneven because she kept changing all these deejay producers who relied too heavily on their sound engineers and session musicians. But it didn't matter so much, because the songs were all infectious. All Madonna needed was more runway, and sure enough, as soon as she moved on to her fourth producer, Reggie Lucas, who was the first real musician to collaborate with her, things started to take off.

I saw Madonna struggling to find a producer, but I knew not to interfere. There would have been no point trying, anyway. The way I've always viewed this game is that once you sign artists, you give them their shot. My job was to support them among the Warner brass, get them money, videos, good sleeves, proper service. If an artist asked for help, whether it was finding a manager, lawyer, producer, dentist, rehab clinic, or whatever else, I was Mr. Address Book. If the artists wanted total control over their music, then fine, but you always let them work *their way*. The only things I ever did for Madonna was stuff like inviting her out to an English Beat gig, thinking she'd connect with their grooves and songwriting. Sure enough, her eyes and ears were glued to the stage all evening, and after the show, I took her backstage to meet Dave Wakeling, Ranking Roger, and the other members of the band. I could tell she went home all fired up, realizing that dance music didn't have to be electronic and linear.

I also asked Marc Almond to put her up in London, which he very kindly did. It was her first reconnaissance mission to scope out the British market and meet up with the local Warner office, where she knew she'd soon need allies to start conquering the world. The one and only thing I *insisted* she do was get a good manager, which she knew she needed anyway. To break out of the club scene and make it as a pop star, Madonna was going to need huge marketing funds from Burbank, which meant having a major-league manager, preferably Los Angeles based. I called up Freddy DeMann, because his partner managed Michael Jackson. I knew Freddy from way back when he worked for Larry Uttal's Bell Records and even before that when he was at Jubilee. He'd shot up in the business since those days, but I asked him if he was interested in meeting our new act, Madonna. "Okay," he replied, "I'm looking forward to meeting *them*."

"Hang on, Freddy. Madonna is a solo artist. She's a *her*."

"Oh, shit, sorry! I thought Madonna was the name of a group!"

"No, expect a pretty young lady. And by the way, Madonna is her real name."

Freddy took her on quite reluctantly, and when he asked us for details and saw her modest record sales, he almost pulled out. "I'm not managing an artist who's only sold three hundred thousand," he scoffed. "I'm Michael Jackson's manager!" His cocky attitude quickly changed when the Jackson father started pushing Michael away from them. Freddy called me up all flustered, suddenly wondering if Madonna would still want *him*.

"Relax," I assured him. "She's smarter than you think. Having you guys all her to herself will actually improve both your chances of things working out." In fact, Madonna was way smarter than Freddy, and all of us in fact. God bless her for that. In later years, the best thing that happened for her as a manager was when young Guy Oseary, a schoolmate of one of Freddy's daughters, came along to assist Freddy. Guy has been Madonna's sole manager for many years and recently took on the task of managing U2 after Paul McGuinness retired.

The only thing that bothered me about Madonna's story was

Mark Kamins, who'd gotten dumped professionally, musically, and romantically. In musical terms, I understood why she'd moved on, but I still felt sorry for Mark, who'd brought her to me. I stayed out of their personal affairs, but I made sure he got looked after financially with a 1 percent override—a symbolic gesture that Warner agreed was appropriate.

Needless to say, none of us could have guessed how big Madonna would explode. She was just a debutante who, in the end, took almost a year to feel her way through that first record while I juggled plenty of other things going on in my life. Throughout late 1982 and early 1983, my father was dying. He'd had cancer for four years, but he'd always put on a brave face. He used to drop into the office to get piles of records that he'd donate to orphanages and youth centers around his neighborhood. Never once did he barge in like the boss's father and order people around. He'd always ask politely, treat everyone with respect, and, if possible, crack a joke before leaving the building. My staff loved him. "I'm sorry for keeping you waiting," my secretary once told him when I was stuck on a long phone call. "I waited forty-one years for Seymour," my father said, smiling. "Twenty minutes isn't going to kill me."

Alas, by June 1983, his cancer had spread to untreatable levels. He was hospitalized and began sliding downhill fast. When his doctor informed us the end was imminent, my sister, Ann, and her husband, Marty, were away on vacation, but Dad held on until they were at his side. I think he wanted us all to be together when he closed his eyes for the last time. He was eighty-two, exactly twice my age.

I'll always associate Dad's last months with the Pretenders' hit "Back on the Chain Gang," which hung in the charts all through early 1983. Now there's a song of pure sincerity sung straight from the heart. Chrissie Hynde wrote it about the death of her beloved guitarist, James Honeyman-Scott, who had been so instrumental in her success. "I found a picture of you"—that line always melts my heart. Isn't that how bereavement feels? Someone you love becomes an old photograph in the bottom of a drawer.

That song would be the Pretenders' biggest ever hit, peaking at number five on the Hot 100 and staying in the charts for a year—the true sign of resonance. As Madonna worked on her debut, the Pretenders' lucky run was quickly eclipsed by Talking Heads, who finally broke into the mainstream in the summer of 1983. Talking Heads had been working their asses off over the previous year to get back on track. To keep fans excited and get some dough into their pockets, we'd released a double album of old live recordings in 1982, while they played a total of seventy shows around the world. The double album's title *The Name of This Band Is Talking Heads* was a deliberate reminder to radio deejays, who kept calling them *the* Talking Heads, that that there was no definite article. It was a subtle relaunch, emphasizing the brand name and repertoire as loudly as possible.

So much touring got the band tighter and more focused than ever before. All the new sounds they'd been developing as producers, all the turmoil they'd put themselves through as a team of strong personalities, all those years of trial and error had reached a collective realization. It was time to whack the ball right out of the park. And by early 1983, as Michael Jackson's *Thriller* exploded and MTV helped pull the record business out of a slump, the world was fast catching up with whatever arty, African-flavored pop Talking Heads had started in the late seventies. Their hour had finally come.

Self-produced over several months in different locations, *Speaking in Tongues* was the name of Talking Heads' fifth studio album, released in June 1983, just before my father died. Jam-packed with funky hooks, its opening number, "Burning Down the House," lived up to its promise and broke into *Billboard*'s top ten. For all of us who'd believed in Talking Heads since the CBGB days, it was such a triumph to witness. With the new record selling better than all their previous ones put together, the band went back out on the road and put on a show like never before.

It began with just David Byrne and a boom box. Then, like a theater production, the show kept evolving through various scenes with different lighting, props, and stage formations. David's suit even got bigger, but the best part was the sheer relentlessness of it all. After five albums, Talking Heads had so many great songs, so much substance, the show just kept punching hard from different angles. As a stage production, it was too impressive not to immortalize for movie theaters and VHS release, so they self-financed the filming of two shows with director Jonathan Demme, the plan being to retain ownership of the movie and make loads of money. They needed a third night's footage, and because the costs of movie-standard filming were so astronomical, Gary Kurfirst talked Warner into contributing some money toward what would become *Stop Making Sense*, their masterpiece film that was eventually released in movie theaters that November.

Talking Heads had become an independent touring machine, possibly the best live band in the world. I had very little to do with them on any operational level, but they were the Sire act I'd most seen since the old days. Not only did I truly love their music as a hard-core fan, Chris and Tina always made a point of inviting me to their shows anytime they knew I was nearby. You could say I became their equivalent of the two old guys in the Muppets, Statler and Waldorf, looking down from my royal box.

After all the years watching them grow, I really did have a commanding view. Obviously, David Byrne was a complete original who *became* every song, like he was in a trance. People always wondered if he was pretending to be so eccentric, if he was an art school fake, but I swear to God, the man is exactly the volcano you see.

Like so many greats in the history of rock and roll, I think he invested so much into his music, he may have suffered in personal ways. He was a solitary figure who put his life's work before his private life, but hey, who am I to judge? I'll always feel an empathy toward David Byrne. Some people are just born black sheep, and it's really not their choice. Don't expect them to turn white with age; they'll only hurt themselves trying.

The relationship between David Byrne and Tina Weymouth wasn't an easy one to fathom, and I was never sure why. Was there some old unrequited love from way back? Or was it just a classic case of a girl getting between two close buddies? I never wanted to ask or know. There's no doubt that Chris Frantz was probably the best friend David Byrne ever had, and I'm sure their brotherly connection must have got trickier when Chris and Tina got married and became a family unit. Onstage, David often turned his back on Tina and in little ways seemed to want to exclude her from the party.

It's true that fans loved Tina, especially all the producers and musicians, who were the toughest customers of all. She always looked gorgeous stepping around with that huge bass over her shoulder. There'd been a few girl bass players in the punk scene, but none capable of nailing down rhythms like Tina. Beside the sweating, rattling spectacle of David Byrne, Tina's feminine presence added both softness and danger, because she was stretching herself in a boy's world. Very often, Talking Heads looked like a string that was about to snap. Backstage, you could feel the tension David and Tina were both under, but they'd pull it off every night.

The magic glue was Chris Frantz, who loved them both and always seemed so relaxed. He sang his heart out as he played some of the tightest, funkiest drumming you'll ever hear in rock and roll. He wasn't singing into a mic; he was just singing along to himself as he played, feeling every inch of those songs, which I think helped him cut his grooves to perfection. He let *the song* find the groove, and maybe there's some undiscovered law about singing drummers. At home, he lived those rhythms with Tina, whom he loved like I've never seen a man devoted to his wife. The bond was mutual; Tina loved him back with her own lifelong devotion, even though they were different as people. Tina had grown up in a family of ten. She had five sisters and two brothers. The Weymouth clan even traveled a lot, so touring the world with a busload of musicians and roadies was second nature to Tina. David was always the main feature, but on the road, Chris was the de facto team captain who kept everyone from stabbing each other in the chest. Chris Frantz was born with a big Kentucky heart and two armfuls of love that just wrapped the whole stage tight.

Jerry Harrison and guest artists like Bernie Worrell could play different instruments and add whatever extra sound or sparkle each song needed, but there was a family spirit behind Talking Heads that, I think, David thrived on rebelling against. It was intense emotional pressure for David to feel so outnumbered by this indivisible family unit, but like a teenager, he could lock himself inside his room, work his songs in front of a mirror, and then storm out for showtime and take his place at the top of the table. Everything would be ready and waiting. The mood would be festive even when he might not be that sociable.

That sweet-and-sour sauce gave Talking Heads such a unique flavor. David's songs were loaded with nervous tension, the verses would build up like tropical thunderstorms and explode into these majestic choruses where peace would rain down over the stage. It was absolutely enthralling to witness, and I'm sure they all fell in cosmic love in those magical moments. I don't know if David Byrne ever consciously realized all this. I don't even know if Chris and Tina did either. Chris and Tina weren't trying to be nice, no more than David was trying to be eccentric. As a band, they weren't trying to be any kind of combustible substance—that's just how the whole thing naturally came together.

The human chemistry behind music is a strange science. Danny Fields always said something similar about the Ramones. For Danny, and I think just about everyone who saw the Ramones up close, the original lineup was always the most explosive. Once Tommy Ramone quit in 1978, the Ramones were never as exciting, even though Marky Ramone was a better individual drummer. Whatever special ingredient Tommy brought, the overall electricity was more heavily charged with his unorthodox whacking. I'm no musician, so I never understood or even trusted technical virtuosity. What do I know as a simple fanatic is that it's boring to watch a band in total control. It's even duller watching a great singer backed up by gun-for-hire session musicians. Pop music is not just notes and beats; the really big vibration that rattles the city walls comes from a real-deal gang walking a tightrope together. Danger is the essence of rock and roll, which is maybe why so many great bands struggled to pull it all off onstage and secretly hated each other offstage.

If you look closely, the history of rock is full of dysfunctional gangs who spent years at each other's throats. Mike Vernon, who'd already seen plenty of fighting between John Mayall and his musicians, witnessed sparks constantly flying during the recording of Focus's breakthrough album. The band's two creative forces, Jan Akkerman and Thijs van Leer, had an extraordinarily tense relationship due to their very different backgrounds and mutual incomprehensibility. Jan was a working-class boy who taught himself the guitar and couldn't read music, whereas Thijs was an upper-class Jew who'd studied classical theory. They both looked at each other's methods with a mix of admiration and disgust and constantly fought about how things should be done. There are so many other examples: Mick Jagger and Keith Richards, Lou Reed and John Cale,

Stephen Stills and Neil Young. Cream was a three-man brawl. I guess tension makes it ring.

Anyway, between Talking Heads, the Pretenders, Madonna, and a whole roster of other stuff that I haven't even got around to mentioning yet, it was an extremely intense period for Sire. Without realizing it until years later, I was probably the king of the castle—in A&R terms, at least. Alongside Talking Heads, Madonna took less than a year to ignite, amazingly fast and roughly the distance between *Speaking in Tongues* and *Stop Making Sense*. Her first record came out in the summer of 1983 and of course didn't jump off the shelves. We had to keep pumping out singles to get Top 40 radio hooked. "Holiday" got inside the top twenty in January 1984 and was technically the first hit. The big bang, however, turned out to "Borderline," the fifth single, later that spring. There really was no stopping Madonna from that point onward.

Considering the club route she'd first taken, "Borderline" was a musical departure that pointed the way into her giant future. Its writer and producer, Reggie Lucas, gave it a modern pop sound, but listen carefully—it's an old-school R&B number that could easily have been done à la Motown with a brass section. Once it started getting heavy airplay in the summer of 1984, all age groups turned their heads and started singing along. "Borderline, feels like I'm going to lose my mind!" You live for these moments when a star is born.

I don't think any artist can be ready for superstardom, but Madonna took it in her stride like she'd been built for nothing else. In fact, she never really changed; it was everyone else who started looking at her differently, me included. She was still living in a small apartment, waiting for her royalties to kick in, a strange situation most rising stars have to live with for a while. When she first met the directors of *Desperately Seeking Susan*, the movie she starred in just as things were taking off, she jumped out of the cab and begged them for the fare, because she didn't have a cent. That's pretty much how she secured the part; she really *was* the character in the script. Some found her a little pushy, but most people loved how she radiated this enormous, youthful lust for life.

It was Madonna who asked Warner if Nile Rodgers could produce the follow-up record, and a very smart choice that was.

By 1983, he'd already seen so much blockbuster success with Chic, Sister Sledge, Diana Ross, David Bowie, Duran Duran, and others, he didn't even need a manager. He just strolled into every situation with a big smile on his face and handled deals personally. When it came to haggling the finer details, Nile took his accountant along, which of course makes perfect sense. If you understand how deals work, all you need is your number cruncher looking over your shoulder to nitpick the small print and ensure everything clicks nicely into your tax affairs. I have immense respect for Nile Rodgers and not just for his hit-making genius; he conducted his business with the same simplicity and success.

Representing WBR was David Berman, Mo's main in-house lawyer, or what we call "business affairs" in the trade. I didn't mind David Berman, but I know Rod Stewart's manager, Billy Gaff, nicknamed him David Vermin. This was a bit extreme in my opinion, but hey, I never got on David's wrong side. Anyway, the contracts man unfairly nicknamed David Vermin offered Nile Rodgers a standard 3 percent royalty as producer, but Nile turned around, smooth as silk, and suggested something more exciting. "Tell you what: I'll take a 2 percent royalty up to two million copies, but after that, I want 6 percent, retroactive."

"What?" said Berman, stunned by the producer's overconfidence. "But Madonna's first record has sold three hundred thousand so far. There's no way it'll sell another 1.7 million."

"Well, I'll take that shot on the next record." Nile smiled.

"Okay," said Berman, thinking he'd just made Warner a one-point savings. In the weeks that followed, there was the mightiest shit storm over that deal. As Madonna's first album started to gain traction, I was sucked into this crisis situation that had moved to the desk of Mo's number-one protégé, Lenny Waronker. I'd always liked, respected, and trusted Lenny Waronker, because he had excellent ears and came from indie royalty. Lenny's father, Si Waronker, was one of the West Coast's greatest-ever music men—the founder of Liberty Records, which launched the careers of Eddie Cochran, Julie London, Henry Mancini, Willie Nelson, Johnny Burnette, David Seville and the Chipmunks, Gene McDaniels, Bobby Vee, Timi Yuro, Gary Lewis & the Playboys, Martin Denny, and Jackie DeShannon, to name a few. Working for the family business in the sixties, young Lenny had also studied under an A&R man and producer named Snuff Garrett, a legend in his own right, and also promotion man turned producer extraordinaire, Tommy LiPuma. Lenny's uncles, Herb Newman and Lou Bedell, had their own indie labels as well. Uncle Herb wrote some fine songs of his own like "The Wayward Wind," recorded by Gogi Grant, and "The Birds and the Bees" by Jewel Akens, both on his own Era label. Lou Bedell had Doré Records, which helped jump-start the career of Phil Spector with the release of his first production, "To Know Him Is to Love Him," as well as some of Jan & Dean's best hits, including "Baby Talk," which, by the way, was produced by two later legends— Herb Alpert and Lou Adler.

Lenny Waronker had received the finest possible music business education from his father, but somehow, he'd gravitated into the orbit of Mo Ostin, who became his career equivalent of a stepfather. I never had the guts to ask Lenny why he never took over Liberty; maybe there was too much tension between him and his father. Mo always claimed that Si was too tough on Lenny, but I believe *tough* is what any record boss father should be. No son and heir will learn how to survive in such a competitive game by being treated differently from everyone else, which was always the problem with Mo's favorite son, Michael. I'd always just assumed that Mo expected Lenny to mentor the Ostin boys, which is why Lenny was promoted into executive roles that didn't suit his A&R talents or temperament—situations exactly like this Nile Rodgers business.

When Lenny Waronker and David Berman showed me the details of the Nile Rodgers deal, I couldn't believe they'd let this happen. "Are you guys crazy?" I gasped.

"But the first album isn't going to make two million," argued Berman.

"Forget her first album. Mark Kamins and Jellybean Benitez are deejays. There was only one real producer on that record, Reggie Lucas, the guy who wrote 'Borderline,' but apart from him, everyone was a learner. With a producer like Nile Rodgers, Madonna is *definitely* going to sell two million."

"Well, then, Madonna will have to pay it," they said bluntly. This meant shortchanging Madonna so that Nile's cut would be sliced out of hers.

"You fuckers!" I exploded. This I knew would start World War III. "Do you know who Madonna's lawyer now is?"

"No, who?"

"Allen Grubman!"

The name sent a shock wave through the room. Allen Grubman was the toughest show business lawyer in New York, who'd beaten the shit out of several major companies in various contentious cases. Mo's boys hadn't yet seen "the Grubman" in Burbank, but they'd heard the stories and knew what to expect. Foolishly, they thought they could handle it.

"You must be responsible for that!" they yelled at me.

"No, I have nothing to do with it. Madonna's dating Jellybean now, and Allen Grubman represents Jellybean. That's how *that* happened."

With a telephone call, a good restaurant, and lots of bended knee, the whole simmering mess could have been settled diplomatically. It wasn't my place to do it for them, but I thought Nile would have accepted a compromise of 4 percent, which still would have been a great deal for him. Nobody, however, had the stomach to call him back and renegotiate. They all ignored it, hoping the whole headache would just go away, which of course it didn't.

When *Like a Virgin* came out in November 1984, it sold six million copies almost immediately. Mo, who hadn't been interested until then, read the numbers and hit the roof. "Nobody is going to take advantage of me!" Oh, boy, did it hurt. Because I'd signed Madonna and was technically her label boss, I had to host another pointless meeting, but with Allen Grubman limbering up in the background, I knew how much shit was going to fly.

Thankfully, I just had to shut up and watch. When Allen Grubman entered the room, it was like a wrestler stepping into the ring. Syd Nathan would have loved him. He was a heavyweight Brooklyn Jew who delivered every legal slam in filthy language and personal insults. At that stage, he wasn't quite the superlawyer he'd later become, representing not only Madonna but Bruce Springsteen, Elton John, U2, Sting, Lionel Richie, and many other superstars. He was still quite young and a bit rough around the edges.

After about thirty minutes, Grubman's machinations got so foul, so devious, so humiliating, Lenny Waronker burst out of the room, physically sick, never to return. Mo was left on his own with David Berman, but the Grubman just kept bouncing them into the ropes, knocking them off each other, which was easy because they hadn't a leg to stand on, legally, morally, or strategically.

Against such straight-talking brute force, Mo's nice-guy tactics were useless. "Allen, we're hoping to build a working relationship."

"Bullshit!" Grubman just kept bulldozing every lame deflection straight back to their weakness. "You thought you'd fuck Nile Rodgers! Had the record sold under two million and he came back whining like you are now, you'd be telling him to go fuck his mother! The artists did their jobs. *You* fucked up. So now you wanna fuck Madonna. You didn't fuck him, you fucked yourselves, and now you wanna fuck Madonna."

Grubman was an astute lawyer who could do all kinds of legalistic pirouettes if circumstances required, but this wasn't legal—this was animal. I'm sure he'd been warned about Mo's techniques by Walter Yetnikoff (chairman of CBS Records) and duly greeted every phony olive branch with a blast of his napalm flamethrower. The more fucks he could squeeze into every sentence, the better. He'd come to gross them out, to repel them into submission. He'd brought his proverbial sledgehammer to teach these tennis-playing Californians the art of disgusting table manners. Any time Mo opened his mouth, it was *bam!* The Grubman kept knocking giant holes into a linguistic sewage pipe and letting raw shit fly all over the boardroom.

When Mo could physically take no more, Grubman stood up to exit the battle scene. Everyone knew the score. From here on in, Warner was going to accept pretty much whatever Madonna wanted. She was in charge now. I almost felt sorry for my groaning, gutted colleagues rolling their eyes around in agony, but they'd brought this on themselves. Warner had to pay what it owed all parties, and from here on in, all future Madonna negotiations would be conducted like a special convening of the UN Security Council.

At the end of the day, Warner got what was coming to it. I'm not saying Nile Rodgers *deserved* so much money; 6 percent was outrageous for a producer in those days. Nile fucked them royally, but he hadn't cheated. He'd simply played his cards and won his bet. Never mind, millions of kids were buying both records, Warner was making tens of millions of dollars in profit. What was there to be depressed about? Nobody died. Great as they were, Madonna was an even bigger success than Prince and Fleetwood Mac. Eighteen months previously, Mo didn't even want me to sign her.

It's amazing how fast situations can change. That stone-broke little blonde who'd come bouncing into all our offices a year before now had the world's biggest record corporation by the walnuts. If any of the Warner staffers wanted to talk to her now, they had to leave a message with either Freddy DeMann or, God help them, the Grubman. At least David Berman and Lenny Waronker had the honesty to admit how they'd screwed up in the first place. "Seymour was the only one who ever believed in Madonna," they told Mo, which was what shut him up.

But only for a while. For someone who'd been so dismissive of Madonna until she was generating millions of dollars, Mo began to take issue with the fact I'd signed Madonna's publishing to my own company, Bleu Disque Music. The irony was, back in 1977, I'd tried to sell 50 percent of each of my publishing companies, Bleu Disque Music and Doraflo, when Mo bought into Sire. He flatly turned me down and over the subsequent years made no effort to hide his disdain for his publishing colleagues in the group. He had so little time for Ed Silvers, the boss of Warner's publishing arm, that very little publishing business ever got passed down from WBR, which was very unusual for a major group.

Finally, Mo ordered me point-blank to hand over both of my publishing companies for the token sum of $150,000, an absolute pittance considering what both catalogs included. As well as Madonna's early compositions, such as "Everybody," "Lucky Star," and others, there were songs from the Ramones, Focus, Talking Heads, and various other Sire acts. This was particularly unfair considering that Madonna and Sire in general contributed a large chunk of WBR's profits that Mo was getting bonuses on. Unfortunately, there was very little I could do. Mo held all the aces, and my greatest fear was that if I played hardball, he'd take it out on my artists. He made a few innuendos about showing me who was boss if I ever stepped too far above my station.

Fortunately for Madonna, she outwitted, outgrew, and outshone us all. I still believe to this day that she would have become a star without any of the other people mentioned above, myself included. The simple truth about Madonna was that she was more naturally powerful than any of us. She was one of a kind, and we were all replaceable cogs in the show business machinery. If there was a trail of whimpering, wounded men along her path to the top, it was only because various guys tried to hold on to her, but as they'd all learn, she didn't *need* any of them. Because, as well as everything else she possessed, she had the very gift that matters most in pop music; she was a brilliant A&R woman who could pick out a great song and sprinkle it with stardust.

I don't care what the begrudgers say, it was her intelligence. Madonna was always the smartest person in the room, even when she wasn't physically there. Whether it's Humphrey Bogart or Marilyn Monroe, sex appeal is never about the actual meat; it's all happening upstairs. When anyone looked at Madonna, they may have seen her curves and pretty face, but what swallowed up the camera was the power in her eyes. That's where all the killer lines resonated from. "Like a Virgin"? Although she didn't write that tune, she spotted it in a pile of junk and made it her own. Try singing that song without laughing or being laughed at. Only Madonna can pull it off. Against everyone's advice, including Nile Rodgers's, who thought "Material Girl" was the better tune, she made "Like a Virgin" her battering ram—album title, opening track, first single, and video. She *knew* what it would do, and she made it happen.

Whether you're Édith Piaf, Elvis, Frank Sinatra, Michael Jackson, or Madonna, it's always been the same business. Strip off all the packaging, wipe away all the bullshit, and get down on your knees with a magnifying glass. There really are only two basic ingredients: artists and repertoire. Right people, right songs.

8. THE KILLING MOON

Until I was an old man, I didn't realize something that should have been blindingly obvious at the time. I never once signed a major deal. The Julius Caesar of the Warner empire, Steve Ross, was now raking in blockbuster returns from the two million Mo had spent buying Sire. I had the A&R equivalent of a triple-A credit rating and could easily have thrown around million-dollar advances. Why didn't I?

The major company sport of poaching big names off competitor labels just didn't interest me. Even when it came to hot new bands, I thought bidding wars were pointless. Why waste a pile of money on one act when half as much money could get three up and running? Bidding wars, especially between indies, always struck me as a form of fratricide. I fought a few tussles over the years, but I lived by the rule that signing acts was a game of first comer. My job was to find great unknowns and hopefully do so before anyone else, and then help them become stars with the tools at hand. My technique for limiting risk was to spread small investments wide—hedging my bets, as British bookies call it.

As success came and kept coming, I had remained and was respected as an indie at heart and have always believed that the tricky business of talent hunting should stick to the old-school rules. You won't get very far buying stars—you have to find them yourself. That's one of the many reasons why I felt so at home and invigorated sniffing around England with all the other underdogs. In the late seventies and early eighties, the American music business got dominated by major corporations and big-money payola. It was costing in excess of a million dollars just in marketing funds to get an act happening coast to coast. This wasn't the case in England, where radio managed to remain accessible, affordable, closer to the street, and far less corrupted by money. The BBC, Britain's public broadcaster, had plenty of high-quality radio and TV shows that supported new bands and enabled independents to reach nationwide audiences. Plus, London had a special position in Europe. English hits generally spread to Holland, Belgium, France, Scandinavia, West Germany, and beyond.

In the eighties, the brand of alternative British rock that became known as "indie" bubbled up from this busy swarm of small, *independent* labels. It's one of the few musical genres that refers to the business rather than the music, but it was just another way of emphasizing the homemade, low-budget, art house character of the market. Like so many genre terms, many musicians found the tag annoying, but it did help sell records and create a communal identity between fans, bands, and their labels. In reality, "indie" was nothing new. It was just a continuation of all the new wave and post-punk of the late seventies, except with bigger hair.

For me personally, the indie chapter began when I signed Echo and the Bunnymen in 1979. They were among a handful of pioneer post-punk bands that included Joy Division, Public Image Limited, the Cure, Bauhaus, Modern English, the Teardrop Explodes, the Associates, and others. On our Korova imprint, Echo and the Bunnymen had been steadily evolving through the post-punk years.

Their second album in 1981, *Heaven Up Here*, yielded a fast-paced single, "A Promise," which we even got into the downtown club scene as a twelve-inch. Then came *Porcupines*, their difficult but artistically ambitious third album in 1982, which gave us "The Back of Love" and "The Cutter."

For four years, Echo and the Bunnymen bubbled under as a cult phenomenon, until in 1984, they produced *Ocean Rain*, a commercially accessible album and arguably their most beautiful. That's when Ian McCulloch started getting famous in Britain and continental Europe. It's also where "The Killing Moon" came from, one of McCulloch's masterpiece songs that I'm sure will be played by English buskers for a thousand rainy Saturdays to come.

The Cure were my second indie signature. They'd started out in 1979 on a Polydor sub-label set up by their manager Chris Parry, a New Zealander and former Polydor staffer. Predictably, Polydor's New York office found the Cure too weird and passed on their American rights, meaning their first records got imported into the States in small quantities through my Jem friends in New Jersey. The weird thing about the early to mideighties was how unadventurous nearly all the American majors had remained. I always think of CBS snubbing the great Leonard Cohen and actually refusing to release his *Various Positions* album, even though it included classics like "Hallelujah" and "Dance Me to the End of Love." Leonard Cohen's lawyer was left with no alternatives but to call up my old buddy Marty Scott and have Jem independently distribute *Various Positions* around the States as a European import. Believe it or not, an edition eventually came out on Passport, our joint venture indie label that I'd had to cash out of when Warner bought into Sire.

The big guy's blunder is usually the little guy's opportunity. Another example was the Cure, who Polydor's New York office refused. I watched them like a hawk and found them very tempting, but I only committed to an American deal in 1982 for their fourth album, *Pornography*, while also negotiating a deal on their back catalog, which Sire subsequently rereleased. We then put out subsequent Cure albums like *The Walk* in 1983 and *The Top* in 1984. There would be bigger things to come from both the Cure and Echo and the Bunnymen, but in 1984, the field was opened up by the biggest indie group of them all, the Smiths.

In that crazy summer of 1983 when my father died and Sire exploded on all sides, I received a call from Geoff Travis, the founder of the Rough Trade store, who by then was running his own record label of the same name. "Seymour, I've just seen this great new band," he announced. "They're called the Smiths, and I think you'll really like them."

"When can I see them?"

"Well, they're playing down here in London in two days, but I know that's short notice."

"Two days? Are you kidding me? Compared to when I signed Depeche Mode, that's plenty of time!"

Geoff Travis was, and still is, an English connoisseur whose taste and knowledge you could trust with your eyes closed. He also grew up in a Jewish family, not that we ever talked about it; I knew music was Geoff's only religion. Behind the counter of Rough Trade, he'd worked at the heart of the whole punk scene, not just selling large quantities of vinyl for such a tiny store but also setting up a distribution network of like-minded indie stores all over Britain. They called their network the Cartel and distributed bands such as the Undertones, Joy Division, the Specials, Cabaret Voltaire, Scritti Politti, the Raincoats, Depeche Mode, Modern English, and hundreds more. Behind all these alternative groups was a new generation of labels such as 2 Tone, Mute, 4AD, Creation, Cooking Vinyl, and of course Factory, whose inspirational founder, Tony Wilson, I always had immense respect for.

Britain's indie community was regionally diverse, but Rough

Trade in London was unquestionably the heart of this nationwide organism that was even starting to spread into continental Europe. Business grew so quickly that by 1980, Rough Trade's distribution wing had to move into a large warehouse, complete with a record label of its own. Geoff Travis's long career had only just begun, and there would be plenty more names to add to his early list of exploits, but even in 1983, there wasn't a man in England who knew more about alternative rock. If Geoff Travis was calling New York about a new band, you'd better sit up straight and grab a pen.

I jumped on a British Airways the following day, and just as Geoff had promised, I instantly loved the Smiths. They were from Manchester and were about as northern as you could get, but again, the songs were so well written, I was confident an American audience would gather round. For a twenty-year-old, Johnny Marr was an incredible guitarist—the kid wrote riffs in his sleep. Coincidentally, one of his biggest influences was the clean sound of James Honeyman-Scott, the Pretenders' just-departed guitarist.

As for the Smiths' larger-than-life singer, Morrissey, he was like a character off a Shakespearean stage—witty, profound, theatrical, yet looking squarely at reality. He was a true original whose lyrics were so well written, an English teacher, a vicar, and a psychotherapist could have spent all night fighting over the meanings. The drummer and bass player at the back, Mike Joyce and Andy Rourke, fit in perfectly, but it was clearly the songwriters, Morrissey and Marr, who were the magical force. In fact, that's what I said when I shook hands on a North American deal with Geoff Travis after the gig. "The whole band were great, but Morrissey and Johnny Marr would stand out anywhere."

In early 1984, Sire released their self-titled first album, *The Smiths*, which did well for an underground debut. I was most moved by "Reel Around the Fountain" with its opening line, "It's time the tale were told of how you took a child and made him old." That debut album was followed by *Meat Is Murder* in 1985. Its eight tracks featured a guitarist's masterpiece, "How Soon Is Now?" which we pushed as a stand-alone twelve-inch. I called it "the 'Stairway to Heaven' of the Eighties," because for a while, it was all you heard in indie record stores. A "guitarchestra" was how Johnny Marr described this method of layering up to ten guitar parts into a type of sonic painting. The Smiths had plenty of melodic pop songs like "Hand in Glove, "What Difference Does It Make?" and "William, It Was Really Nothing," but thanks to "How Soon Is Now?" the Smiths had a heavyweight classic, which won the unanimous respect of American alternative rock fans.

For their third album, *The Queen Is Dead*, which they began making in the summer of 1985, Morrissey and Marr wrote an absolute beauty that's probably Morrissey's most popular anthem, "There Is a Light That Never Goes Out." His lyrics were so effortless, so hard hitting, they had to have been *lived*. Any time it comes on the radio, my heart sinks for whatever inner torment Morrissey was going through at the height of the Smiths' adventure. It reminds me so much of situations I'd been in myself, secretly in love with a straight friend you knew you'd never have.

Brilliant as they were, the Smiths unfortunately weren't made to last. Geoff Travis always says it's because they never had a manager to guide them through the choppy seas of success. They did try but kept firing the unlucky candidates, always expecting Johnny Marr to resume his old duties as the band's temporary problem solver. Marr now admits that his coke and alcohol consumption at the time were partly to blame for the unmanageable chaos the Smiths were becoming, which included the bass player's worsening heroin habit. I don't doubt any of this for a second. However, from hanging out backstage and reading their body language, I've always wondered if maybe Morrissey harbored a deep unrequited love for Johnny Marr, which I suspect Johnny Marr felt and couldn't handle. That was always my gut feeling, and I wasn't surprised when, years later, Morrissey confessed he was living with a man. It's none of my business, of course, but I'd add Morrissey and Marr to the very long list of mysterious love-hate relationships that created some of the best songs ever written.

The Smiths suffered a tragically young death, but they'd at least left behind five classic albums. Without any singles on the *Billboard* Hot 100, we ended up selling about half a million copies of every Smiths album in North America, which wasn't exactly the big time in that period of booming sales, but it's nonetheless a measure of how wide their cult status grew. American fans adopted the Smiths solely by word of mouth without any payola or marketing trickery. In fact, they only played a sum total of thirty shows in the United States, basically one small tour in June 1985 and twenty dates in August 1986.

That glorious stretch between 1985 and 1986 was really the midsummer moment when this "indie" fashion broke out of the British underground and infected America with a new bug. In November 1985, Echo and the Bunnymen released their biggest hit single, "Bring On the Dancing Horses," which became their MTV anthem. Their cause was helped by my old partner in the Korova label, Rob Dickins, who was handed a life-changing promotion to run Warner's UK record company. With power and budgets at his disposal, Rob invested in the classy video for "Bring On the Dancing Horses" that gave Echo and the Bunnymen the look of a major-league band.

We released a longer twelve-inch version for American clubs and put the track on a compilation album called *Songs to Learn & Sing*, which we intentionally didn't present as a greatest hits because all these superbly written songs from the early eighties *hadn't* been hits. Hooked by the video, hundreds of thousands of new listeners were duly introduced to ten other Echo and the

Bunnymen underground classics, enabling fans to delve deeper into the actual albums. It sold about three hundred thousand copies in North America—healthy numbers, and it's why Echo and the Bunnymen are still regarded as a big-haired, mideighties "indie" band, even though they'd really been short-haired art rockers from the late seventies.

Talking of big hair, the Cure took the longest, most meandering route to the top. It pains me to confess, however, that through no fault of their own, they're among my personal disappointments and for all the wrong reasons. Inside the American record industry, the term *indie* meant something else entirely. Among those familiar with the corrupt ways of American Top 40 radio, "indies" were shorthand for independent promotion men, basically the payola brokers who controlled the airwaves. As you can imagine, their controversial existence created a lot of fights between band managers and major company executives who were the only ones able to pay the exorbitant fees.

A case in point was the Cure's manager, Chris Parry, a tough character who believed brute force would get his band these all-important "promotional" funds. His behavior didn't bother me, but Lenny Waronker was a gentle Californian who just couldn't stomach the abuse Parry kept heaping on him. It got so embarrassing, I felt obliged to cut the Cure loose, a terrible mistake I soon regretted. Sire had given the Cure their first big push, so Parry didn't waste any time moving his artists to another label in the Warner group, Elektra, whose even-tougher boss, Bob Krasnow, had no issues with either bad manners or indie promotion. A seasoned pro like Krasnow, who'd actually got his first break working for King's San Francisco branch, had little trouble breaking the Cure at the ripe moment, causing me further embarrassment.

I still regret that mistake, because as the mideighties progressed toward the nineties, I could see Mo stirring cauldrons in the background. Sire had become so successful, I kept getting the distinct sensation that whenever possible, my signatures were getting moved around the group to ensure WBR remained the jewel in the Warner crown. Sire was never going to outgrow its parent company. Mo's concern seemed to be more about his son Michael, by then WBR's main A&R man. Under no circumstances could the chosen heir be made to look like a lightweight beside me or anyone else at Warner.

Michael Ostin definitely wasn't stupid. His curse was that he didn't have to work as hard as everyone else. The smartest artists, producers, and managers all befriended Michael, knowing he was the inside lane to special treatment. Madonna wound up on Michael's desk, as did other big names he never signed himself. In fairness, he had supported Madonna's cause relatively early on, but you get the picture—he was the boss's son. The other problem I encountered in the mideighties was that some of these English artists suffered from what I can only describe as a *cultural allergy* to playing the game by American rules. Especially the North of England groups. I hate to say it, but all those Irish and working-class attitudes that were so strong in places like Liverpool and Manchester may have infused the souls of the musicians with some magic ingredient. Unfortunately, when it came to the dirty work of saying cheese for the camera, some of these northerners just didn't want to sell themselves.

Ian McCulloch, Morrissey, and Johnny Marr were natural-born stars who I think had always dreamed of fame. Like their bandmates, however, there was something about America they just couldn't warm to. They were happy to fly into New York or San Francisco and play prestigious venues to hip crowds, but when it came to touring cities that played ice hockey or doing interviews with provincial deejays who'd introduce them as "punk rock" from "Manchester, England," these proud northerners recoiled in horror.

Without even realizing it, they hated the very traits about Middle America that Londoners hate about the North of England—the parochialism, the funny accents, the awkward gushing small-town hosts always shower on visitors.

I know that Los Angeles label A&M experienced similar problems with Human League, who were from Sheffield, which is about as far north as you get before England becomes Scotland. After Human League's single "Don't You Want Me" blew up on American radio, A&M's publicists spent weeks hustling for a precious slot on a nationwide TV show. When they got it, the Human League singer, Philip Oakey, turned around and declined. He just couldn't do American showbiz and all the smiling, dancing, glitzy self-promotion that goes with it. He felt he was whoring himself. It's what we love about the English, their sincerity, their extreme artistic principles, but my God, if you're in the business of gambling hundreds of grand to get songs on Top 40 radio in the hope that people will buy records, you just want to slap these artistes in the face with a wet fish.

There were no such hang-ups inside the ranks of Depeche Mode. They came from London's outer suburbs and accepted from day one that to break America, you had to play the game by local rules. Both the band and their producer, Daniel Miller, cultivated friendly relationships with the marketing staffers in Burbank and made a conscious effort to be liked and trusted as reliable, can-do partners. Funnily enough, Depeche Mode's cause was helped by me dropping the Cure. As a sort of thank-you gesture for supporting him, Lenny Waronker announced to his staff, "We're dropping the Cure. Instead of spending money on two Sire groups, we're gonna give a bigger push to Depeche Mode, who I think are better anyway."

In August 1985, Depeche Mode scored their first American hit on the *Billboard* Hot 100, "People Are People," which peaked at number thirteen. But even that wasn't enough to launch them nationally. As the old expression goes, success does not have an elevator; you have to take the stairs. They kept writing, kept pushing their sound into new territory, kept adding American cities to every tour, kept playing every show like it was their last. No matter where they played or what they had to do to promote their shows, they worked their leather trousers off until their breakthrough American album in 1987, *Music for the Masses*. That's when they began filling arenas in forty cities around North America. But to get there, they needed millions of dollars in marketing, promotion, and tour support, which they never would have been given without first proving how much they *wanted it*.

But of all the English indie groups on Sire, the most pro-American had to be the Cult. Their singer, Ian Astbury, didn't just have stars in his eyes, he had red-and-white stripes as well. Long before he was famous, he'd lived in Canada and then returned to England, where he formed the band dressed up as a Native American. Originally called the Southern Death Cult, they'd been evolving through the early eighties as underground goth rockers until, in the summer of 1985, they released their classic anthem "She Sells Sanctuary," which launched them in England.

They were signed to a UK indie named Beggars Banquet, with whom I already had a relationship though its sister label, 4AD. Even still, to secure the Cult's North American rights, they were a rare instance when I had to fend off intense competition from Chrysalis and others, which I made an exception of doing, because I knew the unbeatable mix of Sire and WBR was perfect for their sound and image. We released "She Sells Sanctuary" as both a seven- and twelve-inch, but brilliant though it was, the sound was a little too spooky to get into Top 40 radio. The accompanying album, *Love*, was the commercial success that sold about 250,000 copies in the States, highly promising for a left-field debut.

Once the Cult got that first taste of American success, they basically moved over. Their following album, *Electric*, was produced by Rick Rubin, who gave them a drier, sharper, more immediate sound. It was such a musical departure, new fans could have been forgiven for never guessing the Cult were actually English. Their true statement of intention, however, was when they ditched their existing English manager for an American heavyweight named Howard Kaufman, a partner of Eagles supermanager Irving Azoff. For a British indie band, this meant business.

Martin Mills, the owner of Beggars Banquet, was so worried about how much the Cult were shifting their focus away from Britain, he flew to Los Angeles to gently win assurances from the band's new manager. "Will you continue touring Europe as before?" asked Martin as diplomatically as possible.

There was a big map of America on the office wall, so Kaufman looked up and smiled. "Oh, yeah, Europe. It's somewhere over to the right of that map, isn't it?"

In the end, everything worked out fine for everyone. With extra muscle from Howard Kaufman and Canadian producer Bob Rock, the Cult's next album, *Sonic Temple*, provided the sledgehammer effect they needed to sell over a million copies in North America alone, launching the Cult as a major global act. Depeche Mode and the Cult became Sire's biggest indie bands, and it's mostly down to big touring, big investment, and playing by local rules, much like U2 did in the same period.

I signed lots of other indie bands through the eighties like Modern English, Aztec Camera, the The, B-Movie, Everything but the Girl, James, My Bloody Valentine, Ride, and others. I signed both Depeche Mode offshoots, the first being Yazoo, who we had to rename Yaz for American editions. Yaz was the brainchild of Vince Clarke, one of Depeche Mode's founders, who then teamed up with Alison Moyet in 1982 to make dance floor hits like "Don't Go" and

"Situation." Stylistically, Yaz were obviously more electronic than "indie," but they came from Daniel Miller's Mute label, which was an independent using Rough Trade's distribution. A few years later, Vince Clarke teamed up with a new singer, Andy Bell, to form Erasure. They gave Sire two top-twenty U.S. hits, "Chains of Love" and "A Little Respect" off their 1988 hit album, *The Innocents*.

It wasn't a conscious strategy to sign so much British music. As in the seventies, I supported what I liked, and a lot of interesting newcomers just happened to be English. For the same reasons, I signed plenty of international bands that I picked up on my travels, many of which I found through my French connections. In the eighties, I'd fallen in love with Paris and bought an apartment on Avenue Carnot, one of the quieter streets that radiate out from the Arc de Triomphe. Hunting for art deco treasure in the flea market was my idea of a perfect weekend, and boy did I fill that beautiful little nineteenth-century Parisian flat so full of vases, paintings, and furniture, it was sometimes hard to move around. Yes, while scoring all these hits, I was a maniac for collecting. After a typical hundred-hour week in New York, I was jumping on planes and sometimes getting up at 5:00 A.M. in Paris to get to the flea market before the crowds arrived.

The living in Paris was easy. I was just a stone's throw from my favorite Moroccan restaurant, Le Marrakech, and Paris being Paris, there was a large choice of outstanding restaurants in all directions. My favorite haunts were a Vietnamese restaurant named Tong Yen and an Italian restaurant named Le Stresa. There were countless French bistros, but my favorites were Chez L'Ami Louis and Le Taillevent, both local. In all these cozy little eateries, I hung out with friends and lovers, and sometimes we'd head out afterward to the hippest club in town, Les Bains Douches, which was just off the Champs-Elysées and also a pleasant stroll from home.

Once you knew your way around and had enough bullshit French to not get ripped off by taxi drivers, Paris was all yours.

There, I discovered and signed various local delights like "Marcia Baila" by Les Rita Mitsouko, a sizzling French pop classic. While at Midem, I heard and proudly signed a mixed racial South African group, Juluka, led by Johnny Clegg, whose international hit, "Scatterlings of Africa," was a landmark anthem containing some words in Zulu, quite a big deal during apartheid, and it reached number one in France and stayed there for three weeks. The eighties for me were a golden age of world pop, and I also discovered and signed Ofra Haza, the Israeli pop diva of Yemenite origin, who became known as the Madonna of the Middle East.

I think it's fair to say the eighties were when my lifestyle became gay. I can't say that I ever really came out. I didn't see the need. Not only did I have two daughters who were still too young to understand, there was something about all that badge-wearing, flag-waving gay-parade ideology that I never identified with. Physically, I was never turned on by the raving queens who were so unbelievably gay, they were almost women. I was attracted to *real* men, the tall, handsome, intelligent hunks that women melted for, too. I had a lot of gay friends, of course, some of whom almost *were* women, but I had no interest in coming out only to close myself off into some frock-wearing ghetto. I was happy living in the real world, if the music business qualifies as that. And yes, my proudest, happiest exploits were with straight men who couldn't resist my charms. It was not simply the physical attraction; it was intellectual also. I loved the company of smart men who had something to say and were living interesting lives.

My mother died in 1986, just three years after my father. As was her way, she put on a happy face throughout her final years, even though she was truly lost without him. It was as if she wanted to lie down beside her husband and close her eyes. In their own private way, they were very much in love, and I still believe they got their happy ending after a long life of work and sacrifice. They say that when your parents die is when you truly become an adult. In my case, however, I think I just let go and indulged the irresponsible boy I'd always wanted to remain. No more kidding myself now. I was a balding, graying, fortysomething man-child who never wanted to grow up. It certainly hadn't been easy as a sexually con-fused teenager in the 1950s, but I can't complain, because unlike so many people I met throughout life, I'd come from a loving family. My folks didn't fuck me up; I got to do that all by myself.

I doubt my folks ever guessed I was gay, which tells you how innocent they were. They were born at the turn of the century and remained old-fashioned throughout their long lives. I kept my sexuality to myself as a matter of respect to them, and to this day, I don't regret that I did. I never saw privacy as cowardice or dishon-esty; I told the truth to anyone who was interested. The reality was, straight people were always more uncomfortable about homo-sexuality than even the most tortured closet queens. I always under-stood and respected that fact of life. Call me old-fashioned, but I don't think we become more enlightened by kissing on subways or by talking the life out of our quirks and kinks. Privacy is a greatly underestimated necessity for living together. Sometimes the best way of winning people's respect is to shut up and keep your bed-room door closed.

Despite all the progress made in the seventies, once AIDS hit, the world suddenly felt a lot less gay-friendly. When my parents died, it was like a whole decade of funerals was winding the clocks backward. It first began mysteriously with reports on TV, and then it started getting closer until you didn't stop hearing friends bawling their eyes out over the phone. There were rumors and an-nouncements every day, funerals every week. Testing positive for

HIV was as good as a death sentence, because in those first ten years, nobody got out alive. When it comes to AIDS, there are only two types of people, and it's not a matter of gay or straight. I know straight people whose eyes well up at the mention of the word. Count your blessings if you only ever saw it as a news story, somewhere far away on a TV screen. Those of us who watched a friend or a brother die in agonizing pain will never forget the horror.

The AIDS epidemic was an apocalypse. In their thousands, people were wasting away and disappearing right in the middle of New York City. They even looked the same: skeletal faces in oversized clothes, ghostlike figures, hidden away, ignored, ostracized, sneered at. It's the mental image of an entire corner of a city, vacated, disappeared, nothing left but old photographs. The sadness of seeing so many young men dying was hard enough to swallow. What made it even worse was that polite society didn't give a damn. In fact, for a lot of people, we were the new lepers who *deserved* this.

HIV had actually been identified in Lenox Hill Hospital while I was there getting my heart fixed. Throughout the decade, I was in and out of hospital like a yo-yo and was basically kept alive by my doctor, Alan Pollock. With all my heart problems and bouts of septicemia, I had to get tested for HIV of course, which was an experience so terrifying, I can understand those who didn't and just waited to get sick. Like every gay guy who'd partied through the late seventies and early eighties, I was convinced I'd be next, but somehow I wasn't. Without drawing you any diagrams, there were certain sexual practices I didn't like, and I can only presume that's how I avoided infection. I was very lucky. I can think of people who weren't promiscuous at all and yet they died. There really was no moral justice to who got infected and who didn't.

Whenever I think of all those faces, I'll always see David Geffen stepping up. That guy has taken so much fire over the years for apparently being the record industry's greatest ever prick. He quietly gave money to people, some he barely knew, so they could die with dignity. Not even close friends—some were faces he'd seen around from the disco days, friends of friends. Death because of AIDS complications was slow and ugly. Victims were too weak to work, many were rejected by their families, and they had no savings or safety nets. Many were dying stone broke, unable to pay hospital bills, facing eviction. I'm sure thousands died on the street or on people's sofas. David couldn't help all of them, but he helped many slip away peacefully without any financial humiliation hanging over their deathbeds.

For this alone, I will not tolerate a bad word about David Geffen. If ever he was rude in business, it was only because he was ten moves ahead of everyone else. It was torture for such a fast mind to sit there listening to everyone dragging out what he'd understood in the first five seconds. He was constantly being held back and sometimes his patience would snap. He's the classic example of the star student who comes first every time, but as a result, can never win in playground situations because of course everyone's so jealous. It's lonely at the top, but make no mistake, the rest of us are better off being barked at by the best. The alternative is mob rule.

I was spared from AIDS, but there would be other tragedies along my journey. Any time a bomb fell through my ceiling, Geffen was always the first person to pick up a phone and help me out of the wreckage. He'd listen and handle all the shit you can't handle when you're depressed or in shock. He'd keep calling back until you were on your feet. To this day, I love and admire him, and I know he did the same for others, always offering concrete help and never once seeking gratitude or public attention as a showbiz nice guy. The man has soul.

Linda was a big fan of David Geffen, although I'm not so sure if her admiration was as reciprocal. He knew she had a heart of gold, but her lack of tact was often toe curling. Once, on the French Riviera, David, Linda, Elton John, and John Reid were in a restaurant when David noticed a handsome waiter looking back at him. Elton and John bailed out early, but David asked Linda to hang around until the waiter finished his shift. Linda never needed much persuasion to keep the night young, so when the place was empty, David asked her to check out if the guy wanted to go out partying. Typical Linda, she arrived back with her arm around the bemused waiter and screamed, "David, he's straight!" then laughed out the door, dragging the guy to who knows what.

There's no doubt that Linda became a lot happier as she found a career and tasted her own success. We had our regular feuds over money and me not seeing enough of the girls, but on the whole, we started getting along better. We'd never be normal friends, but we did become abnormally friendly considering what we'd been through. As well as the Ramones, she'd managed Steve Forbert for a while, but in the mideighties, she wound up in real estate simply because she knew so many rich people who talked endlessly about their Central Park penthouses and beach villas in the Hamptons.

Despite what real estate agents like to pretend, it's not an easy life. The killings are big, but even the best go through barren patches when they sell nothing for months, sometimes a year. Linda was determined and quickly earned her reputation as the real estate broker to the stars. Over the years, her clients included Harrison Ford, Sting, Madonna, Sylvester Stallone, Elton John, Billy Joel, Christie Brinkley, La Toya Jackson, Steven Spielberg, Liam Neeson, Andrew Lloyd Webber, Michael Douglas, and many others. In fact, Sylvia Miles, the actress who played the real estate broker in Oliver Stone's *Wall Street*, took Linda out to lunch to study her accent and mannerisms. Linda had become the caricature.

I was becoming one myself. Because everyone knew how much I loved music business history, I was asked to be a founding member of the Rock and Roll Hall of Fame, alongside Ahmet Ertegun, lawyers Allen Grubman and Suzan Evans, and *Rolling Stone* co-founder Jann Wenner. There was already a Country Music Hall of Fame in Nashville, and a Songwriters Hall of Fame, so it seemed natural to some of us who'd reached the upper slopes of the rock industry that we should build some kind of mausoleum for our own community. Cleveland of course ended up being the site. Yes, Memphis could have fit the ticket, and New York would have gotten the tourists, but the city of Cleveland was the only credible candidate to engage aggressively and put up the millions of dollars needed to build it. They *wanted* it more than anyone else, and in the end, that always makes the difference. Cleveland was where Alan "Moondog" Freed first aired his seminal radio shows and where the term *rock and roll* was arguably popularized.

Although I was only forty-three, I always considered the launch of the Rock and Roll Hall of Fame as a rite of passage. This was the beginning of the rest of my life as a sort of music business elder. I'd never been to college, so it was a particular honor for me to contribute to these formal meetings. We all had to do our own private research, prepare notes, debate inductees, and basically map out the story of popular music, both behind the scenes as well as musically. That genealogy is largely taken for granted today, but in the mid-deighties, it was far from clear who were the branches and who were the leaves.

Ever since I was a kid, I'd always felt that black music was the big event of the century. My first records were mostly R&B, the first label I worked for was King, the first record Sire produced was an R&B singer, Mattie Moultrie, and when I invested in Blue Horizon, one of the first projects I supervised was recording the Memphis Country Blues Festival in 1968. Even with all the white bands I'd signed in the late sixties and seventies, from the British bluesmen to Talking Heads, there was always a connection to black music. So, when hip-hop arrived, I felt like I'd missed an important train. It was the one new genre that completely eluded me, and I have to say, for a few years in the mideighties, that failure really bothered me.

I began looking laterally at the first wave of hip-hop, and the one detail that struck me as strange was how all the pioneers had come from east of the Mississippi. *Can there really be no rap in Los Angeles, San Francisco, and Seattle?* I wondered. The answer, as so often, came from an unexpected source. In 1986, I got a call from a character named Ralph Cooper, the son of a tap dancer, actor, and band leader of the same name. Many years previously, I had become friendly with the father, even though there were two generations between us. He'd lived a full and fascinating life, he'd performed at the Apollo in the swing years, he'd been in Hollywood movies, where he'd been nicknamed "the Dark Gable" because he was black and so handsome. Anyway, his equally handsome son was the last person I expected a hot tip from, but A&R is as random as pigeon shit. Ralph junior told me to urgently check out an artist named Ice-T. Once I heard the words *rap* and *Los Angeles*, I dropped everything and investigated.

I hate to use the term *blown away* so often, but it's the only way to describe the shock and awe of a direct musical hit that really does feel like a ten-ton bomb going off between your ears. I didn't know anything about hip-hop, but I immediately connected with Ice-T's lyrics and realized as I kept listening what I'd been prejudiced about. On a subconscious level, I'd considered rap a threat to R&B in the way that I believed that authentic country music from the thirties to the sixties was cheapened by all the "countrypolitan" dreck that followed. The intelligence of Ice-T's word games, however, made me look at the genre as something in and of itself. Rap had nothing to do with R&B; it was black poetry.

When I finally met Ice-T and his young Bolivian manager,

Jorge Hinojosa, I couldn't believe he hadn't been signed by anyone. In that meeting, I was asked a very simple question, which I don't think was meant as any kind of personality test. "What is it about me that you like?" asked Ice-T, which is a great way of putting a record exec on the spot.

"I think you tell great stories," I replied tentatively, "but you know what? At the risk of losing you, there's something about you that makes me think of calypso." Ice-T looked back at me a little confused, like he'd only heard the reference but no actual calypso records. "Can I play you something?" I asked him.

I had to rummage around my legendarily messy office, which was always jam-packed with records, magazines, and antiques. This probably wasn't the meeting Ice-T's razor-sharp manager was expecting, but they sat there watching me. The first calypso record I played him was the 1956 hit "Jean and Dinah" by Mighty Sparrow, a song about the troubled prostitution market after Trinidadian independence. With its great lines about "the yankee's gone, sparrow take over now," it's a humorous yet poignant portrait of a particular time and a place. The next record was Lord Kitchener's 1978 hit, "Sugar Bum Bum," which can only be described as a tribute to the "fat behind" of a lady called Audrey. As all this sexually charged West Indian music poured into the room, Ice-T sat there smiling beside his manager. Calypso was weird prehistory for a young rapper, but he suddenly grabbed me. "I want to sign with you!"

It was an unorthodox way of recruiting Sire's first great rapper, but he'd asked me an honest question, and I gave him an honest answer. Ice-T knew I wasn't pretending to be an expert on his scene, but he at least saw that I understood the irony in his lyrics—which not everyone did. There was a tendency in rap's early days for white onlookers to take rap more literally than the artists meant it themselves. I'm also sure Ice-T thought I was half-nuts, but the fact I came from Brooklyn, I think, added to the growing affinity between us. We both came from humble beginnings, and yes, that usually does create a certain trust. Needless to say, Ice-T went on to sell many millions of records.

Warner's sales sheets were now full of Sire monsters. Symbolically, moving into 75 Rockefeller Plaza in 1988 marked Sire's ascension into big business. Our new office was on the twentieth floor and had such a commanding view of the plaza, even I started looking forward to Christmas. As every New Yorker knows, Rockefeller Plaza is the site of a giant Christmas tree that every tourist and Midtown family flocks to see as a sort of annual winter pilgrimage. Every year, when the lights flicked on for the first time, whoops of joy would ripple around the office, and we'd all rush to the windows. We were looking down on the very epicenter of Christmas, knowing that Santa Claus would deliver millions of our records to kids all over the world. Call me sentimental, but there's no business like show business.

And the smash hits just kept coming. That year, my big Canadian star was k.d. lang. Before making any records, she'd started out as a Patsy Cline tribute singer and gradually began writing songs of her own. On first listen, I was hooked by her incredible voice and signed her up to a long and successful relationship. One of the artist development managers out in Burbank, Carl Scott, was a huge fan and deserves due credit for supporting k.d.'s cause. People say she was the world's first lesbian pop star, but of course, there were others long before k.d. who had no choice but to keep their sexuality private. I'm proud to have helped such a beautiful voice reach such a large audience, albeit for reasons entirely musical. I honestly wasn't attracted to gay artists; I just didn't let their sexuality get in the way of my ears. I hear what people have inside. I never judge musicians on anything but their music.

The icing on the cake was a surprise at the end of the decade. Nearly every one of the British indie musicians I'd ever signed, including a few American bands like the Replacements, had grown up listening to the songs of Lou Reed. For a guy who'd struggled so much in his early years in the commercially unsuccessful Velvet Underground, Lou Reed had grown into the prophet of the indie generation. Thanks partly to Sire's success with all these alternative rock bands in a period that was otherwise synonymous with cheesy pop, I got a phone call sometime in 1988 from Lou Reed explaining that he was sick of RCA, who were also sick of him. He'd been floundering through the eighties and was in urgent need of a new label, new collaborators, a new plan. And that's how Lou Reed's so-called New York trilogy knocked on my door.

As a rule, I never signed established stars, but Lou Reed was the one guy you'd make an exception for, especially considering he was the one asking. I'd met him socially many times since the seventies through Danny Fields, so when he walked in sporting a curly mullet, we just got straight down to business. People always talk about Lou Reed's grumpy character, but I always found him cordial. He didn't want anyone's fawning, but if you talked to him normally and let him be, he was friendly enough. I suspect that, like Bob Dylan's, Lou's bad reputation was both provoked and diagnosed by bug-eyed journalists who'd drive him crazy with pseudointellectual questions until he'd snap. He was just a quiet, brooding type who liked to observe. As with his song lyrics, there was nothing he appreciated more than simplicity and straight talk. The thing we both absolutely loved was old-school Brill Building pop. Get him onto old fifties classics, and he was in his element.

He was born in Brooklyn just a month before I was, so I'd always regarded him as a peer. He was our local hero, but I never let my admiration get the better of me. Unfortunately, the people at WBR didn't like him, but that's because they didn't understand where he was coming from. I suspect it was mutual. At the time, Lou's second wife, Sylvia, was technically his manager, although I didn't get the impression she was in charge of much except chores. I never really understood her role in his business. All I know is that Lou was allergic to corporate bullshit. He didn't want to deal with any junior staffers or Warner go-betweens; he insisted on coming to me for everything. I didn't mind—I was actually quite flattered—but his presence did make me nervous. If he was dropping by in the afternoon, my mornings always felt a little intense.

On one occasion, he called in with some demos, but we couldn't get the stereo working. After what felt like an eternity of fumbling around, my executive assistant, Risa Morley, came to the rescue, but Lou asked her to leave the room when she got his tape playing. He was a touch paranoid, but the only opinion Lou ever wanted was mine, which again was flattering but somewhat pointless. I was never going to tell Lou Reed to add a piano or change a syllable. It was his privilege to make songs whatever way he wanted and mine to ensure everything got paid for, pressed, and publicized.

Did I worry that he had a reputation for drug use? Nah, he obviously had a way of functioning and working anyway. All I cared about were the end results, which was an album called *New York*, hailed by critics as a return to form. Next came his collaboration with John Cale, *Songs for Drella*, their tribute to the departed Andy Warhol. That record got even bigger plaudits. Then *Magic and Loss*, another concept album about friends dying. I never expected Lou Reed to make another "Perfect Day." I knew that, like myself, he had serious mileage on the clock and was writing about old men's concerns, but he kept his promise to pull off something worthwhile. His most loyal fans appear to agree this New York trilogy was the highlight of his later work.

Lou Reed was the icing, but there was a cherry on top, Brian Wilson, who I hadn't chased around with a checkbook either. His signature came together even more spontaneously. I first met him backstage at the second Hall of Fame induction ceremony in

March 1987. It was my idea for Brian Wilson to induct Leiber and Stoller, whose songs I knew were a huge influence on his teenage imagination. We were both standing in the wings awaiting our cues to deliver a speech. I don't know who was more terrified, him or me, but by encouraging each other, a bond was formed. After years of addiction, reclusion, and suffering from mental illness, he was clean and now only beginning to show his face in public. I'd always loved his music and still think he was the greatest ever pop songwriter of that whole post–World War II era. He seemed sweet but very fragile, and I just wanted to help him climb further out of whatever hell-hole he'd slid into for so long.

While chatting afterward, I told him about a former Sire artist and friend of mine, Andy Paley, whose dream I knew was to collaborate with his number-one hero, Brian Wilson. In his excitable, almost childlike way, Brian ordered me, "Call him right now. I want to talk to Andy. Let's do this." We found a phone booth in one of the emptier corridors of the Waldorf Astoria. I used my credit card, and for about one hour, Brian Wilson and Andy Paley just kept talking and talking about music. I had to stand there like a voyeur, waiting to get my credit card back. It was all a bit insane, but I guess we were both feeling the adrenaline of the after-show.

That phone call developed into Brian Wilson's solo comeback. I secured them a $200,000 budget, which was extravagant in those days but easily spent if you were hiring only the best musicians and taking your time as Brian Wilson liked to do. I just couldn't stay away and spent a few weekends in Brian's home, hanging out for meals and listening to them play from a respectful distance. The only dark shadow hanging over an otherwise happy adventure was Brian's minder, the notorious Eugene Landy. He was the so-called doctor who treated Brian for schizophrenia. In fairness, Landy had probably saved Brian's life, but along that long, slow process of recovery, Landy began to abuse his powers as a psychotherapist. He took over Brian's life, including his business interests, and even registered some of Brian's compositions under his own name. Dr. Eugene E. Landy, as he called himself, was a sicko who should have been thrown in jail. Brian's adorable brother Carl was the most concerned of all, as was Brian's girlfriend, Melinda, now his wife. We were all working carefully as a team to help Brian out of the mental grip of this absolute monster and con man.

As soon as Lenny Waronker started hearing demos and tales about me sunbathing in Brian Wilson's garden, he was like a boy staring into the window of a toy store. Lenny loved the Beach Boys, so when Brian and Andy ran out of money, he stepped in and encouraged them to keep going with what seemed like unlimited support. In the end, the record turned into a million-dollar folly, by far the most expensive production on Sire's books, but nobody in Burbank seemed to mind. In California, helping Brian Wilson was considered as a noble deed of community service. As everyone could see, Brian's only chance of a second life was to earn back his shattered self-confidence through work. Simply titled *Brian Wilson*, the record was a cast of thousands that disappointed some fans. Never mind, it did succeed in helping Brian Wilson seize back some of his old self.

As the eighties drew to a close, I guess I'd finally reached the very top. Sire still had the biggest star in the world, Madonna, and as an A&R man, I was one of the hottest names in the business. On a personal level, between Brian Wilson and Lou Reed, I had also reached the best minds of my own war baby generation. To be honest, it was an eye-opener to see just how much these heroes of mine had to overcome. Their struggles probably fueled their imaginations in the first place.

Ambition is basically dissatisfaction with who and where you are. You're born with demons that you have to harness before they kill you. For a long time, I thought it was my sexuality, but there was definitely a lot more to whatever kept me running and hardly sleeping. Some forms of obsessive and extreme behavior can produce momentary relief. My way of scratching the itch was chasing hits. I was like a shark. Stop moving and I'd die. I knew I was a hopeless case who just couldn't sit still or get enough action. But what d'ya do? Get a Dr. Landy? Or just keep running with your precious madness?

9. CRAZY

I'd be holding a telephone receiver in my right hand, talking to an artist or a manager or a label in London. With my left hand, I'd be signing off paperwork that my secretary was simultaneously peeling off my desk. In the background, a staffer at the door would be mouthing something about an important call on line two. In the middle of this mayhem, a fresh stack of demos would arrive. And all day long, the phones just kept ringing on every desk.

This was my life in the eighties and early nineties. Morning was London time, evening was Burbank time, lunchtime was everybody-go-nuts time. My daily mission at Sire was to keep up with a level of international success that had grown fantastically out of control. Like Space Invaders on the final level, the aliens had gone apeshit. My life was to keep shooting and dodging bullets, just *keep going*, to stave off the inevitable *Game Over* for as long as I could.

My reward was seeing how many bestsellers on WBR's sales reports were ours. Considering Sire was basically me and a team of seven or eight people, we had a ridiculous success rate, probably the highest of any record label our size at the time. But it all came at a personal cost. For a guy who was in and out of cardiac wards, I was putting a lot of coke up my nose. I'm embarrassed to admit it at my ripe old age, but that's how I kept rolling. The rhythm was so intense, even my staff didn't have time for private lives, and considering the action they were getting, I doubt they even had much patience for normal civilian company. Sire was work, play, breakfast, lunch, and dinner. It was parties, gigs, traveling, everything rolled into one big fat life that most young New Yorkers could only dream of.

The days were so long and fast, none of us saw much of our apartments, which only really served as a locker and a bed. You'd have a suitcase wide open on the floor, with half-unpacked clothes pouring out. That was your portable wardrobe. I was such an elusive creature in my own home, the NYPD could have conducted exams in my kitchen. It was like an uninhabited snow world of footprints and eerie silences. Student detectives could have been assessed on their forensic skills by matching every half-drunk coffee cup in the sink to the unopened letters piled up on the table.

You came, you slept, you showered, and off you buzzed back to the bright lights, happy as a gnat on a midsummer's night. If you went out to a gig until two, which you did several times a week, you had to be in the office the next morning at nine. Standing up at your desk, you'd man the decks until Burbank went home, which was about ten at night in New York. Every day took forever, because your main job of finding new acts and promoting new releases was constantly being interrupted. With the amount of Sire bands on tour, people were always looking for tickets or backstage passes, including the odd surprise like James Brown asking to see Madonna. There were lunches, events, Hall of Fame business, helping people out. You took all these calls, because no matter how busy you were, you had to remain friendly.

The only way to make the space to actually listen to demos, read magazines, and snoop around for fresh product was to put in these manic eighteen-hour days. So, if you had to be in London the following day, you couldn't waste a good day by taking an afternoon flight. Hell no. You squeezed a full day into ten hours and then grabbed a night flight. You continued working on the plane and arrived frazzled for a full day's work in London, typically followed by a gig. You just kept going because it's true, folks: the early bird really does catch the worm.

And no matter where you went, those ringing telephones followed you everywhere—London, Paris, Los Angeles, Sundays, vacations, religious holidays, visits to the hospital. In my usual Chinese restaurant in London, the Gallery Rendezvous, they'd kindly put a telephone on my table and allow me to work away while eating. Flights were my only out-of-reach moments, so I'd use the undisturbed silence to get certain chores out of the way, like expenses. One of my little quirks was to stuff my receipts into a barf bag, where they belonged. Planes were perfect for dictating letters to my main assistant, Risa, who'd often travel with me. Possibly the most crucial part of my job was to rally support for my artists, so thanks to the invention of the fax machine, my trick was to write what I hoped would be inspirational memos to Mo and other WBR people, many of which I'm sure were written in vain.

I'm sure Mo hated receiving these two- or three-page word bombs. It suited me, however, to come across as the mad professor. All I ever wanted was money and green lights, so in roundabout ways that weren't obviously confrontational, I had to keep reminding Mo that I had more musical vision than he ever did. If Mo could save face by telling his colleagues I was insane, but to shut me up with whatever I wanted, it was a fair bargain. I'd earned a reputation inside Warner as the company maverick, and I knew that soldiers on the battlefield all felt honored to be formally addressed and shown how their daily missions mattered to the overarching war effort.

When my faxes arrived into various departments around the Burbank complex, I'm sure staffers thought that I was doing blow while writing these giant monologues—and it's true that my writing skills occasionally needed an extra lift. Few, however, could question my knowledge, my sincerity, and above all, Sire's track record of pointing the way. To get my outcast artists the attention they deserved, I had to stir things up and motivate troops who weren't under my direct command. In the age before emails, a carefully written and nicely typed-up letter carried far more weight than a phone call. Plus, of course, my letters got passed around.

In the middle of all this sleepless activity, Linda kept bursting into frame and adding to the chaos. If I was late on paying her money, she'd torture my assistants until I coughed up a check. "Where's His Majesty?" she'd whine at them in that Bronx drawl that sounded so much like her mother's. An integral part of working for Sire was coping with my ex-wife, which, to their credit, they all did with good humor. Although they wouldn't tell me until years later, my staffers said what they all found so weird was how Linda and I would insult each other, but just as sincerely, we'd start laughing and smiling together when we met up socially, which we did often. Ours was an incomprehensible love-hate relationship that somehow never died. There was such static between us, innocent bystanders felt their hair spiking upward.

I remember one New Year's Eve when Irving Azoff sent us tickets to a Bette Midler show only hours before it was to start. They were Irving's tickets, and at the last minute, something had come up. Miraculously, we only arrived ten minutes late, exceptionally punctual by our low standards. Bette Midler was already onstage and saw us pushing past people to reach our seats. "Well, there they are, late as usual," she announced midperformance, "that famous tag-team duo, Seymour and Linda Stein, better known as the Battling Steins."

Even long since divorced, our fights were still the talk of the town. Once, at the turn of the nineties, there we were again, the odd couple, sitting in the back seat of a cab, moving through some sunny New York afternoon. We'd been divorced for fifteen years, but bound by history and two daughters who'd become young women, I still had to endure Linda's legendary nagging. The blow I did in those years probably didn't help. The last thing you need when you're nicely coked up is your ex-wife screaming in your ear.

Linda was the psychological equivalent of a food blender. To be fair to the mother of my daughters, however, she never turned her back on me, even though I constantly did disappearing acts on the girls. Beneath her stormy skies, there was a homely loyalty that I objectively didn't deserve. If I forgot Samantha's or Mandy's birthdays, Linda would order flowers and put my name on the card, and any time I was in hospital, she was always the first to rush in. At the end of the day, for a guy who'd reached the top, I was a resounding failure at simpler things. When Samantha and Mandy came bounding into the office, my assistants, who were all young ladies themselves, could see how much they just wanted to spend time with their father. Alas, time was the one thing I just did not have enough of. Sire ran on my complete devotion. *It* was my baby. I was like a long-departed father who had another family now.

For thirty years, I'd been a professional music junkie. I craved the thrill of the game more than I craved anything else. The only people who could stand my foot-to-the-floor company were other record business characters, because all we wanted to do was get the freshest, purest new stuff into our ears. Thing is, as long as you stuck together and kept finding the goods, you were forgiven for your otherwise difficult personality.

The big gathering of our species was Midem, the record industry's largest trade fair, in Cannes, just outside Nice on the French Riviera. It took place in late January or early February, along the exact same stretch of hotels where the Cannes Film Festival was held three months after we'd gone. The action spilled out from the conference center—or the Palais des Festivals, as it's called—down along La Croisette, Cannes's spectacular beachfront. With its palm trees and landmark hotels overlooking the Mediterranean, it was a glamorous location for such a pack of badly dressed mutts as the music business. For me, it was like going to a bank and taking out cash. In the early days, deals made at Midem saved Sire's ass on a number of occasions, and even in the Warner era, it remained *the* place to meet up, collect demos, and share news.

It's every A&R man's fantasy to think he can keep catching lightning in a bottle by chasing distant thunder into the hills of Tennessee. Let's be honest, if you do it twice in your entire life, you're among the most privileged. The secret to my longevity was that I loved getting out of New York and catching up with my contacts. I felt happiest when I was on the move, new scenery flashing past, on the way to hook up with my brethren. Most of the time, you wouldn't find the next Elvis, but by turning up and keeping your friendships alive, lucky breaks occasionally skidded out of a lunch or dinner conversation and spilled onto your lap.

It always amazed me how few American competitors I'd bump into at Midem. It's an indication of how insular the American record business was and arguably still is. You certainly never saw Michael or Mo Ostin there. Most years, it felt like only a few of us had first picks over the entire European harvest, both indie and major. The two hotels to stay in were either the Carlton or the Majestic, both big Edwardian buildings on the seafront. The slightly cheaper alternative was the Martinez, which had the funkiest bar and generally got the biggest crowd at night. Room 130 at the Carlton was often reserved for me; it was a suite with a balcony facing the sea. I needed a room big enough to serve as a private office, because getting through the lobby or down to La Croisette, I was constantly being accosted by demo-wielding indies.

For those three or four days, the lobby of the Carlton was a crowded trading floor, and if you hung around and watched, you'd see major deals being struck between familiar faces. Everyone was swarming around in all directions, and because there were no mobile phones in those days, we were leaving each other messages with the hotel concierges or in a big letter box at the conference hall. Between your various meetings, you'd tour the stands and say hello to your favorite labels, but the actual trade fair was so noisy, you generally arranged to see your most important contacts in a hotel or at Felix, the popular lunch spot.

In the hills behind Cannes, there was a beautiful medieval town called Mougins. On the road up, hidden among eucalyptus and olive trees, there was probably the Riviera's best restaurant and inn, Le Moulin de Mougins. It was run by a famous chef, Roger Vergé, and was *the place* to have dinner during Midem. That's where you'd bump into all the big players, including the likes of Atlantic president Doug Morris or Sony Music chairman Tommy Mottola or Elektra boss Bob Krasnow. The clientele during Midem, however, was mostly made up of European moguls and indie bosses, as well as Allen Grubman and well over a hundred other American attorneys and, in fact, lawyers from all over the world. We all table-hopped, and even those who would peel back the table linen and chop out lines of coke on the wood surface were not frowned upon. The waiters were used to high-tipping deviants like us, and with typical French indifference, they got on with their jobs and let us do ours.

After dinner, everyone would slowly gravitate back down to the hotel bars along the Cannes seafront, especially the Martinez, where I could barely get a drink or sneak off to the toilet for the number of people trying to shove demos down my throat. The thing about Cannes is that as well as the huge film festival and Midem, there were other trade fairs around the year for TV production, advertising, duty-free products, and other prestige industries. That whole stretch of coast has long been a popular hangout in summer for the superrich, who'd moor their yachts and visit the high-class casinos and designer boutiques. It was like a French mix of Miami Beach and Las Vegas, with its own back line of drug dealers, escort girls, limo drivers, hustlers, and party people feeding off the nonstop action.

If you were gay, Midem was like Christmas, because you were chatted up constantly by local guys, both gay and straight, usually artists, deejays, TV presenters, publicists, or other colorful showbiz characters, whose English was sometimes so limited they got to the point in about ten words. There's nothing like a serious language barrier to cut straight through all the nonsense, and a few times, my evening plans cartwheeled off into some hotel room. Still, I generally managed to mix business and pleasure in the right order. Believe it or not, I was one of the best behaved at Midem. The more adventurous miscreants among us would actually stay in the handful of rooms they had in Le Moulin de Mougins. If you wanted to lose your mind on gourmet cuisine while burning holes through your pockets and nostrils, up in the hills was where you played.

It was nearly impossible to get much sleep anywhere, so for all the jet-lagged, coked-up insomniacs, the last refuge was this hellhole of a nightclub called La Chunga, possibly the ugliest dive on the French Riviera. I was dragged in once or twice and avoided it like the bubonic plague. For three nights every year, all the record dons, with nowhere left to go, flocked inside like bats into a bell tower. There they'd keep drinking, snorting, and shouting in other's ears until the fear of sunrise scared them back into their coffins.

As a community, we were all half-nuts and constantly trying to outbrag each other, but I think our common ailment created an unspoken empathy. We may have been competitors, but we helped each other professionally, and even in personal ways, we were the only stepbrothers most of us would ever have. We knew each other's struggles, we'd been playground rejects and failed husbands, we'd all been broke or had worse problems. We were all stuck in the game with no way back to normal civilian life, not that any of us wanted out. We all suffered from a similar personality disorder, which we could easily see in each other, but weren't ready to face in ourselves.

All of that glued us together as a community. Like a flock of squawking birds on a rock in the hostile Southern Ocean, we were safer together. It's your long-standing personal relationships that'll land you big fish and keep you out of court. I was never sued, which is surely amazing. My sword and shield were a telephone and a freshly updated address book. You needed ears to prosper, of course; the rest ran on your relationships.

In February 1990, I was in Cannes for our annual gathering when I bumped into Jill Sinclair, the wife of British superproducer Trevor Horn, a great team. While chatting in the aisles of the Palais, we decided to meet up a few days later in my London office to listen to Trevor's latest creations. Midem was great for collecting demos from overseas producers who you'd only get to meet once a year, but it was not an ideal place to listen to music.

Jill and Trevor, whose imprint was ZTT, were probably the most successful husband-and-wife production team in pop music. Trevor Horn was the genius of "Video Killed the Radio Star" fame, but as a producer for acts such as Frankie Goes to Hollywood and Grace Jones, he'd become a notorious perfectionist who always spent months, sometimes up to a year, sculpting his pop master-pieces into surefire hits. On paper, he boasted one of the highest batting averages in the game, but considering the amount of time and money he'd spend on each production, people in the business used to joke that he *had to* score smash hits just to recoup.

His perfectionism might have driven him insane had it not been for his wife, Jill, who added discipline and business drive. She was tough, she was respected, and she always made sure Trevor's hard work paid the bills. Whether it meant negotiating on his behalf, screaming at Trevor to stick to deadlines, or chasing up money from labels, she was the great woman behind the great producer.

At Midem, Jill played me a track from one of their techno-pop groups, 808 State. It just wasn't my cup of tea, but I had the perfect excuse. I knew 808 State was a studio group from Manchester whose U.S. rights had previously been licensed to Tommy Boy, a New York hip-hop label that had recently joined the Warner group. Tommy Boy founder Tom Silverman was a colleague of sorts, so to let Jill down easy, I explained as politely as I could, "I'm pretty sure Tom Silverman already played this for me. Isn't he putting it out?"

"No," she hit back firmly. "We don't want to do business with Tommy Boy anymore. It's available."

"Well, Jill, it's a bit of a tricky situation for me," I said and pointed to her big bag. "Surely, you must have something else in there. Can you not play me something new?"

"Well, there is something Trevor's been working on, but it's nowhere near completion. It's actually for our new deal with Rob Dickins, and I know Trevor would kill me for playing it. Even Rob hasn't heard it yet."

As any A&R man worth his weight in gold discs will tell you, you can often smell an important demo just from the sparkle in someone's eyes. It's the one they don't want to play you. Whatever tape Jill had at the bottom of that bag was probably Trevor Horn's latest all-in gamble to pay off an advance he might have already spent in the studio. Trevor was a perfectionist. I had to hear it, but convincing an iron lady like Jill Sinclair was going to require more than just begging. "You do realize," I began, "that Rob Dickins has serious problems in the Warner family right now. Bob Krasnow at Elektra hates him. So does Mo. It's even worse at Atlantic, where Doug Morris can barely speak to Rob."

"Really?" said Jill, looking concerned.

"Yeah, it's not his fault, but it's getting very messy. If you ask me, the Americans can't handle an A&R man running the British office. They used to be able to sign up British acts directly. The London office never had anyone that good, and now they're all upset. Anyway, listen, Jill, I love Rob Dickins. We go back to 1979 when we set up the Echo and the Bunnymen label. I know how he thinks; if he hasn't heard your tape yet, it's not committed to anyone, and he won't mind me hearing it. And under the current circumstances, I might even be the solution to his American problems. And yours."

A seasoned dealer like Jill Sinclair knew I was twisting her arm, but she had the instincts to know I wasn't lying. In America, where radio promotion costs hundreds of thousands of dollars, boardroom politics often decided the fate of many a great record. She reached into her bag and handed me a tape, which I slid straight into the deck. "I can't leave this with you," she warned. "It's nowhere near finished, but it'll give you an idea of what Trevor's doing right now."

As the intro rolled into its killer groove, it was like one of those scenes in a James Bond movie, where a mountain opens up and Blofeld's rocket appears. It was an early mix of "Crazy" by Trevor Horn's latest discovery, Seal. Everything screamed success; the synth riff, the panoramic space-rock sound, Seal's suave voice, the spooky melody, but most of all, it was the message of the chorus that sent a shiver down my spine on first listen. We're never gonna survive unless we are a little crazy? Yes, sir, I'll toast to that. *L'chaim!*

"Jill, this is a monster! Sign it to me and you have my absolute promise I'll make sure it gets a major push in America."

"Okay, listen, I'm going to make you a conditional promise that you can get first call when Trevor's finished. But it'll need Rob's blessing first."

"Can I talk to Rob? I'll tell him I forced you to play me something new."

"Okay, do that, but go softly."

"Don't worry, Jill, I've been in this game a long time."

When I got hold of Rob Dickins, he heard my enthusiasm bubbling down the telephone line. In the back of his head, I knew he was weighing up Sire's cool factor with whatever headache he was experiencing with the bigger American label bosses in the Warner group. The alternative to letting little ol' Sire release Seal was to run the risk of Mo, Bob Krasnow, or Doug Morris burying the record or just doing a halfhearted job. Stranger things happened in that era of big suits and even bigger egos. Bob Krasnow and Doug Morris had ears, but they didn't particularly foresee or even welcome the electronic sound bursting out of England, certainly not in the way that Rob Dickins did. Of all the Warner labels, Sire was objectively the best imprint to break such an unfamiliar UK sound.

"Okay, Seymour. I'm good with that," replied Rob, "but it's ultimately Jill and Trevor's call."

As was his way, Trevor Horn took almost a year to finish the whole album, by which stage guess who was stirring it up in the background? None other than Mo Ostin, of course. When the following Midem rolled around, "Crazy" had just been released in England and was making a storm. Its American license hadn't been signed yet, because as far as I was concerned, it was a done deal. On the promenade in Cannes, however, I bumped into Chris Wright, the cofounder of Chrysalis. Chris happened to be a good friend of Trevor's and Jill's and ran over to me.

"Jill Sinclair's been looking all over for you," he said. "She's really upset. Mo Ostin's pushing her hard to give Seal to Irving Azoff's new label, Giant, which she absolutely does not want to do. Go find her immediately. If you can't find her, she told me to tell you that she gave you her word and she needs you to keep yours."

My head went into a rage. Los Angeles was waking up, so I called Mo and asked him straight out, "Why are you trying to screw me like this?" In his best nice-guy voice, Mo started pleading with me not to pursue Seal. "Look, I've just lost Geffen," he said in reference to MCA's purchase of Geffen Records from right under his nose. "So, I thought that signing a deal with Irving Azoff would be the solution. Please don't fight me on this, Seymour."

"Mo, I heard that demo a year ago and fell immediately in love with it. I'm not giving this up."

"Please, Seymour, I'm just trying to give Irving a break. We've got to pull together and do what's best for the whole group."

"Are you suggesting that Irving Azoff can't find his own hits? Right now, he's far more successful than both of us."

I was so pissed off. Not only was it seriously rude to conspire behind my back, Mo's meddling made no financial sense. Warner owned all of Sire but only 50 percent of this new Giant Records venture. I had nothing against Irving Azoff, but if Mo didn't believe in his talents to make Giant as successful as Geffen Records, he should have never invested in the first place. Needless to say, Mo kept *being nice* while not budging an inch, and because he was my superior with the power to torpedo the deal, I eventually made up my mind that if I couldn't have this record, I'd figure out a way to get back at him.

I called Bob Krasnow and arranged for Jill to play Trevor's record. He called me back saying he liked the record and would pursue, and then a couple of days later, he called again cursing. "What the fuck did you just get me into, Seymour?"

"What, is Mo's leaning on you, too?"

"No! You told me this was Trevor Horn's record. Why didn't you tell me it was from Rob Dickins?"

"Hang on, Bob. Surely you know Rob's done a license deal with Trevor and Jill for ZTT, but only for England. Jill and Trevor decide who gets it for the States. Forget Rob Dickins—it's a Trevor Horn production."

"Seymour, don't you get it? If Rob Dickins is behind this, it can't be good. That asshole is incapable of making hits. Everything he touches turns to shit."

"Oh, c'mon, Bob. You know that's not true."

When Bob Krasnow was obsessed about some pet hate, there was no point even arguing. Luckily for me, Jill Sinclair was so fed up with everyone's bullshit, she put her foot down and made it crystal clear to one and all that Seal was promised to Sire, end of story. I was incredibly grateful for the way she withstood so much pressure from Mo, who, being the strongest king of the whole empire, tended to win wrangles such as this. Jill was steadfast and strong, and for that, I cherish her memory and often think of her.

About a fortnight after the deal was signed, I received a call from Trevor Horn about Seal. In passing, he mentioned he was flying out to Los Angeles for some session and asked if I had any leads on hot recording studios in the city. It wasn't my domain, so I suggested he ask either Lenny Waronker or Ted Templeman, who formed the nucleus of WBR's unbeatable production team.

"Oh, I think I'll just ask Michael Ostin." Trevor sighed. "He's given me some useful addresses in the past. By the way," continued Trevor, changing his tone, "keep this to yourself. The one other person we would have considered for Seal was Michael Ostin. I don't know why, but for some reason, he just never stepped forward."

Thank God, I thought and kept my mouth shut.

"And maybe you don't know this either," continued Trevor, "but the last person we were going give Seal to, or anything else of ours, was Irving Azoff." He then described ZTT's near-death experience being sued by Frankie Goes to Hollywood with Irving Azoff allegedly pulling strings in the background as the band's manager. Trevor was right—I didn't know. I should have remembered, but I guess you can't catch every snippet of gossip. The irony, however, almost made me crack up. The mighty Mo Ostin trying to shove Trevor Horn's nemesis down Jill Sinclair's throat? Was the old pro that out of touch? If Mo had just stopped meddling in everyone's business and let his son get involved, the result might have turned out very differently.

When I said goodbye to Trevor and hung up, I leaned back and smiled to myself. The smarter people around the music business were starting to wake up to what I'd been saying for years. Behind his nice-guy mask, Mo Ostin was a dictator, and like all aging dictators, years of purges, nepotism, and fast-tracking the wrong people into the wrong places would be his downfall. There comes a twilight in every dictator's life when having it too easy for too long makes him sloppy.

I'm happy to report, the battle for Seal was worth fighting. In May 1991, Sire released Seal's self-titled album in the United States, and by September, "Crazy" had climbed to number seven on the *Billboard* Hot 100, a major North American hit all summer long whose spacey sound really did herald in the druggy, electronic feel of the nineties. In its wake, I signed up Primal Scream and the Farm, all ambassadors of this new ecstasy scene bursting out of England. Once again, I was surfing a new wave into the next decade of pop music.

Little did I know what craziness was about to engulf the entire company. Above Rockefeller Plaza, dark clouds were gathering.

Rumor had it that Steve Ross was terminally ill. He'd been the guiding hand behind Warner's spectacular rise throughout the seventies and eighties into an entertainment superpower, which he merged into Time Warner in 1989, the world's biggest media conglomerate. As his prostate cancer became untreatable throughout 1991, he sensed some kind of succession war was going to erupt and, in Steve Ross style, decided to fire the first shot himself.

From his deathbed, Ross directed a surprise coup while his healthy young rival and cochairman, Nicholas J. Nicholas, was on vacation. Apparently, Ross got the idea watching TV. In August 1991, the last premier of the USSR, Mikhail Gorbachev, was at his holiday home in the Crimea when his political opponents struck in Moscow. Nicholas had been the former Time boss with whom Ross had clashed on so many decisions since the controversial merger. Ross's farewell coup succeeded in ousting his younger archenemy, but it didn't bode well for the times ahead. Ross at least chose a nicer man named Jerry Levin to become his cochairman of Time Warner, which effectively made Levin the sole successor.

Once Steve Ross was lowered into the ground, which was in December 1992, we were an unhappy family of spoiled brats staring right into a power vacuum. Because Levin had risen up through the Time hierarchy, he didn't know much about Warner's various businesses, least of all music. As a result, the existing Warner Music chairman, Bob Morgado, suddenly found himself enjoying new freedoms and powers that he was never allowed under Steve Ross. If you're to believe most historical accounts of what can only be titled *The Fall of the Warner Empire*, Bob Morgado usually gets blamed as the catalyst for the years of civil war that followed. I don't quite agree. Bob Morgado was certainly a tough personality who took no prisoners, perhaps too tough for his own good, but all the years of pent-up tension go back to what seemed to be Mo's secret desire to step upstairs into some powerful corporate position, leaving Michael Ostin in charge of Warner Bros. Records. When destiny did not go according to Mo's liking, it must have been very hard for him.

Steve Ross had paid Mo handsomely and made him a very powerful man. And maybe because Mo was so wealthy, he thought he could get rid of Bob Morgado if he pushed. Morgado, however, was a politician himself and got so sick and tired of Mo's sense of entitlement, he teamed up with Doug Morris to give Mo the treatment many people felt Mo had long deserved. Doug Morris, who'd been president of Atlantic and its de facto boss for over a decade, was promoted by Morgado in 1994 to a new position as chairman of the Warner Music's U.S. companies. Mo was so shocked and insulted that he'd have to report to Doug Morris, he officially announced to the press he wouldn't be renewing his contract at the end of the year. This was typical Mo; he made it look like he was leaving while giving himself a few more months to possibly fight back. In reality, Morgado and Morris had already decided to turf him out. *They* didn't renew *his* contract.

For the rest of my life, I would be chastised by former Warner staffers who'd say I was too hard on Mo, that he was a lovely man with a sunny disposition, that Mo built the greatest record label in the history of America. Sorry, I don't believe the nice guy mythology. Oh, yes, the man clearly had a rare talent, and yes, WBR was a truly great record label that defined the seventies and enabled me to enjoy the best years of my life. But if Mo was such a nice guy, he'd have shared more of his bumper bonuses with me and the others who helped build Warner's, right? And if the company was really such a family, he'd have secured his succession, he'd have made sure his flock were set up safely without him, because that's what noble fathers do, right? So, go easy on the Californian bullshit; Mo was just as selfish as any of us old schoolers from the east. When Linda organized a big party for my sixtieth birthday, I saw his face come through the door and couldn't believe he'd actually turned up.

"Mo, I didn't expect you here," I said, caught off guard.

"I made a lot of money out of you," Mo said, smiling. He knew how much it hurt me to hear these words, and yet it appeared to be a compliment. Typical Mo.

With Mo and Lenny gone, the vacuum left by Steve Ross was even bigger. We did, however, have younger talent coming up from elsewhere in the family, especially Rob Dickins, who I thought was by far the most interesting of the younger bucks. At that point, he may have been the hottest executive at any of the majors. The thing about Rob Dickins was that, unlike any of the other contenders for a promotion, he'd actually built something of his own and was in his prime. He had world-class acts like Simply Red, Enya, and Seal. He worked with Trevor Horn and William Orbit, the producers who in many ways captured the sound of the nineties. In mainstream pop, Rob had brought Cher and Rod Stewart back from the dead, proving that he could score winners in every genre and age group. And because he came from publishing and had great ears, Rob was a different kind of boss who kept his hands free to handle all the label's creative heavy lifting.

Creative people usually aren't good managers, but Rob had excellent instincts when it came to team building. For the company's everyday nuts and bolts, he hired the brilliant Max Hole, who was such a rock-solid organizer, he went on to run Universal Music Group International. Rob found the best promotions and press duo Britain has ever seen, Moira Bellas and the Boston-born Barbara Charone. He also brought in Paul Conroy, another great all-rounder from the new-wave days who went on to run Chrysalis and later Virgin. You'll always know a leader by the quality of his recruits, and Rob's gang was the meanest of the younger generation.

The underlying reason I think Rob Dickins was so unanimously hated by his American counterparts went back to the way Nesuhi Ertegun had been running Warner's international division since the seventies. Nesuhi, who'd died in 1989, was a diplomatic and talented fellow, but he was a peacemaker who let the Yankees ride roughshod over the foreign companies, especially the UK office, which had been a puppet until Rob Dickins took over. Rob didn't take anyone's shit. He turned away lots of American dreck and was every bit as determined and discerning as any mogul in the game to find his own winners. But because he was a younger Englishman in an American group, it was easy for the older Yanks to paint him as an upstart troublemaker.

Mo thought Rob was arrogant, Krasnow and Rob clashed over their very different tastes, but I think Doug Morris had a special ax to grind. When it comes to global corporations, it's amazing how one little incident between two men can be like a grain of sand fucking up the clockwork of destiny. In the decline of Warner Music and all the chain of events that affected my own fate, I always think of Rob's biggest artist, the Irish singer Enya. It had nothing to do with Enya personally, but her success in the late eighties forced Rob to make some tricky moves that came back to haunt him in the midnineties when civil war broke out.

Back in 1986, just a year after Rob Dickins took the reins in London, he gave the American rights for Enya's debut record to Doug Morris at Atlantic. That record didn't happen, so Rob licensed Enya's second album, *Watermark*, to Geffen Records, which was half-owned by Warner at that precise moment in 1988. Geffen's promotional team were on a roll and broke Enya wide open, selling over four million albums in the States alone. Then Geffen suddenly sold his label to MCA in 1991 just as Enya's third album was ready for release. To keep Enya in the Warner family, Rob Dickins had to, once again, find a new home for Enya's American operations. That's exactly when my Seal episode also happened.

Rob wanted to move Enya to WBR, but because he had such a terrible relationship with Mo over all the WBR titles he felt weren't suited to the British market, Rob called me up trying to get me to lure Lenny Waronker out to England to meet Enya.

"What do you think I should do?" asked Rob.

"It's not my place to tell you what to do, but if you really think Lenny Waronker is the right choice for Enya, you're going to have to put your hand in your pocket and pay for her and her manager to go out and meet *him*. But before you do, Rob, listen to me—Doug Morris is gaining so much steam right now, I actually think you should call him up and say, 'Look, Doug, Geffen broke Enya, but that record was way better than the first, so please just take the ball they've given you and run with it.' Because if you don't try to put things right with Doug Morris, he's never going to forget."

Instead of going back to Doug Morris and stitching up the old wound, Rob stuck with his hunch to make Lenny Waronker Enya's new custodian in America. Enya did live happily ever after with WBR, which is what helped get her music into movie soundtracks and sell millions more records without ever touring. Rob had made all the right choices commercially, but politically, I'm sure Doug Morris never forgave the snub, and if there's one thing an alpha male like Doug Morris will remember, it's watching everyone else score smash hits with an artist that was snatched out of his hands.

Considering Doug Morris was doing about $900 million at Atlantic at the time, this Enya business should have been no big deal in itself, but the simmering resentment bubbled over in 1994, straight after Mo got the chop. Bob Morgado saw Rob Dickins had immense talent and offered him a life-changing promotion to take Mo's place. It was Rob's dream come true—I'd never seen him so happy—but behind the scenes, I can only imagine that Doug Morris was seething. Morgado should have never taken this step without first consulting Doug, who was by then the head of Warner Music Group in the States.

I imagine many onlookers thought it was risky to put an Englishman in charge of such a large American major. I nonetheless supported Bob Morgado and still believe Rob Dickins would have taken WBR into interesting and successful musical territory, and just as importantly, would have hired a new generation of talented staffers. Rob had the ears, the judgment, the experience, and the audacity to do in the States what he'd done in the UK. He was exactly the young conqueror to fill the giant vacuum left by Mo. I've always believed that Brits are among the best music men because they take a more global view of music. It is not surprise to me that the heads of the three remaining major record groups today are all Brits—Lucian Grainge at Universal Music Group, Max Lousada at Warner Music Group, and Rob Stringer at Sony Music.

Alas, poor Rob wound up in a New York hotel waiting and waiting for days while Bob Morgado and Doug Morris remained and battled it out. Because of Morgado's missteps, Rob Dickins was never given Mo's old crown. Instead, one of Doug Morris's former colleagues from Atlantic, Danny Goldberg, was appointed. Surprisingly, Goldberg didn't think it was necessary to relocate to WBR's headquarters in Burbank, and he spent most of his relatively short tenure as chairman of WBR based in New York.

Decision-making was difficult because there were so many problems happening all at once. The other drifting ship was Elektra, where Bob Krasnow was shown the door. Like Mo, Krasnow knew his game was up. I'd never had an easy relationship with Bob Krasnow. Then again, I don't think many people did. He was a great A&R man who had turned around Elektra in the mideighties. He knew how to get what he wanted, but he'd earned himself a bad reputation for overspending, doing too much coke, and making other people miserable. For a while in the early nineties, horror stories about Bob Krasnow were a stock genre of music business comedy. But let me reiterate, Kraz had incredible ears, among the best ever in the business.

The last straw was when Krasnow and some guests took one of the Warner jets down to South America. Krasnow eventually picked up some hookers and flew off into the sunset, leaving his guests stranded. I'm sure Elektra paid for their airline tickets home, but their story grew more legs than a millipede. Morgado was already fed up with Krasnow's chicanery and had made up his mind to throw him out with Mo.

With Mo and Krasnow out on their asses and Rob Dickins sent back to London under a black cloud, things got very complicated for me. Since 1978, Sire had been owned by and plugged into Warner Bros. Records, which never made sense to some onlookers, because by this stage, I was based in Rockefeller Plaza beside Elektra and the Time Warner corporate headquarters. To make his mark, Doug Morris began thinking about structural changes that he felt should have been made long before. It wasn't simply a question of geography; in the eighties, he'd turned Atlantic around through label acquisitions and all that "economies of scale" stuff that consisted of making juicier profits by getting one office to handle several catalogs.

He had a close relationship with one of his protégées, Sylvia Rhone, an attractive black lady originally from Harlem, who had been working at Atlantic. To everyone's astonishment, Doug gave Sylvia the CEO position at Elektra, and I was offered the dubious honor of being its president, which in reality meant I was just a nominal number two and Sire would cease to exist as a stand-alone label. Like the East West and Nonesuch imprints, Sire was to be rolled into Elektra.

When this absolute shock of a plan was unveiled to me, the first person I called was Allen Grubman, which tells you how I felt. Grubman advised me to shut up, grit my teeth, and bear it. He did his own checking as I did mine, and we both came to the bleak conclusion that I had no viable move; it was wind up on the scrap heap or just roll with Doug Morris, who was clearly on a path of conquest. Once we moved our attentions to the nitty-gritty, there were all kinds of legalistic pitfalls to the plan. For starters, Madonna would never move to Elektra. I'd been slowly losing her anyway, but now it was definitive.

In 1992, I'd helped Madonna and her manager, Freddy DeMann, set up their own Warner sub-label, Maverick Records, 50 percent of which was still owned by Sire. Mo was dead against it, but I supported Madonna and made sure she got her way. It pains me to admit that Mo's fears about Maverick, at least at the beginning, were largely founded. This was all well before the signing of Alanis Morissette and others. Apart from Madonna's own *Erotica* album, which was a huge hit, her label had signed artists who'd achieved moderate, or slightly better than moderate, success. So, with all the changes happening, I'd basically have to kiss goodbye to that investment as well as Madonna herself. I understood she didn't need me anymore and would just stay where she was, working through her LA label straight into WBR's promotional machinery, where she was still their main act, bigger even than Prince.

I'd also lose Depeche Mode, who, for the same general reasons, wanted to remain plugged straight into WBR. To make things even messier, Sire's main manager, Howie Klein, was offered a golden opportunity by Danny Goldberg to run Mo's old Reprise sub-label. Although Howie was a great talent in other ways, I felt he didn't have the ears to run a label, but I couldn't get in the way of his big break without looking like an evil prick. His departure spelled double trouble for the carcass that Sire was fast becoming, because Howie was a popular character who'd worked closely with most of Sire's artists. I knew that some might want to follow him to Reprise, which of course would be a way of staying part of the Burbank network that my artists had previously been going through for promotion and marketing. So, while I was supposed to be schmoozing my remaining artists into this visibly smaller Elektra offshoot, it was like a flashing exit was knocked through the back wall behind me.

I don't think there was any conspiracy to fuck me from all sides, even though that's what effectively happened. The whole Warner Music group was in the grips of major turmoil, and Sire, being a lot smaller than WBR, Atlantic, or Elektra, was understandably not a priority. The chaos was more a case of every man for himself, rather like a game of musical chairs, except with fifty-year-old men trampling in all directions around a boardroom table as Doug Morris and Bob Morgado fought over who got to press the buttons. Maybe because I was an outcast who hadn't really grown up into the kind of suit-wearing corporate executive that Doug Morris had become, I was one of the schmucks left standing with his dick in his hand.

On the corporate chessboard, Sire was basically sacrificed, with all its artists going to WBR. I'm sure my critics will say that by then I was losing my edge as a talent spotter, but I don't agree. You never lose your ears; what you do lose is your winning streak, your aura, or in my case, my biggest artists, including Madonna, and most of my staff.

Fortunately, God, in his infinite wisdom, gave us the Jewish lawyer. Allen Grubman engaged with Doug Morris on my behalf and negotiated me a huge advance, which, I have to say, definitely softened the pain. Apart from the money, everything else about the deal stank, but it was a simple choice of stick with Sire or find a job elsewhere. I tightened my gut and moved into the office next to

Sylvia Rhone, and to be fair, things were okay in the beginning. I fought off competition from Sony to sign a very successful band called Spacehog, which raised everyone's spirits.

Spacehog were a gang of Leeds boys who'd relocated to New York and proved to be very much a cool item in that midnineties Brit-pop period. They were fronted by two handsome brothers, Royston and Antony Langdon, who were so popular with the ladies, they managed to date Liv Tyler and Kate Moss, respectively. Their debut album, *Resident Alien*, sold over a million copies and provided a Top 40 hit single "In the Meantime," just as groups like Placebo, the Dandy Warhols, Suede, Supergrass, and Pulp started blowing up around the world. We'd caught the wave just at the right time.

I definitely tried to make something of the Elektra-Sire double bill. I soon discovered, however, that although Sylvia Rhone had definite talents and a certain charm, she had whirlwind traits that in the long run made her difficult to work with. She was always glamorous in designer outfits, and often accompanied by one or two assistants and a driver. Underneath all that glamour, she was one tough executive who had her own agenda. It quickly became obvious to me that my appointment was totally Doug Morris's idea and not necessarily Sylvia's.

Not surprisingly, across the whole Warner Music group, Doug filled all the key positions with former colleagues who worked under him at Atlantic, all of whom he had been grooming for executive positions for years. Apart from Sylvia, another of his protégés was Val Azzoli, who'd been appointed as Doug's successor at Atlantic. With his curly hair and big, affable face, staffers used to joke that Azzoli was straight out of a pizza place. Then, of course, there was Danny Goldberg, for the most part running WBR out of Atlantic's office in New York, which was a big change for its Burbank roots.

As the weeks turned into months, one plausible theory was that Doug Morris put me underneath Sylvia Rhone as a type of safety net. Sylvia did have ears, she knew how to work hard, and she'd handled hot product before. The problem for me was that she'd come up through Atlantic, where she'd worked with acts like En Vogue. Her natural habitat was black pop, as proven by the acts she had future successes with, like Ol' Dirty Bastard, Busta Rhymes, and Missy Elliott. So Doug must have thought I could help Sylvia with her inherited roster of indie acts (many of which had been brought in during the Krasnow years) such as Björk, Moby, the Cure, Inspiral Carpets, the Prodigy, and Nick Cave, as well as metal heavyweights like Metallica, Mötley Crüe, and Anthrax. Plus, of course, Elektra's back catalog carried all the original founder's folk and psychedelic acts. The great Jac Holzman, who started Elektra in the fifties, had signed the Doors, Love, Tim Buckley, the Stooges, and MC5, thanks to Danny Fields and many others.

None of it made sense considering the stakes were so high. Warner Music was the biggest record group in the United States, controlling 22 percent of the market. It was also Time Warner's most profitable division, earning $900 million annually on $4 billion turnover. So, it's not like our civil war didn't have consequences on hundreds of bands and, arguably, the health of the whole music industry. There's nothing journalists and readers love more than a boardroom massacre, and because we were the biggest gang on the block, every national newspaper was reporting the latest whacking in the turf war. As well as office gossip at every water cooler and worried managers calling up nonstop, we had journalists crawling through every keyhole. Bob Morgado and Doug Morris were barely on speaking terms, and everyone knew the next big casualty was only a matter of time.

With all the bad press affecting Time Warner's share prices, our corporate guardians couldn't sit on their hands any longer. Investors wanted a head on a stake, and at that point, Bob Morgado seemed to be the common denominator in all these feuds. Bob Morgado should've backed off and given Doug Morris free rein. Instead, Morgado had fallen out with every last label chief, which didn't make him look good in the eyes of the corporates. Outsiders, however, didn't understand the personalities he was dealing with. As I kept trying to remind everyone who bothered to listen to me, all this power lust had been fomenting for years.

I'll never forget the scene on May 2, 1995, when my office door swung open and a pizza deliverer appeared carrying three boxes. "I didn't order these," I told the kid, who stared back at me, clueless. It was then that I was overwhelmed by giant stench of cheap industrial cheese wafting through the door behind him. I walked into the main office and almost vomited. Pizza boys were crawling around like ants handing out boxes to every desk. "What's going on?" I asked. And that's how I learned that Bob Morgado had just been fired. Sylvia Rhone was so over the moon about Doug winning the war, she ordered in pizza for every one of the hundred-plus staffers.

God, I hated that office and everything we did in those lost years. A while later, Sylvia celebrated O. J. Simpson's acquittal with another office load of stinking pizza, which struck me as even weirder. Hadn't a woman and her lover been murdered? But these, dear reader, were the naughty nineties in all their tacky splendor. Hubris had taken over. There was too much easy money, too much cocaine, and no way of feeding all these hungry egos who I'm sure look back today and cringe at their own appetite for power and excess.

Warner Music was officially a madhouse, and crazy as it sounds, for the first time in many years, I suddenly felt a lot saner than everyone around me. The midnineties were when I stopped taking cocaine, and apart from a wobble here and there, I had mostly emerged from my wild years. Seemingly, I wasn't the only bemused witness of this corporate tragedy. The boss of HBO, which was then part of the Time Warner group, was handed Morgado's responsibilities and took a long, hard look at some of the people around me. His unlikely name was Michael Fuchs, and because he had his own TV empire to command and kept working out of his regular HBO office, everyone in the Warner labels wrongly presumed he was just an interim caretaker, pending Doug's total ascension.

Just weeks after Fuchs was nominated, Doug Morris strolled into a meeting at HBO on a hot June morning expecting his Warner Music U.S. chairmanship to be expanded to the entire world. Fuchs instead presented a draft press release announcing that Doug Morris was fired. After what I can only presume was total shock followed by screaming, Doug was escorted by security guards back to Rockefeller Plaza to clear out his desk.

I was in a Hall of Fame meeting, where I received a call from Sylvia Rhone wailing down the phone, "Doug's just been fired!" She kept calling back, borderline hysterical, like it was the end of all our lives. She had a hotline into Doug's mind and probably knew all the details of whatever motivated Fuchs to pull the trigger. Sylvia knew I was with Ahmet Ertegun and begged me to interrogate him. "Do you think Ahmet had something to do with this?" she seethed. I don't believe she meant it. She was frantic and upset.

"Of course not," I said. "Doug's always been respectful of Ahmet. I can assure you. He's told me that himself."

I pulled Ahmet out of the meeting and told him what was going on across town. He shrugged with one of his Turkish smirks that could have meant anything. Doug Morris had been Ahmet's protégé, who'd done a solid job throughout the eighties of making Atlantic hot again, which in turn had enabled Ahmet to enjoy a long and happy period as the elder statesman of a freshly restored super-power. I was certain by the expression on his face that Ahmet had not played any part in this coup or even knew about it.

Sylvia Rhone was never the same after that day. It was obvious she depended on Doug. Doug was her mentor, and what of it? He was a damn good one. Who am I to talk? Where would I be without all the mentoring I received from Syd Nathan, Jerry Wexler, Ahmet, and the others? Full-blown paranoia followed her every move. She began imagining that rivals were out to get her, which I can promise wasn't the case. Not only did Elektra's biggest acts prefer her to Krasnow, there'd been too much bad press for her to be added to the list of casualties. She held on for another few years, but the fall of Doug Morris was instant curtains for Danny Goldberg, who lasted only nine months as WBR boss. I must admit, I really enjoyed those last few months working with Doug. He was totally hands-on. I was well into my fifties and thought I knew everything, but I learned quite a bit from Doug. I was not at all surprised to see him move on to become head of Universal and finally Sony, after a rocky start running his own Rising Tide Records.

Fuchs needed to stabilize the chaos. His problem was there wasn't enough talent in the ranks capable of stepping up and making a difference. In another panicked compromise, the keys to the Burbank castle were handed to Russ Thyret, the only old boy left. The bright idea was to get WBR back to something resembling Mo's old crew, and it's most definitely true that in his prime, Russ had been a great promotion man, responsible for bringing Prince to WBR. While he was a really great and dedicated music man, it seemed to me that, like many other others, the hard-charging lifestyle of a music executive had taken its toll on him.

As we'd all eventually learn, the same old story just kept repeating itself. I say this as someone with a certain distance from events. Like all the protagonists, I had an ego and a habit of irresponsible, self-ish misbehavior. I was certainly no choirboy and had consumed my share of blow, (which by this time I had all but cut out). The difference was that I didn't harbor any dark fantasies to take over labels or companies that other people had built. All I'd wanted from life was to keep sailing the good ship Sire into my own personal sunset. But by letting them all do what they were going to do anyway, with or without me, I was one of the very few who survived.

To stay in the game, I knew I just had to keep signing hot new acts. The problem was I'd lost so much clout, staff, the ability to secure budgets, and, perhaps worst of all, my little halo as Warner's indie maverick that what used to be so easy had now become much more difficult. You're only as good as your name, and ours had become toxic. Warner Music Group was in deep trouble. Sadly, Warner was in disarray. I wasn't there, but Steve Baker and Howie Klein were far from ideal choices to run Warner and Reprise. Klein was not a star at A&R. He had strengths, but that was not one of them. He was good at marketing and promotion. Steve Baker was one of the smartest and best at A&R, and an all-around music man. The problem was, in my opinion, he didn't want all the responsibilities heaped upon him. I'm not sure, as I was not there at the time. That said, to this day, I would trust his ears more than most.

For example, people always ask me why the song "Seymour Stein" by an indie band named Belle and Sebastian came out on another label. The truth is, I wanted to sign Belle and Sebastian and chased them all the way to Scotland. I showed up at gigs, charmed them, took them out to dinner, but I felt so bad about the *Titanic* I'd be luring them onto, I eventually let go when a hot little indie named Matador Records offered them a deal. At the lowest point of my career, I was very honored and still am that any artist would name a song after me. Whenever it comes on, I drift back to that lost period in the mid- to late nineties and can almost smell the pizzas. I love the line "It's a good day for flying," because it really was.

I got so fed up and depressed about everything, I decided to do what to my father would have done. I jumped on a plane full of orthodox Jews to visit the tomb of Rebbe Nachman in the Ukrainian town of Uman. Such a trip had suddenly become possible because, since the old Soviet Union had collapsed, Jewish pilgrimages were no longer illegal. I'd been invited by a holy man, Rabbi Jesse Kramer, who was the son-in-law of my old Talmud Torah teacher, Rabbi Leo Rosenfeld, long since dead. Kramer and his followers from the family synagogue were all dressed in their black suits and hats. I must have looked like an embarrassing schlub tagging along in my T-shirt and sneakers, but they welcomed me into their experience. I needed companionship and some kind of higher fix I wasn't getting from music. We sang and laughed and prayed ourselves into trances. It wasn't the tomb itself that did it for me, it was the people and all the happiness stirring around Rabbi Nachman's legacy.

I'd been thinking for months about leaving Elektra, which I'd never wanted to be involved with anyway. No matter how nominal my new title was, Elektra to me would always be the baby of its founder, Jac Holzman, a long-retired mensch whom I subsequently lobbied hard to get inducted into the Rock and Roll Hall of Fame. Luckily, there was a reliable old nuts-and-bolts man in Elektra's engine room who campaigned for my rehabilitation. His name was Aaron Levy, Elektra's chief operating officer, more of a treasurer and fixer than a record man. I'd first met him in the early seventies when he ran Paramount Records. He was a veteran by the late nineties, nearing retirement, but Aaron was one of the few sane people left, and I'm pretty sure he spoke to the men upstairs about what was really going on in the asylum below.

Thanks to Aaron's help, I was eventually thrown a lifesaver by the Time Warner chairman, Jerry Levin, who I got to know better than I'd ever known Steve Ross. Because Levin had risen up through the Time hierarchy, he'd long been regarded suspiciously as a hapless outsider by the Warner Music family. But I understand why Steve Ross made him his successor. Jerry genuinely cared and learned about our business. In our conversations about Warner Music's problems and in particular our international operations, which he felt I had an eye for, I told him to hire Roger Ames, London's PolyGram boss. Roger was an old pro and everything we needed: good ears, good manager, business literate, internationally minded. To my surprise, Levin called me up a few weeks later and announced, "I've just hired Roger Ames to run international!" To lure him over to New York, Warner had to buy out Roger's stake in London Records for a juicy $200 million. The price tag was more than a little heavy, but Roger's arrival marked the long-awaited turning point in Warner's misfortunes.

It also provided an urgently needed change for me, because Roger didn't want London Records rolled into Elektra as Levin had first suggested. He specifically demanded that London be teamed up with Sire. After a bit of haggling, the end result was London-Sire, another label merger. It was smaller than Elektra, and at face value, it was lower than where I'd come from, but I much preferred small and felt more at home in a transatlantic experiment. For a year, we put out interesting British electronica from the likes of Aphex Twin, Paul Oakenfold, Orbital, the Avalanches, and other innovators of that Y2K period.

Roger Ames shot up the ladder faster than even I imagined. Within months, Levin made him CEO of the entire Warner Music

Group. That's when the right people started being placed into the right slots.

As for me, London-Sire was an expensive experiment at a time when the industry began tanking and when corporate flab all over the Warner Music Group, which we were still carrying from the bad old days, was being trimmed into shape. Following about two years of limited commercial success, Levin called me to his office.

"Am I going to be fired?" I asked him straight out.

"No, Seymour," he replied with a smile. "You're too emblematic. We want you to sit back for a while and slowly revive Sire as a stand-alone label, except this time, within Atlantic. You'll have your own label and office attached to Atlantic's. You can feed into them for promotion and marketing, but you're basically on your own again."

Not only had I been saved by the kindness of Steve Ross's chosen heir, everyone from the old days was long gone. I was maybe old, washed up, and diminished, but I was the last man standing. And so, like a bearded veteran hobbling back from ten years of civil war, I returned to where I'd started. Well, almost. Sire had been stripped of its entire back catalog in the nineties; I was just a little office with an assistant. Nominally, however, I was good old Mr. Sire again. No double-barrel bullshit—just me and the Sire flag. Call me simple, but all I ever wanted was to keep sailing my own boat into the great unknown. Looking back, I honestly don't know how I made it through. I guess I didn't know what else to do. My kids had grown up and were *ignoring* me, living their lives as twentysomethings were supposed to. All I had was my art collecting and the Hall of Fame.

What kept me going, I think, was my Brooklyn spirit. Even when things were rock bottom, I always knew it wasn't the end of the world. I was still in play and doing okay considering. If my ego was as inflated as my worst critics claim, I would have slammed doors and taken a big executive job at another company. I didn't. Because it wasn't a career I ever wanted, it was a full and long life. Mine was always about the story, the adventure. I held on to Sire because, folks, this precious life we're given is about knowing where you belong and surviving as long as you can. The good times are only a bonus. I'd enjoyed more than my fair share. How could I be ungrateful? There's an old proverb that I've whispered to myself through every dark moment: "And this, too, shall pass."

10. THE SONG

October 30, 2007, was a date that would be etched into our memories, cited again and again in countless articles, police statements, and courtroom dispatches. I was leaving a Broadway play when Mandy rang my cell phone. The words came out like a bolt of lightning: Linda was dead. In the ensuing blur, all I remember is running for a cab, and—miraculously for Broadway at ten in the evening—one was there. As my heart began to sink, I told the driver, "965 Fifth Avenue."

Mandy happened to be working in New York that week and was staying at her mom's. When she'd opened the door at around ten, the apartment was in total darkness. Sensing something wasn't right, Mandy went from room to room until she found Linda on the floor, facedown, cold and hard, with her head hidden in a hoodie. Luckily, the light was so dim, Mandy didn't see the pool of blackened blood or that Linda's head was bashed in. She knew her mother was dead but thought it was a heart attack or some natural cause. In a state of panic like *The Scream* painting, Mandy ran out of the room and dialed 9-1-1.

When I reached Linda's building, the cops were everywhere.

Both Samantha and Arlene, Linda's sister, as well as my assistant, Rodney, had already arrived and were pushing their way through the police cordons. We stood there in total shock waiting to see Mandy, who was being questioned by detectives. There was never any doubt that Linda was dead; we knew they were taking her directly to the morgue.

We had barely taken in our new reality when the media started banging our doors down. In Jewish tradition, funerals should be within forty-eight hours of death, so we began organizing a ceremony in Linda's childhood synagogue in Riverside, unaware of what mayhem we were inflicting on ourselves and this neighborhood temple. All our friends flew in from around the world and squashed in, many of them having to sit on the floor, as packs of journalists pushed around mourners, clambering for photos of crying celebrities. We were moved by the huge turnout, but we were totally unprepared for the maelstrom it became.

Samantha and Mandy read their eulogies, but when the crowds dispersed, they went looking for answers. Mandy was particularly anxious, because she'd just been questioned a second time by the cops, who kept repeating the same questions to the point of exhaustion. They went straight to the hospital to ask the medical examiner what was the cause of death, and it was then they were presented with the gruesome evidence of a brutal murder.

Someone must have leaked the news to NY1 and 1010 WINS. All the newspapers quickly followed. REALTOR TO THE STARS BLUDGEONED TO DEATH ran the headlines. MANHATTAN MURDER MYSTERY was one newspaper title in London. If it bleeds, it leads, and this one had celebrity names to tag on and play with. All the movie and pop stars Linda had sold apartments to were reeled off in glamorous whodunnit stories beside photos of Linda with the Ramones or Elton John.

It took ten long days for the killer to be identified, but that only marked the beginning of a tortuous cat-and-mouse game. The cops questioned us all, and even I was worried that my alibi sounded lame. We were all starting to look at each other funnily until they hauled in Linda's personal assistant, a twenty-six-year-old woman, Natavia Lowery.

After the confession, the cops uncovered evidence of her repeated theft and reckoned she'd stolen at least $30,000 in the two months she'd occupied the job. In one particularly bizarre sting just three weeks previously, Lowery forged Linda's signature on a check and called American Express, pretending to be Linda. This was how she raised the necessary $4,000 to get into the premiere of *American Gangster*, apparently in an attempt to meet Denzel Washington. Yes, Linda's new assistant was a reputed psycho with a history of pathological lying and cheating, including accusations of stealing a friend's identity and embezzling from a church. Confronted with so much damning evidence, Lowery confessed to the murder on camera. Sniffling but not really crying, she claimed that Linda had insulted her and blew pot smoke in her face. In a fit of rage, Lowery said she grabbed a three-foot stick that Linda used for yoga and hit her six times.

The autopsy, however, depicted a far more gruesome death. Linda's last moments must have been pure horror; she was whacked twenty-four times with a blunt instrument, possibly this stick that Lowery had described but never revealed the whereabouts of. If that wasn't disturbing enough, Linda was sixty-two and had just pulled through a long and hard battle against breast cancer. Then, just weeks before the murder, a tumor had been identified on Linda's brain; it was benign but obviously a source of major concern. Lowery knew that Linda was lucky to be alive, which only added to the grotesque horror of it all.

Our nightmare spiraled into a three-year saga as Lowery re-canted her confession, claiming she hadn't been given a lawyer. Because the weapon was never located and because no DNA was found on or around the body, Lowery and her lawyers walked into the ensuing murder trial pleading guilty to the theft but claiming innocence to the murder.

It was blindingly obvious to anyone sitting in the gallery the accused was guilty as hell. I mean, seriously? You calmly confess to a murder *on camera*, no signs of any undue police pressure, and then you turn around and claim your rights were violated, and, uh, you didn't mean what you said? By changing her story so many times, Lowery only succeeded in illustrating her pathological dis-honesty, her complete stupidity, and, worst of all, her total lack of remorse.

I can only presume that once Lowery's lawyers explained the finer details of her legal situation, she was given a tiny glimmer of hope to wriggle out and save some face in her own family's eyes. She told her family that Linda's murder was a high-society con-spiracy, because hey, who cares about evidence when you can make people believe *the system* is rigged? At one point, Lowery got so caught up in her own impossible lies, she looked at Mandy and seethed, "You know you did it." Lowery's family wanted to believe their daughter was innocent, but in playing along with her denial, they made fools of themselves, whining to the press about corruption.

On a purely human level, I had some sympathy for her parents, but their behavior revealed so much about themselves. Both the crime and the ridiculous defense came back to Lowery thinking Linda was richer and more powerful than she really was. Thirty grand in two months? A hole that big could not have gone unno-ticed for too long. Linda was a real estate agent, not the Bank of El

Dorado. Okay, we Steins knew plenty of stars, but that doesn't mean you have the New York justice system in your pocket.

I shouldn't be too harsh on the parents, because in my own way, I was useless during that murder trial. I only turned up for a few sessions even though I should have been there to shoulder my daughters, who turned up every day. Mandy in particular got dragged through the mud by Lowery's lawyers, who tried to insinuate she had reasons to kill her mother. I just couldn't stomach that courtroom. Once I saw the defense happily playing along with Lowery's games, I was waiting to hear she'd changed her story again, was pleading manslaughter, and for her lawyers to keep shooting in all directions, claiming that Linda could drive a person to violence. Had Linda's stormy character become the issue, I knew I'd have been the first mug put under the spotlight. The whole thing wasn't going to end well for any of us. Lowery was going down, but I knew she'd claw at us as she slid.

If there's one thing people love in the United States of America, it's a celebrity murder. I think every country does, but we've taken the serious business of crime and law to theatrical extremes. We've got our fugitive live chases, our perp walks, our televised courtrooms. Our culture has been so forged by westerns, cop shows, and twenty-four-hour news channels, our criminal justice system has become a branch of the entertainment industry. You could probably say the same about our political system, too.

The more cameras you point around a situation, the more its protagonists are likely to lie or crack under the pressure. The whole thing becomes a stage performance. There's a reason why defense lawyers line up to take on a big-news case. Win or lose, it's how they get a name for themselves. Even Mandy had to fire her first lawyer, because, like an agent representing a character in TV show, he started shooting his mouth off to the press machine.

The journalists can be just as selfish. Like a pack of piranhas in a bucket of bloody water, there's nothing like a group of cameramen fighting each other for the best image. The more of them there are, the worse they behave. I saw scenes of invasive disrespect toward Mandy and Samantha that would make you lose faith in humanity. They were darting around from door to door, getting in and out of cars, trying to avoid being photographed. You couldn't avoid the cameras and would see yourself in the papers the next day, looking like a rabbit in the headlights.

Justice was at least delivered. It took an hour for the jury to convict Lowery on all counts. Linda was killed in the afternoon when only Lowery was in the apartment. The building was far too secure with camera surveillance for any intruder to come in unobserved. Even discounting the recanted confession, the jury agreed with detectives that absolutely everything pointed to Lowery. Security cameras showed how she left the apartment with her trousers inside out, probably to hide the bloodstains. She then walked down the street and withdrew $800 from a cash machine with one of Linda's credit cards.

We'll never know the precise details of how the fight was sparked, but I can almost imagine the scene. I'd say Linda discovered something and went berserk. She probably had no time to think or telephone the cops; she most likely flipped out and called Lowery every name under the sun. Even if she did, it's still a piss-poor excuse for murdering an old lady who's just caught you emptying her bank account. No matter how brash and rude Linda was capable of being, she didn't deserve to be beaten to death.

I left that nightmare with a lasting lesson about people. Okay, so Linda was "crazy" when it came to partying, insulting cab drivers, squeezing *fucks* into a sentence, smoking pot on the streets of Manhattan. Yes, she was sometimes a handful, but she was not a sicko by any psychiatric definitions. Linda was mostly bluster and show.

She had a kind heart, she stood by all of us, she raised money for charities and genuinely cared about other people's problems. Linda remembered everyone's birthday, and I'm sure she was kind to Natavia Lowery. It's as if Lowery never computed the gravity of her actions. It was her blankness, her numbness that I found so disturbing.

The true lunatics in this world aren't the big screaming personalities or the artists diving off stages. They're the silent ones who feel nothing except envy. They're so invisible, so blind to their own danger, you don't even see them coming. Life is cheap for those who are already half-dead inside. Linda opened her door to a wolf in secretary's clothing who thought she'd landed the keys into a self-service candy store. Bearing in mind that she had been accused of fraud and embezzlement, Lowery should never have been recruited by Douglas Elliman and the temp agency who sent her to Linda. Don't these agents do any background checks for the fees they charge?

When I think of Natavia Lowery and her family's angry statements to the press, I am drawn to the image of the late, great Leonard Cohen standing in his own courtroom hell. Leonard Cohen's manager and erstwhile lover, Kelley Lynch, had emptied his bank accounts during his long sabbatical in a Buddhist monastery. When Lynch was ordered to pay back the money and sentenced for subsequent charges of harassment, Leonard Cohen was granted his wish to deliver his own personal message that, to me, resonated louder than the judge's hammer. "It is my prayer," said Cohen, "that Ms. Lynch will take refuge in the wisdom of her religion, that a spirit of understanding will convert her heart from hatred to remorse, from anger to kindness, from the deadly intoxication of revenge to the lowly practices of self-reform."

When the camera crews ran off to the next tragedy, we finally had the space to mourn in solitude. Once I felt Linda gone forever,

I realized how much I loved her. I know it wasn't the love that Linda had dreamed of as a young woman, nor was it the type of love I'd felt for others. But Linda was the woman of my life, the costar of my movie. It wasn't just the children we'd brought into existence; for thirty-five years, we remained connected by a hotline that was never severed, even when the proverbial phone bills lay unpaid. Linda's mile-a-minute company always woke me up and got me punching on my toes, and although I bitched about her, I enjoyed the electrifying effect she had on me. We were like Bonnie and Clyde. That photo of us standing outside the Roundhouse in 1976—look what sparks fly when you rub two sharp Steins together.

I wish I could say that Linda's murder was the greatest tragedy to befall our family. Just two years after the case was wrapped up, Samantha began getting migraines and was diagnosed with brain cancer. For two years, she underwent heavy treatment in the Memorial Sloan Kettering Cancer Center on the corner of Central Park and 106th Street. As her condition worsened and became more desperate, she tried experimental treatment in the Duke Cancer Center in Durham, North Carolina. Tragically, it was all in vain. Samantha died in February 2013 at the age of forty, leaving behind an eight-year-old daughter, Dora, named after my mother.

There are many hard knocks you can overcome—heartbreaks, heart surgery, divorce, public humiliations, even the murder of your ex-wife. But there's one pain like no other. Burying a son or daughter runs against the laws of nature. It doesn't just break your heart; it breaks your will to carry on. Linda's murder had hit us like a train, but at least she'd lived to sixty-two. At least her daughters had grown up. In time, we were able to tell Linda stories and laugh about the old days. When Samantha died, there was a silent emptiness around her grave that never turned to acceptance or laughter. Just to see that eight-year-old little girl staring into the hole where her mother was gone forever. My heart turned to stone.

For months, I couldn't even cry. I bumped into people on my rounds, and they'd extend their condolences. Every time I was reminded, I just froze into a dead silence, a zombie, lost to emptiness. And when the tears eventually welled up early one morning, I don't think I've ever wailed like that in my life. No human can cry from the pits of the soul like an adult who has lost his child. You ask the sky why this happened. And there is no answer. It is the most damning sentence this life can hammer down.

What made the pain so bad was that Samantha did not have an entirely happy life, and I know I'm partly to blame. Being raised by nannies was tough enough, but discovering that I was gay I think affected the girls to a certain degree. But I always thought, in truth, they were both very supportive and ahead of their time in accepting gay dads. To be fair, they always had gay friends, they were open-minded New Yorkers, and most of Linda's friends were gay. Samantha and Mandy grew up around a lot of gay men. But it's one thing to accept that friends and surrogate uncles are gay, another to find out your own father prefers men.

As a kid, Samantha was positive, always busy, always popular at school, she was a natural-born crowd stirrer who inherited her mother's organizational skills. But as she entered the crazy mirrors of adolescence and college, she felt that life had given her a bum deal. And like so many young adults make the mistake of doing, she began asking herself those pointless questions: "Why me? What did I do to deserve this?" She developed eating disorders, which I now realize may have been an attempt to get my attention. They say it's a cry for help, generally directed at the family. Unfortunately, this wasn't a distress flare I understood or could answer. And the more I didn't address her problems, the deeper she slipped. This was during my own wildest years in the late eighties and early nineties when I was living my own life to the max. I knew she was suffering, but I just didn't know how to reach her. Even Linda was stumped. Mandy, too.

Samantha slipped out of reach in personal ways, until, thank God, she started taking control of her demons. There was only one person who could help her, and it wasn't her strange daddy or her crazy mom or her kid sister; it was herself. With counseling, better company, clearer thoughts, stricter self-discipline, she figured her way out of the labyrinth she'd gotten lost in. Like so many people who've been to hell and back, she came out strong. Everyone enjoyed Samantha's company, she had principles, she listened, she was kind to others. When she died, I noticed that she hadn't touched a penny of her mother's inheritance. It's just a detail, but I've always admired those who can resist the cheap thrill of spending; it's a sign of good character. Samantha was no snob, no brat, no rich kid. She knew the true value of people and things.

The only happy thought that I've clutched onto like a piece of broken raft is the absolute joy Samantha felt to bear a child. Baby Dora was the culminating triumph of her whole life's journey, the fruit, the treasure found at the end of her soul searching. From the moment she knew she was pregnant, her eyes lit up and remained sparkling with a mother's pride for the last eight years of her life. Even when she was very sick, that love continued burning like a beacon. Samantha accepted her own destiny better than those of us who loved her. I guess that as she walked her own spiritual path into the inevitable, Dora provided the happy ending to an otherwise cruelly brief life. Her time had not been in vain. The circle of life was respected, and motherhood brought her the gratitude and meaning that she'd been missing for so many years. So, little Dora, when you grow up and we are not around, always remember that you were bathed in your mother's love and wrapped in the warm coat of my mother's name. Should doubts ever whisper in the darkness, call on your foremothers for guidance and you will never be alone.

And I say to my three grandchildren, I don't know if this book clearly expresses that, despite ups and downs, double-dealing, naivety, and lack of experience on my part and all that goes with it, I wouldn't have traded my life in music, which I love, for just about anything else in the world. It's been a bumpy ride, but an exciting one. It is one thing to discover a great song, record, or artist and watch it slowly climb the charts, become a hit, and the artist or band you believed in become famous as a fan. Double, triple, quadruple all that, and it doesn't bring you anywhere close to the joy and satisfaction of being part of it. I have enjoyed occasions like this for many years, and I am most grateful to the artists and to God for this ride I've been on for so many years, and old as I am, I'm still in no hurry to get off.

And what about my remaining daughter, the light of my life, Mandy, who's lived through so much heartache? The childhood she endured, finding her mother dead like that, her only sister dying at forty? If ever there was someone in this story who graduated through the School of Hard Knocks, who has *survived* through a forty-year assault course, it's Mandy. She's my connection to much of the past. She's the light that warms me every time I visit her in Los Angeles and watch her play with her two young daughters, Leia and India.

Now I'm the grandfather at the Thanksgiving table and proud of it. I give thanks to the mothers whose love matters so much in a child's self-confidence. My own success owed so much to my happy, selfless, kindhearted parents and my big sister, Ann, who loved and encouraged me like a mini mom. I know I was the difficult child, the black sheep, and I thank my family for accepting me as I was. They were the supportive record label, and I was the troubled artist whose strange talent only they recognized, accepted, and kept believing in. That's where it all began.

But beware of love alone; it's not enough. A teenager needs to learn a trade before his own dreams drive him to insanity. How lucky was I to have lived in an era of mentors and apprenticeships? Where did we lose that great old tradition of showing youngsters real jobs and careers to follow? I know I was given more than I ever gave back, and maybe that imbalance was the failure of my generation. The postwar era created so much great music and pop culture, we were a rare crop, but in growing so big, we sucked the soil around us barren. So, dear reader, please don't write me off just yet—my chores are not done. We oldsters must keep handing down our toolboxes and our trade secrets. Dignity in transmission. This chapter has a few more pages left to figure out.

All that's now left is me, Mandy, and my three granddaughters. The other survivor is Sire, which I run out of an office in midtown. Sire is not the smoking hit factory it once was, but it's my own little corner store, still open for business, and helping young artists make music and prosper. Over the last fifteen years or so, I've been releasing records from the likes of Kill It Kid, Cold Fronts, Residual Kid, Lottery Winners, Sugarmen, and Paul Shaffer. I've even just worked on a Cindy Lauper album. I'm still doing what I do and will continue working for as long as I can. It was never "work" anyway. Not in the way most people mean the word. Sire was always a way of life, a vocation, a necessity, a privilege.

You should see me now: I'm a bit of a rambling wreck (sans

Georgia Tech) held up by a cane and a stubborn determination to keep going. People joke about high mileage, but mine really is fifty-plus years of jet lag. I'd love to be able to put a number on the air miles I've clocked up; I'm sure it's in the same league as Apollo astronauts. As for the amount of gigs I have seen, how I'm not deaf is a mystery. Yes, I'm out there with all the obsessive-compulsives who sacrificed family and even sleep for a hobbyhorse that has kept galloping through the decades. At the age of seventy-five, I'm not done yet. I love going to the office every day and traveling the world.

You may cross my path in airports. Whether it's happening in Los Angeles, Liverpool, Bombay, Toronto, Tel Aviv, New Orleans, Beijing, Hamburg, Brighton, or Chicago, I'll make it on time. You'll see me in Cannes during Midem, in Austin, Texas, for SXSW. You'll find me in Trinidad for Mardi Gras, or sitting on the shores of the Dead Sea in winter, or shuffling around Sotheby's on a rainy Thursday. You'll see me in the corner of my favorite restaurants in London and Paris. You'll even see me still walking to work every morning down the streets of Manhattan. Please say hello. Please play me your songs. For as long as I've got time on this earth, I've always got time for a good story and a great song. My ears are forever young.

The world I live in today is not the same as the one I entered. When I visit boomtown cities in India and China, I can feel the same infectious, self-confident energy that I felt in London in the sixties or New York in the early eighties. Power moves around, and with it, the mojo strikes kids as randomly as lightning storms. You can feel an artistic storm ready to burst in the developing world; in Israel, too, there surely must be Palestinian and Israeli musicians somewhere out there who will inspire a generation.

Last year, I unexpectedly lost two close personal friends who were also Sire artists, actor Bill Paxton, who recorded two amazing singles, both with sensational accompanying videos: "Reach" with video directed by Academy Award winner James Cameron; and "How Can the Labouring Man Find Time for Self-Culture," directed by Rocky Schenck. Also tragic was the passing of Tommy Page, who in 1990 had a number-one hit on Sire, "I'll Be Your Everything." Both deaths shocked and saddened me immensely. I'm still not over them.

I am grateful for the extra-large helping that has been heaped on my plate. I have been able to do what I love. What more can a man ask for? My happiest moment in recent years, and possibly the ultimate feather in my fedora, after being inducted into the Rock and Roll Hall of Fame several years earlier, was being inducted into the Songwriters Hall of Fame in 2016. I couldn't believe seeing my name on the roll call, because it's a club that record men aren't invited into. I never wrote a song nor was I allowed to be a publisher. But its gatekeepers, Linda Moran and Charlie Feldman, invited me in because I was one of the few record industry deans who always believed, hard as cast iron, that musical brilliance boils down to songwriting. I was always skeptical of producers who claimed that sound mattered most. For me, it's always been the *what-you-have-to-say*. Listen for yourself. Behind every pop masterpiece, there's always a killer song. It's the source of the magic and always will be.

Having listened to so much music over the years, I've reached the simple conclusion that the greatest music in history is the stuff that's made it into the public domain. I refer to our most familiar melodies and lyrics, our hymns and bedtime lullabies, our social rituals and national anthems. They are bigger than national treasures; they're humanity's greatest hits that have outlived all statutory limits of copyright. These are the people's songs that have been immortalized by the test of time.

I refer to the great classical airs and folk monuments. The

beauty of "Silent Night," "Adeste Fideles," "It Came Upon a Midnight Clear," and "The First Noel" get me excited every time I hear them at Christmas. I'm Jewish, of course. I don't celebrate the holiday, but that doesn't mean I don't love the music. One of my personal favorites is the "Song of the Volga Boatmen," a true masterpiece guaranteed to send you tumbling back through time to nineteenth-century Russia. Or "Kol Nidre," the heart-melting vow that begins the solemn ceremony of Yom Kippur every year. It can be chanted orally, or it can be played by musicians without its words. Like all truly great songs, its magic can be evoked in so many ways. "Hatikvah," the Israeli national anthem, meaning *the hope*, is another stirring beauty that envelops you from its unmistakable opening line. Its long story began in nineteenth-century Russia as a wistful, prayer-like poem about the dream of every Jew to return to the ancestral homeland. Before Israel was even a vague possibility, it brought solace to millions of Jews in times we can barely imagine. If you want to understand Israel, listen to it carefully.

Our own national anthem, "The Star-Spangled Banner," is one that always brings a lump to my throat. We almost chose "Columbia, the Gem of the Ocean," whose melody I love, but I think we missed an opportunity to not have adopted the fourth and final stanza of "The Star-Spangled Banner" in the standard shortened version. "O thus be it ever when freemen shall stand, between their loved home and the war's desolation. Blessed with victory and peace, may the heaven rescued land praise the power that hath made and preserved us a nation. Then conquer we must, when our cause it is just, and this be our motto—'In God is our trust.' And the star-spangled banner in triumph shall wave, over the land of the free and the home of the brave."

The strange thing about all these old songs, and too many others to mention, is how they unleash a sort of genie into the air. You don't put these songs on like a record; they only fit serious occasions in the way that prayers are reserved for collective rituals. Of all the songs ever written, there's a special place in my heart for "La Marseillaise," the French national anthem. I first discovered it as a boy watching the famous scene in *Casablanca* when Rick's Café erupted into song to drown out the Nazi soldiers singing their beer-hall dreck. *Casablanca* was released the year I was born, which I guess makes it another great war baby to add to my long list. I never understood the lyrics of "La Marseillaise" until they were explained to me years later, but its sheer emotional power hit me in the chest and continues to floor me every time.

The song was originally written in 1792 as a citizen's call to resistance at a time when revolutionary France had just declared its republic. The neighboring Prussian and Austrian empires were poised to invade and stamp out these new ideas of rights and citizenry. The song was actually written in Strasbourg, right where the imperial armies were coming. Like all great songs, it was personally felt—it was *lived* by its authors from the front line of human experience. "Tyranny is out to get us," go the lyrics, roughly translated. "Its bloodstained banners are risen." Then, as the melody moves into its melancholic middle section, it asks, "Can you hear it in your countryside? The thunder of ferocious soldiers who'll march into your homes. They're coming to slit the throats of your daughters and your wife." In its final melodic pivot from pain to hope, it lifts the roof with its great battle cry: "To the guns, citizens!" Whenever I hear it, I feel like jumping on a horse, pulling out a sword, and screaming, "Charge!"

In times of peace, France's fainter hearted wondered about the song's bloody imagery, but you can see how it fit so perfectly into *Casablanca*, when the bloodstained banners of tyranny had once again marched into people's lives. I never thought I'd see it, but the song came back to life when I was in Paris conducting the interviews for this book following a series of terrorist attacks throughout 2015 and 2016. A wave of evil psychos claiming allegiance to ISIS went on a killing spree, murdering writers, music fans, Jews, youngsters, families at the Bastille Day fireworks display. It was the most grotesque outburst of extreme violence France had experienced since Nazi occupation.

Suddenly, those old lyrics resonated like the year it was written, mystifying the very people who'd been hearing it for years. France happened to be hosting the European soccer championship that bloody summer, and before every match involving the home team, "La Marseillaise" raised the sky and, I think it's fair to say, stole the show of the whole sporting event. In bars and village squares, the whole country sang along, tears in their eyes, feeling every word. They didn't want this senseless bloodshed, but in equal measure, they knew they had to stand up for what they believed in. It was like Rick's Café in real life.

These are the great mysteries of music. A song can unite and lift a divided and demoralized nation in ways that no political leader can. Never let it be said that music is just entertainment. Most of the time it *is* just entertainment, but when bigger things need to be said, when humanity needs to see clearly, music is the higher language that designates the righteous.

Looking back into the last century and beyond, I've come to realize that music is like a river flowing through the ages. Sometimes it's a flood, sometimes it's a stream, but as long as there are people roaming this earth in search of happiness, it will never dry up; it just keeps winding through new landscapes with new tributaries loaded with new musical genres and ideas coming along all the time. We can feel it flowing through our lives, but only some can tap into it. David Byrne tapped into that river. The Ramones,

Talking Heads, the Pretenders, Madonna, the Replacements, Chrissie Hynde, Depeche Mode, the Smiths, Seal, k.d. lang, Ice-T, Ian McCulloch, they and many others all did in their own different ways. But even the very greatest artists of all time cannot *move* the river. Not Dylan, not Hank Williams, not Duke Ellington, not Mozart. The river follows only the story of humanity, and we are all just travelers down its banks. Every great song that was ever written or recorded is like a bottle of distilled life. Uncork any one and you will be magically transported to a time. You will breathe its air and see through its eyes.

Sixty-plus years in the music business, and I keep hearing the same old groan: that pop music isn't what it used to be. If you really believe that every generation is getting dumber, I'm afraid you're just over the hill. Every crop of kids thinks it's more clued in than the previous one, and as they get older and their parents die, they turn their contempt to youngsters. The truth is there's always great stuff happening, albeit in small amounts. You just have to go out and find it. There are always budding geniuses locked in rooms, locked inside *themselves*, out of sight and unappreciated until they're given a stage and world full of love. You can't stop it. That big river just keeps rolling onward, right where the absolute present and the timeless world meet. Right now, teenagers are dancing round fires along its banks and howling at the moon. They're just as happy as you and I were at their age. And the reason they don't care if we like or dislike their songs is because they are coming of age. They are addressing their own future that we're not part of.

Long ago, I pitched my tent somewhere back down that riverbank. For years and years, I've kept walking, just trying to stay close to the kids. The faces come and go, and sometimes the songs are hard to understand. It's not easy keeping up with such a fast-moving language. But I'll tell you this: it's still the best place on earth. That magical water keeps us young in spirit. It's what's keeps my heart still pounding. Rest assured, there's great music still to come and always will be.

Keeping our spirits high is the only way to get through life. So, make the most of what you have. And do it now while you can.

APPENDIX

People in My Music Life

At age seventy-five and still actively involved in music, looking back, I realize that one of the main reasons for my success, and the joy and happiness derived, was because I decided at such a young age, without even knowing what it entailed, that being in the music business was the life for me. Meeting so many people while still in high school, working afternoons at *Billboard*, was a major factor.

I would be remiss if I didn't make mention of as many people as possible that I can recall whose paths I crossed along the road, especially in those early days, from the mid-1950s to the mid-1960s. Some were people I might have met just once or twice, others much more, and some with whom I've worked closely.

I've assembled this list rather quickly. Many of these people are also mentioned in the book. It's been a great musical ride through many eras and genres, and I wouldn't trade it for anything.

I hope I haven't left anyone out, and if so, I apologize.

<u>King Records</u>: Syd Nathan (Cincinnati), Zella Nathan, John Kelley, Mary Lou Smith, Al Miller, Johnny Miller, Eddie Smith (amazing engineer), Milt Dragul, Al Rogoff, Arnie Orleans, Sonny

Thompson (Chicago), Rudy Toombs, Nat Tannen, George Levy (New York), Hy Penzell, Lefty Stevens, Jack Pearl (King lawyer)

Publishers: Lester Sill, Ralph Peer, Julian and Jean Aberbach (Hill & Range), Freddy Bienstock (Carlin), Irving Mills (Mills Music), Lou Levy (Leeds Music), Don Kirschner and Al Nevins, Jon Platt (Warner-Chappell), Bill Lowery, Wesley Rose, Joe Santly and Georgie Joy (Santly-Joy), Harry and Gene Goodman (Regent and Mark Music), Goldie Goldmark (Sheldon Music), Joe Csida (Trinity Music)

INDIE LABELS

New York

Atlantic Records: Ahmet Ertegun, Jerry Wexler, Nesuhi Ertegun, Herb Abramson, Miriam Bienstock

Cadence: Archie Bleyer

Bang Records: Bert Berns

DynoVoice/NewVoice Records: Bob Crewe

Carlton Records: Joe Carlton

Musicor Records: Aaron Schroeder

Rainbow Records: Eddie Heller

Kapp: Dave Kapp

Sue Records: Juggy Murray

Fire/Fury Records: Bobby Robinson

Enjoy Records: Danny Robinson

Kama Sutra Records: Artie Ripp, Phil Steinberg, Hy Mizrahi

Baton Records: Sol Rabinowitz

J&S Records: Zell Sanders (Bronx)

Diamond Records: Phil Kahl, Joe Kolsky, Wes Farrell

Herald/Ember Records: Al Silver

Scepter/Wand Records: Florence Greenberg, Luther Dixon, Marv Schlacter

Apollo Records: Ike and Bess Berman

Laurie Records: Robert and Gene Schwartz, Allan Sussel, Doug Morris

Jubilee: Jerry Blaine, Herb Abramson

Coed Records: Marvin Cane

Beltone Records: Les Cahan

United Artists: Mike Stewart
Amy/Mala/Bell Records: Larry Uttal
Smash Records: Charlie Fach (where I first met Quincy Jones)
Canadian-American Records: Gerry Granahan, Hutch Davie (originally based in North Dakota)
Hull Records: Blanche Casalin
DCP Records: Don Costa, Teddy Randazzo

Chicago

Chess: Leonard and Phil Chess, Marshall Chess, Max Cooperstein (ace promotion man)
Vee-Jay: Vivian Carter, Jimmy Bracken, Ewart Abner
Mercury: Irving Green, Irwin Steinberg
National Records: Al Green, Herb Abramson
Chance Records: Art Sheridan

New Jersey

All Platinum Records: Joe and Sylvia Robinson
T-Neck Records: Isley brothers (Kelly, Rudy, and Ron)

Philadelphia

Cameo/Parkway: Bernie Lowe, Dave Appell
Jamie/Guyden Records: Harold Lipsius, Harry Finfer
Essex Records: Dave Miller
Chancellor: Bob Marcucci, Pete DeAngelis
Swan Records: Bernie Binnick, Tony Mammarella, Dick Clark

Pittsburgh

Calico Records: Herb Cohen, Nick Cenci

Cincinnati

Fraternity Records: Harry Carlson, and, of course, King, Federal, De Luxe & Bethlehem

Detroit

Motown: Berry Gordy, Barney Ales, Smokey Robinson
Golden World: Joanne Bratton

Fortune Records: Jack and Devora Brown
Anna Records: Harvey Fuqua, Gwen Gordy

Minneapolis

Soma: Amos Heilicher

Seattle

Dolton: Bonnie Guitar, Bob Reisdorff

Houston

Duke/Peacock/Backbeat: Don Robey

Nashville

Dot Records: Randy Wood (Gallatin); Nicki Addy (New York office)
Starday Records: Don Pierce
Excello Records: Ernie Young

New Mexico

Nor-Va-Jak Records: Norman Petty (Clovis), one of the few true geniuses. Discovered and/or was first to work with Buddy Holly & the Crickets, Roy Orbison, Waylon Jennings, Buddy Knox, Fireballs, String-A-Longs, and many others.

San Francisco

Autumn Records: Tom Donahue, Bobby Mitchell, Sylvester "Sly Stone" Stewart

LA

Liberty Records: Si Waronker, Snuff Garrett
Imperial: Lew Chudd
Specialty Records: Art Rupe
Modern: Bihari brothers (Jules, Saul, and Joel)
Aladdin: Eddie and Leo Mesner
Era Records: Herb Newman
Doré Records: Lou Bedell
Keen Records: Bob Keane

4 Star Records: William A. McCall, Jr., Clifford McDonald, and Richard A. Nelson
Exclusive Records: Leon Rene
Class Records: Googie Rene
Dootone Records: Dootsie Williams
Philles Records: Phil Spector, Lester Sill

New Orleans
Minit Records: Aaron Neville
J&M Recording Studio: Cosimo Matassa

Shreveport
Jewel/Paula Records: Stan Lewis

Memphis
Sun Records: Sam Phillips, Shelby and John Singleton
Stax/Volt: Jim Stewart, Estelle Axton
Hi Records: Joe Cuoghi

Miami
TK Records: Henry Stone and Steve Alaimo

Massachusetts
Rounder Records: Ken Irwin, Bill Nowlin, Marian Leighton-Levy

Mississippi
Ace Records: Johnny Vincent (Jackson)

Virginia
Legrand Records: Frank Guida (Norfolk)

BRILL BUILDING / 1650 BROADWAY FOLKS

Doc Pomus
Otis Blackwell

Mort Shuman

Dion DiMucci

Neil Sedaka and Howie Greenfield

Barry Mann and Cynthia Weil

Gerry Goffin and Carole King

Johnny Marks ("Mr. Christmas")

Bob Feldman and Jerry Goldstein

Neil Diamond

Tommy Boyce

Bobby Hart

Toni Wine

Tony Orlando

Frank Slay

Hank Medress and Mitchell Margo (the Tokens)

Kenny Vance, Jay Black (Jay and the Americans)

Joel Diamond

Al Kooper

Hal Fein (Roosevelt Music)

Brooks Arthur

Stanley Catron

Auction Houses

Sotheby's: Roberta Louckx, Pittman Shay, Ben Doller, Jodi Pollack, Lydia Cresswell-Jones, Philippe Garner

Christie's (London): Victoria Wolcough, Martin Beisly

Bonhams (LA): Scot Levitt

Rago Arts (New Jersey): David Rago

Swann (New York): Nicholas "Nico" Lowry, Todd Weyman

Freeman's (Philadelphia): Alasdair Nichol

Neal's (New Orleans): Lisa Weisdorffer

And the folks at all the great auction houses in Paris:

    Millon

    Aguttes

    Tajan

    Artcurial

    Félix Marcilhac

Bukowski (Stockholm): Eva Seeman

Dorotheum (Vienna)

ACKNOWLEDGMENTS

The year of *Siren Song*'s publication figures closely with Sire's fiftieth anniversary, and also just a bit over my sixtieth year in the
music business. Looking back on where and when my great journey
in music began, I recall memories, adventures, good and bad times,
and most importantly of all, the people who helped me along the
way. Some of them, but unfortunately not all, are mentioned in
these paragraphs. First, my parents, David and Dora, my daughter
Samantha, who passed away in 2013, my granddaughters Dora
Wells and Leia and India Logan, my late ex-wife, Linda, my sister,
Ann, and her husband, Marty Wiederkehr, my cousins Arland and
Kay Weisberg, Herman Weisberg, my nieces Susan and Robin
Katz and their husbands, Barry and Jonathan, and their offspring,
as well.

Also, my GP, Dr. Alan Pollock, who has kept me alive and well
over many years, in spite of myself, and George Goldner, who I
worked for at Red Bird Records with Jerry Leiber and Mike Stoller.
Most of all, my daughter Mandy, a constant source of inspiration
and the driving force who helped pick and secure most of the great
photos in this book, selecting great photographers like **Bob Gruen**,
Roberta Bayley, and **Bobby Grossman**.

My success in music is due directly to the mentors who taught me and handed down what they learned about music, and, in particular, great songs and artists and the courage to be a leader and not just follow along. Fortunately, perhaps because I began my quest (career) at such a young age, I had many mentors, mostly indie record label founders and folks I was fortunate enough to meet at *Billboard* when I first worked up the courage to visit their offices when I was no more than thirteen or fourteen years old. Some of them are mentioned on the pages that follow.

Some of their careers stretched back to the 1920s. Chief among them, in addition to Tom Noonan and Paul Ackerman at *Billboard*, were Syd Nathan of King Records, Jerry Wexler, and Ahmet and Nesuhi Ertegun at Atlantic Records.

Finally, Jerry Lieber, Mike Stoller, George Goldner, Ellie Greenwich, Jeff Barry, Shadow Morton, Steve Venet, all at Red Bird Records. Super important, because that is where I first met Richard Gottehrer, with whom I started Sire Records several years later. Red Bird was on the 8th floor and Richard's company, with his partners Bobbly Feldman and Jerry Goldstone, FGG Productions, was on the 9th floor. We'd often meet riding the elevators up and down to work. We were partners in Sire for the first seven years, and they were among the roughest, but some of the best as well.

Sire's first assistant was a young Englishwoman, Helen Glatt, who I brought over from Red Bird. She was followed by many great women on both sides of the Atlantic to whom I owe so much: Risa Morley, Sandy Alouete, Geraldine Oakley (Lines), Maxine Conroy (Forrest), Karen Rooney, Ellen Zucker, Deirdre Allen, Ellie Smith, Susanne Emil.

Over the years, there were others at Sire who stood out: Paul McNally, Randy Miller, Ken Kushnick, Michael Rosenblatt, Kenny Ostin, Mark Kamins, Lyle Preslar, Craig Winkler, Steve Savoca, John Montgomery, Larry Demellier, Phil Greenop, and Selwin

Turnbull. There were folks at the various labels from whom Sire licensed music. At EMI: L. G. Wood, Roger Ames (whose credits I always touted and who eventually became my boss at WMG for several years), and David Croker. Among the artists, Climax Blues Band, Renaissance, Barclay James Harvest, Stackridge, Kevin Ayers, and others that helped keep Sire's doors open. At the Rough Trade store in London: Geoff Travis (the Smiths), Peter, Judith, and Steve (I never knew their surnames) and Daniel Miller at Mute Records, whom I met there and who entrusted Sire with Depeche Mode, Erasure, Yaz[oo], Silicon Teens, and the Normal. At Beggar's Banquet and 4AD: Martin Mills, Ivo Watts-Russell (the Cult, Modern English). At Creation Records: Alan McGee (Primal Scream, My Bloody Valentine, Ride). At Transatlantic: Nat and Sarah Joseph (the Deviants, the Johnstons) and others from my early UK days—John Gillespie, Neil Slaven, John Reid, and Phil Greenop.

Prior to hooking up with Warner Bros. in 1977, we were distributed by several labels: London Records, where we had fond memories of working with Herb Goldfarb, Mimi Trepel, and Diana Weller. At Polydor Records, with Jerry Schoenbaum, at Paramount with Tony Martell and Aaron Levy. At British Decca, with Hugh Mendl, a great music man who signed Moody Blues and, together with Dick Rowe, the Rolling Stones, Geoffrey Milne, and Sir Edward Lewis. At ABC, there was a great, old-school music man and mentor from back in the days of the Decca branch in Chicago, Jay Lasker, and a support team that included Charlie Minor and Dennis Lavinthal.

At Warner, the most supportive over the years have been Dion Singer, Michael Nance, Craig Kostich, Lenny Waronker, Ted Templeman, Carl Scott, Liz Rosenberg, Tom Ruffino, Andrew Wickham, Steve Baker, Bob Regehr, Bobby Shaw, Bob Merlis, Michael Hill, Peter Standish, John Esposito, Steve

Margo, Tom Draper, Benny Medina, Brian Bumbery, and most recently Robin Hurley, James Steven, Nicole Smith, and Bob Kaus. In Warner's UK office: Rob Dickins, Max Hole, Paul Conroy, Moira Bellas, Barbara Charone, and currently my close friend and associate Serene Sass. Across the Channel in Warner France: Neeky Kergraisse. Eliah Seton, and everyone at ADA, the greatest indie distributor in the world. Finally, Jon Platt, not just a great publisher but a great song man.

Labels Sire was closely involved with: Blue Horizon Records: Mike and Richard Vernon (Peter Green's Fleetwood Mac, Chicken Shack, Duster Bennett, and some of the greatest blues artists of all time); Jem Records: Marty Scott (Nektar, Synergy); Real Records: Dave Hill (the Pretenders); Hansa Records: Trudy Meisel (Boney M), who also hooked me up with the wonderful folks at Ariola/BMG, including Hartwig Masuch and Kate Hyman. Also, Dag Haeggqvist at Sonet.

My lawyers over the years, and in particular, my current attorney, friend, and advisor Jess Drabkin. I'm not being at all modest when I say, without his help, understanding, and support, this book most probably would never have been written. Also, the legendary Allen Grubman, Alan Stein—no relation—who was Sire's first lawyer and guided Richard and me through uncharted waters, Jim Mosher, Rick Streicker at Warner's, Sire's in-house lawyer, Jonathan Brett, and my family lawyer and cousin, Arland Weisberg, and his wife, Kay (some family photographs taken by Arland's late Brother Brian are included in this book), and my accountants, Peter Fairley and Anand Viswanath at CohnReznick.

Other dear friends and supporters in and out of the industry: Danny Fields, Linda Moran of Songwriters Hall of Fame and her husband, Mike Moran, one of Elvis' key engineers at RCA Victor, Charlie Feldman at BMI, Jerry Blavat (the Geator with the Heater),

Ian "Molly" Meldrum, legendary Philadelphia disc jockey Freddie Gershon, Bill Paxton, Brett Ratner, Mandar Thakur, Tony Wilson, Dave Pichilingi, Li Hui at Modernsky in China, Atul Churamani, Blaise Fernandes, Viraj Sawant, Jimi Wang, Mohammed Hamzeh, Paolo Della Puppa, Shep Gordon, Christine Semba/WOMEX, Jeremy Hulsh, Ed Peto, Mark Potter, Eric and Wanda Ramos, Gary Kurfirst, Sat Bisla, Guy Oseary, Jorge Hinojosa, Andrew Loog Oldham, Linda Ramone, Hilly Kristal, Arturo Vega, Frank Barsalona, Suzan Evans and Rabbi Chaim Kramer, Martin Elbourne from Great Escape and Glastonbury Festival, Sat Bisla from MUSEXPO, Jasper Donat from BRANDED, Michael Gudinski and Michael Chugg in Australia, and Neill Dixon from Canadian Music Week.

Special thanks to my personal assistant of nearly thirty years, Rodney Richardson, one of the most brilliant people I've ever known, from whom I've learned so much about art. Rodney helped me build up an amazing collection and, more importantly, kept me healthy in spite of myself. Together, we shared many exciting and important adventures and talent searches over the past thirty years. Also, on those trips, we met so many great international music men and women.

Also, my previous assistants, Jean-Michel Coletti, who went on to have a career at Warner Music France, Ron Maida, and Alistair Coia. Also, current Sire staffers Robin Hurley, Eric McLellan, Mike Kain, and Teasha Edwards.

There are so many people whose paths I have been privileged to cross during my sixty-year career in music. I've listed many of them in the appendix to this book, which also contains a list of the auction houses that are some of my favorite places to spend time.

—Seymour Stein

Gareth Murphy would like to acknowledge the help and support of:

Elizabeth Beier, Jeff Capshew, Chris Frantz, Brian Powers, Risa Morley, Rodney Richardson, Michael Rosenblatt, Ken Kushnick, Danny Fields, Andy Wickham, Arlene Adler, Mandy Stein, Richard Gottehrer, Craig Lyon, Marty Scott, Maxine Forrest, Geraldine Lines, Ann Wiederkher, Arland Weisberg, Sandy Alouete, Rabbi Chaim Kramer, Mike Vernon, Richard Vernon, Jean-Michel Coletti, Daniel Miller, Geoff Travis, Martin Mills, Nicole Williams, Jennifer Donovan, Mark Fowler, Don Bajema, Ivo Watts-Russell, Judith Azoulay, and James Azoulay-Murphy.

INDEX